Contextualizing Theology in the South Pacific

American Society of Missiology
Monograph Series

Series Editor, James R. Krabill

The ASM Monograph Series provides a forum for publishing quality dissertations and studies in the field of missiology. Collaborating with Pickwick Publications—a division of Wipf and Stock Publishers of Eugene, Oregon—the American Society of Missiology selects high quality dissertations and other monographic studies that offer research materials in mission studies for scholars, mission and church leaders, and the academic community at large. The ASM seeks scholarly work for publication in the series that throws light on issues confronting Christian world mission in its cultural, social, historical, biblical, and theological dimensions.

Missiology is an academic field that brings together scholars whose professional training ranges from doctoral-level preparation in areas such as Scripture, history and sociology of religions, anthropology, theology, international relations, interreligious interchange, mission history, inculturation, and church law. The American Society of Missiology, which sponsors this series, is an ecumenical body drawing members from Independent and Ecumenical Protestant, Catholic, Orthodox, and other traditions. Members of the ASM are united by their commitment to reflect on and do scholarly work relating to both mission history and the present-day mission of the church. The ASM Monograph Series aims to publish works of exceptional merit on specialized topics, with particular attention given to work by younger scholars, the dissemination and publication of which is difficult under the economic pressures of standard publishing models.

Persons seeking information about the ASM or the guidelines for having their dissertations considered for publication in the ASM Monograph Series should consult the Society's website—www.asmweb.org.

Members of the ASM Monograph Committee who approved this book are:

Robert Gallagher, Associate Professor of Intercultural Studies and Director of M.A. (Intercultural Studies), Wheaton College

Paul Kollman, Associate Professor of Theology and Executive Director Center for Social Concerns (CSC), University of Notre Dame

RECENTLY PUBLISHED IN THE ASM MONOGRAPH SERIES

Lila W. Balisky, *Songs of Ethiopia's Tesfaye Gabbiso: Singing with Understanding in Babylon, the Meantime, and Zion*

Kevin George Hovey, *Guiding Light: Contributions of Alan R. Tippett Toward the Development and Dissemination of Twentieth-Century Missiology*

Contextualizing Theology in the South Pacific

The Shape of Theology in Oral Cultures

RANDALL G. PRIOR

FOREWORD BY
ROGER SCHROEDER, SVD

PREFACE BY
ILAITIA SEVATI TUWERE

American Society of Missiology Monograph
Series vol. 41

PICKWICK *Publications* · Eugene, Oregon

CONTEXTUALIZING THEOLOGY IN THE SOUTH PACIFIC
The Shape of Theology in Oral Cultures

American Society of Missiology Monograph Series 41

Pickwick Publications
An Imprint of Wipf and Stock Publishers
199 W. 8th Ave., Suite 3
Eugene, OR 97401

www.wipfandstock.com

PAPERBACK ISBN: 978-1-5326-5857-0
HARDCOVER ISBN: 978-1-5326-5858-7
EBOOK ISBN: 978-1-5326-5859-4

Cataloguing-in-Publication data:

Names: Prior, Randall G., author. | Schroeder, Roger, SVD, foreword. | Tuwere, Ilaitia Sevati, preface.

Title: Contextualizing theology in the South Pacific : the shape of theology in oral cultures / by Randall G. Prior; foreword by Roger Schroeder, SVD; preface by Ilaitia Sewati Tuwere.

Description: Eugene, OR: Pickwick Publications, 2019 | American Society of Missiology Monograph Series 41 | Includes bibliographical references and index.

Identifiers: ISBN 978-1-5326-5857-0 (paperback) | ISBN 978-1-5326-5858-7 (hardcover) | ISBN 978-1-5326-5859-4 (ebook)

Subjects: LCSH: Christianity—Oceania. | Christianity—Vanuatu.

Classification: BL2620.M4 P6 2019 (print) | BL2620.M4 (ebook)

07/09/19

To those who pioneered *The Gospel and Culture in Vanuatu Movement*

and

to those everywhere who live *with one head and one heart.*

**Promoting Theology
in the
South Pacific**

Contents

List of Illustrations | ix

Foreword by Roger Schroeder, SVD | xi

Preface by Ilaitia Sevati Tuwere | xiii

Acknowledgments | xv

List of Abbreviations | xvii

Introduction | 1

    Outline | 5

    The Particular Context—Vanuatu | 6

    A Personal Excursus | 12

1. Tracing the Movement of the Contextualization of Theology | 16

    Context-free Western Theology | 16

    The Tide Begins to Turn | 19

    Moving Towards an Agenda of Contextualization | 22

    Adopting the Formal Language of Contextualization | 26

    Is all Theology Contextual? | 40

2. The Contextualization of Theology within the South Pacific | 42

The Beginnings | 42

Six Catalysts for Contextualization within the South Pacific | 44

Two Further Stimuli to the Contextualizing of Theology | 63

The Momentum is Sustained | 68

Summary | 69

3. The Voice of South Pacific Islanders: On the Definition, the Content, and the Methodology of Theology | 70

The Definition of Theology | 72

Summary Comments on the Definition of Theology | 91

The Content of Theology | 92

Summary Comments on the Content of Theology | 115

The Methodology of Theology | 117

Summary Comments on the Methodology of Theology | 141

4. Methodology: The Key to Contextualization: Three Fundamental Issues | 143

Primary Orality | 144

Not Enlightenment | 156

The Separation of Theological College and Local Church Community | 159

5. A Case Study: The *"Gospel and Culture in Vanuatu" Project.* | 163

The Need for the Contextualization of Theology in Vanuatu | 164

The Evolution and the Form of the Experiment—Stage One | 169

The Evolution and the Form of the Experiment—Stage Two | 181

The Evolution and the Form of the Experiment—Stage Three | 216

The Next Stage | 221

New Directions in An Ongoing Case Study | 223

6. Conclusions | 224

Bibliography | 235

Index of Names | 255

Index of Subjects | 257

Illustrations

Map of Vanuatu | xviii

The Ten Drawings of Graham Louhman | 170

Foreword

WHAT A WONDERFUL JOURNEY is charted out for us in *Contextualizing Theology in the South Pacific*! Randall Prior situates himself and us at the beginning of such a pilgrimage at a 1979 conference in New Hebrides (Vanuatu). Around that time of political independence, the local church described itself as having "Two Heads and Two Hearts." They possessed, on the one hand, a colonial mindset with Western cultural presuppositions, and at the same time, their rich traditional Pacific Island culture and life.

I am reminded of my experience of arriving in Papua New Guinea (PNG) a month after its independence, when a catechist asked me, "The government has independence; when will the church gain independence?" He, as a Roman Catholic, was not proposing that PNG have its own pope, but rather that Christianity there needed to shift from being a foreign "import" to being an indigenous local church in its own right.

Prior has provided us with an in-depth and fluid description of such a process within the Pacific Island context with a focus on theology. In the first two chapters, he presents comprehensive reviews of the recent developments in the contextualization of theology in general and in the South Pacific in particular. Prior then gets to the heart of the book in chapter 3 where he invites the reader to listen to the voices of Pacific Islanders regarding their own definition, content and methodology of theology. Prior goes further into the latter often overlooked topic of methodology in chapter 4. Finally, he is able to offer in chapter 5 a very helpful, detailed and insightful case study from Vanuatu, drawing upon his privileged position of having accompanied the local church through its development of a contextual theology over many years, especially through his involvement in the "Gospel and Culture in Vanuatu" project.

After reading Prior's doctoral dissertation as an external examiner, I was hoping that he would be able to share these fruits of his years of experience and theological studies with a wider audience. This rich description of the coming-to-age of Pacific Island contextual theology will be a wonderful resource for theologians and church personnel in Oceania. Furthermore, it provides a conversation partner for doing comparative contextual theology studies—a field that is just opening up—around the world.

As a final point, when I finally had the opportunity to meet Randall Prior for the first time in person over lunch when I happened to be in Melbourne in 2016, I realized more clearly how his studies and writing reflected a life-long commitment to the Christians of the South Pacific and Vanuatu. And he is now inviting us to join him in this journey!

Dr. Roger Schroeder
Louis J. Luzbetak, SVD Professor of Mission and Culture
Catholic Theological Union at Chicago

Preface

IT IS WITH GREAT pleasure that I write this very brief Preface on the very kind invitation of Dr. Randall Gregory Prior the author of this book. And I'm sure I am speaking on behalf of all churches in the region of the South Pacific—its leaders and especially writers, students and theological teachers, to thank Dr. Prior for the publication of his book dealing with contextualizing theology in the South Pacific.

The shape and scope of this academic work is clearly set out in the Introduction and is followed through from beginning to end with integrity. Special reference is made to Vanuatu where the writer has lived and worked for some years. Dr. Prior has obviously worked very hard handling a mass of materials.

The aim of this work as indicated at the beginning is to "explore the contextualization of theology within the distinctive cultures of the South Pacific." In many ways this work is a helpful introduction of the history of the ecumenical movement worldwide, with special reference to the development of contextualization of theology in this region of the South Pacific. It traces the beginning of this global development within the ecumenical movement back in the 1950s and how this has impacted the shape of theology in the context of the South Pacific. For the reader to understand this impact, Dr. Prior has allowed the voices of the South Pacific Islanders themselves to become the basis of this examination. And he has made an acceptable and useful presentation of these voices in this work.

The author has an excellent knowledge of contextualization of theology in general, its beginning and development including the South Pacific with particular reference to Vanuatu. He has relevant research skills and principles and has the ability to engage in independent critical reflection and analysis.

Dr. Prior has indicated quite correctly at the beginning that "while there has been significant progress in the contextualizing of the 'content' of theology in the South Pacific, the 'methodology' of such theology has been given little attention." And he moves on to explain this methodology by prescribing four questions: WHO does theology? WHAT is the primary location for theology? What FORM does it take? What is the PURPOSE of theology? He then moves on to address these questions in chapters 3 and 4 in this work. Chapter 5 specifically addresses the Vanuatu context. The investigation made above by the author of this work is a new development of scholarship in the process of contextualization of theology in the South Pacific. This new development is handled with critical reflection and is useful for future work on doing contextual theology in this part of the world.

Again I must say *vinaka vakalevu,* many thanks for sharing your thoughts and experience about the subject of contextualizing theology in the South Pacific. It has also helped us to better understand the present process of contextualisation both in our own contexts and the rest of the world.

Rev. Dr. Ilaitia Sevati Tuwere
Retired Methodist Pastor & Theological Lecturer in Fiji, the Pacific & Aotearoa-New Zealand after 47 years of service (1970–2017).
Present Address:
41A Baverstock Road, Flatbush, Auckland 2016, New Zealand.

Acknowledgments

IN 1983, AT A time of national euphoria and cultural renaissance in a newly independent Vanuatu, I began a five-year ministry appointment in the indigenous national Presbyterian Church. This ministry landed me in a cultural world dramatically different from my own. I was compelled to become a student of that world and of the church in that world. After departing Vanuatu I remained involved with the church in matters of local theological education, and have returned on countless occasions. The passing of time has served to deepen my appreciation of the culture and to enrich my relationships with the people in this distinctive part of the world. Therefore my primary acknowledgement is to the people of Vanuatu who, for over thirty years now, have lavished me and my family with gracious hospitality and enabled us to find a treasured home among them.

Secondly I owe a huge debt to Lawrence Nemer, SVD, who supervized the dissertation that resources this book. Larry has given his life to the vocation of missiology and is highly regarded in that field. He is a gentle and humble man who has the rare gift of combining graciousness, wisdom and scholarly depth. He has never wavered in his support, encouragement and advice.

The theological community of which I have been a member has also been instrumental in facilitating my research. The Uniting Church Theological College (now Pilgrim Theological College) has been my most immediate theological community since 2003. This community supported my periods of study leave and allowed me to make numerous trips to Vanuatu. The United Faculty of Theology, to which the Uniting Church College belonged until the end of 2014, provided a wonderful collegial

---

community of Jesuit and Anglican scholars who inspired and transformed my research and teaching.

The University of Divinity (previously the Melbourne College of Divinity) has been my sponsoring tertiary institution. I count it a privilege to have done my research under the umbrella of this specialist Australian University.

The Dalton-McCaughey Library, belonging to the Jesuit Province and the Uniting Church in Australia, has been a great scholarly resource. It is reputedly the best library of theology in the Southern Hemisphere. The library staff have gone out of their way to assist me at every point. The libraries of the Yale Divinity School and the Pacific Theological College have also been indispensable to my work.

While it may be routine to offer acknowledgement to family, no-one deserves such appreciation more than my own wife, Heather, and my children, David, Ben and Sophie. Together we made our home in Vanuatu. While they have gained immeasurably from their time in that world, I am aware of the huge costs they have borne.

The comments made and encouragement received by Roger Schroeder, SVD, and Illaitia Sevati Tuwere have been definitive for me. I am deeply grateful to both of these scholars. The academic critiques offered by Ian Weeks and John Flett were instrumental in sharpening my analysis and ideas. I am grateful too for the proof reading done and suggestions made by John Cleghorn and Jo Ellen.

Finally, I offer my sincere thanks to James Krabill and the American Society of Missiology Monograph Series Committee who recommended my work for publication. It is offered in the hope that it makes a genuine contribution to the ongoing challenges to the contextualizing of theology in the South Pacific, and potentially more broadly. I thank the reader for taking the time to consider whether this hope has been accomplished.

Abbreviations

EATWOT	*Ecumenical Association of Third World Theologians*
IMC	*International Missionary Council*
LMS	*London Missionary Society*
MATS	*Melanesian Association of Theological Schools*
MJT	*Melanesian Journal of Theology*
PCC	*Pacific Conference of Churches*
PCV	*Presbyterian Church of Vanuatu*
PJT	*Pacific Journal of Theology*
PTC	*Pacific Theological College*
PTE	*Program on Theological Education*
PWMU	*Presbyterian Women's Missionary Union*
SPATS	*South Pacific Association of Theological Schools*
TEE	*Theological Education by Extension*
TEF	*Theological Education Fund*
WCC	*World Council of Churches*

Map of Vanuatu[1]

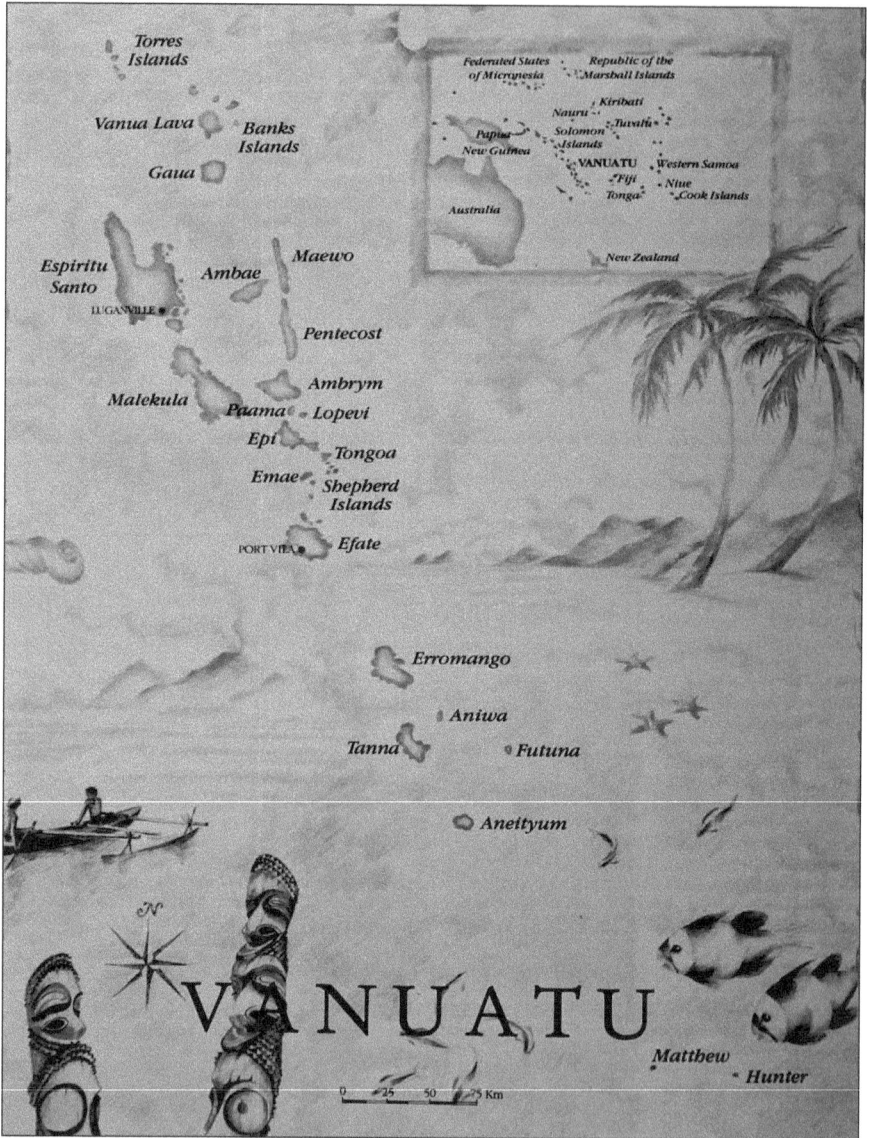

Introduction

In April 1979 in the South Pacific Island nation of the New Hebrides,[1] a two-week workshop on the topic of "Culture and Faith" was held. It was part of a series of such workshops convened around South Pacific Island nations between 1978 and 1983, sponsored jointly by the Australian Council of Churches and the Pacific Conference of Churches, and facilitated by the Rev. Cliff Wright.[2] For the church in the New Hebrides, it came at an historic moment. It was just one year before the declaration of national independence in July 1980, after seventy-four years of joint colonial occupation by Britain and France. The fact that the church and its leaders were the pioneers of the independence movement, and would soon play a definitive role in the post-colonial government, generated a unique atmosphere among workshop participants. There was a strong sense that it was timely for the church to examine closely the relationship between the colonial inheritance of the Christian faith and their own changing local cultural context.

The content of the workshop was mirrored in the sub-title chosen for the final report, "Two Heads and Two Hearts."[3] This title was evocative. It indicated that workshop participants had reached the conclusion that the Christian gospel introduced by the nineteenth century mission movement had been appropriated in such a way that it had not become integrated

1. The New Hebrides is the pre-independent name of the country now known as Vanuatu.

2. Cliff Wright was an ordained minister of the Methodist Church of Australia. Through the 1960s, he was Director of Christian Education for Victoria and Tasmania. In that role he had travelled across the South Pacific as a delegate at various meetings and conventions.

3. Wright, *New Hebridean Culture.*

1

with the cultural context of the lives of the people. In fact, adherence to the Christian faith and embodiment of cultural tradition seemed to exist concurrently, even where there may be clear contradiction between the two. It was as if they formed two parallel lines. For example, people may be paralyzed by the fear of evil spirits, while also speaking of the victory of Jesus over such spirits; people may offer worship to ancestors while also declaring that God alone is worthy of worship; people may make use of black magic as a form of control over others, while also claiming that only God may have such control; people may carry a light when walking after dark, not to illuminate the pathway but to ward off evil spirits, and at the same time confessing that Jesus has rendered evil spirits powerless; people may hoard fetishes in their homes as assurance of personal safety, while also acknowledging that they are safe in the arms of Jesus.

This workshop in the New Hebrides illustrated a reality that was apparent across the whole of the South Pacific: "Most people in the island communities of the Pacific have been torn between two worlds. It is as though in the one head there are two heads, one Christian and one traditional, and in the one heart two hearts with love for both the Christian and custom ways."[4]

This dual reality is by no means unique to South Pacific experience; it is recognized also in other regions of the world.[5] In his landmark publication, Roman Catholic missiologist Robert Schreiter reflects on two quite different theological approaches to mission, one that assumes the pre-existent presence of Christ within a mission situation, and one that suggests that Christ is absent until being brought into that situation by the missionary. With the latter approach Schreiter notes that

> One consistently runs the risk of introducing and maintaining Christianity as an alien body in a culture. The word of God never receives the opportunity to take root and bear fruit. What results in many instances are dual systems of belief, wherein the older system continues alongside Christianity, with each being selectively used by the people as needs arise. This is the case in many parts of Latin America and Africa today.[6]

In dealing more specifically with such situations of duality, he comments,

4. Fugui and Wright, *Christ*, 5.

5. See Bediako, *Jesus*, 51; Sanneh, *Translating*, esp. 157–66.

6. Schreiter, *Constructing Local Theologies*, 39–40.

> In dual systems a people follows the religious practices of two
> distinct systems. The two systems are kept discrete; they can
> operate side by side. . . . Conversion to Christianity has usually
> meant putting all other religious systems aside, but in these in-
> stances significant parts or even the entirety of a second system
> is maintained.[7]

Schreiter is describing precisely the pre-independence reality as
referred to in the 1979 New Hebrides workshop report, and in the more
general situation across the South Pacific Islands as summarized by Fugui
and Wright. The core problem is that the introduction of the Christian faith
from the colonial world into the South Pacific, through the decades of the
missionary era of the nineteenth century, created a situation whereby it was
never integrated into the cultural identity of local communities; in fact it
remained *dis-integrated*. Despite the widespread acceptance of the Christian
message, it failed to take root within the cultural context of the people; it
was never truly incarnate or contextualized.

What is true in relation to the Christian faith, is also true in relation to the evolution of Christian theology within the South Pacific. The
pursuit of Christian theology has been dominated from the beginning by
Western influence and by Western cultural presuppositions. As such it has
remained culturally alien to the South Pacific in both its content and its
methodology. A chorus of voices affirm this viewpoint. By way of example, Feleretika Nokise, in his survey of the fifty-year history of the Pacific
Theological College, remarks that the earliest forms of theological education were established by the missionaries "as a crucial component of the
overall evangelization policy of each mission society." This policy, he says,
was "to serve the imposition of Western civilization and Christianity."[8]
Again, this has been the experience in other areas of the missionized
world beyond the South Pacific.

However in the period following the Second World War there has
been an evolving international reaction in the Third World against such
Western dominance, giving rise to a movement committed to the contextualization of Christian theology across the diversity of non-Western cultures.
This international movement began to impact upon the South Pacific in
the 1960s, was taken up more deliberately during the 1970s, and became
firmly established in the 1980s. Through this period there was a growing
recognition of, and discontentment with, the inadequacies of the inherited
missionary theology, and a corresponding emphasis on the need to localize

---

7 Schreiter, *Constructing Local Theologies*, 145.

8. Nokise and Szesnat, *Oceanic Voyages*, 7–9.

theology within the indigenous context of the people. Over the last four decades that task has been the focus of much attention by theologians and leaders of South Pacific churches.

Nevertheless, despite the serious attention given to the contextualization of theology in the South Pacific, it has been a constant struggle to achieve this goal. This struggle has been due essentially to the persistence and force of the Western cultural presuppositions that were handed down from the missionary era. They have thwarted attempts to contextualize theology and have continued to define the shape of theology. Thus the vision of the 1980s, namely to achieve a contextualization of theology appropriate to the cultures in the South Pacific, and serving the faith and witness of local church communities, remains largely unfulfilled nearly four decades later.

What lies at the root of this ongoing struggle has been a failure to recognize how extreme is the fundamental clash between the categories that define these two different cultural contexts—Western and South Pacific—and what is actually required to achieve a contextualizing of theology, one that is free from the shackles of Western culture, and at home within South Pacific cultures. The struggle has been exacerbated by a further failure to consider adequately the important distinction in theology between matters of content and matters of method—the contextual content of theological discourse on the one hand, and a contextual methodology[9] for doing theology on the other hand. The clash of cultural categories impacts forcefully on both, but more persistently and subtly on a contextual methodology. Only the clear recognition of this reality will provide the key to finding a way through the obstacles to a form of contextualization that is genuinely grounded within the cultures of the South Pacific. Accomplishing this task lies at the heart of this book.

In forging this pathway, I will identify the principal factors internal to the cultures of the South Pacific that clash with the Western cultural and missionary heritage. I will establish that there are three such factors. The first of these is the fact that the cultures of the South Pacific are primary oral cultures and not primary literate cultures.[10] The second is that the cultures of the South Pacific do not share with the Western world a heritage of the era of the

---

9. For the particular approach to methodology in this book, see the explanation given in chapter 3.

10. The term "primary" indicates that a culture is not exclusively either oral or literate. Nevertheless, there are very clear distinctions to be drawn between those that give primacy to orality and those that give primacy to literacy. For a formative work on the differences, see Ong, *Orality and Literacy*.

Enlightenment.[11] The third is inter-connected with the first two, namely the cultural anomaly created by the separation of theology and local church.

All three factors create profound dilemmas for establishing a contextual methodology for theology in the South Pacific. Without such a contextualization, the Christian faith will risk remaining dis-integrated from the culture and life of the South Pacific peoples—"two heads and two hearts."

OUTLINE

In order to provide a coherent background for this work, chapter 1 will trace the evolution of the recent international movement of the contextualization of theology, including the formal adoption of the language of contextualization. The book then moves into chapter 2 for a more focused examination of how this international development, together with other coinciding influences, acted as catalysts for contextualizing of theology to become an inescapable agenda for the theologians and leaders of South Pacific churches.

These first two chapters of the book thus set the foundation for a much closer examination of the distinctive character of the contextualization of theology as it has unfolded within the South Pacific. Chapter 3 then addresses this more specific investigation. This will be done in a particular way, namely by attending to the voices of South Pacific Islanders themselves. Because the self-conscious and focused pursuit of contextualization of theology for the South Pacific is one that is to be determined by the indigenous peoples, it is important to examine how they themselves have experienced and given shape to it. The theological voices are numerous and passionate, and deserve investigation.

In approaching this investigation, I do so under three headings. First, I identify how South Pacific Islanders have defined theology. Secondly, I map the specific content that has been given to this theology. Thirdly, I examine the methodology that has been evident. Although the three elements are intertwined, it is necessary to make a distinction between them in order to provide a more precise understanding of the strengths and limitations of the way in which theology has so far been contextualized within the South Pacific. It also paves the way for identifying the critical issues that lie at the foundation of the ongoing struggle for a more genuine contextualization of theology.

It will be the particular matter of the methodology of theology that emerges as the critical stumbling block to the contextualizing of theology in the South Pacific. The issues that create this stumbling block, and how they

11. For a clear statement of the meaning and impact of the Enlightenment, see Bosch, *Transforming Mission*, 268–79; Newbigin, *Foolishness*, 1–41.

are to be addressed in order to break through the barrier towards a more grounded and sustainable form for contextualizing theology, will then be addressed extensively in chapter 4.

Having established what is required for the development of a contextual methodology, chapter 5 turns to the examination of the case study known as the "Gospel and Culture in Vanuatu" project. The project deliberately sought to address the challenges illuminated so strikingly by the 1979 workshop and to develop a theology that was culturally localized, accessible to and owned by the indigenous people. It is this project that will be examined for its effectiveness in theological methodology, one that is grounded within the cultural context of the people, and one that therefore can be considered as a model for the contextualization of theology.

The final chapter of the book sets out the conclusions for the shape of the contextualization of theology within the oral cultures of the South Pacific, with implications for people of primary oral cultures beyond the South Pacific.

THE PARTICULAR CONTEXT—VANUATU

Vanuatu is located in the South Pacific and comprises eighty-three islands, sixty-six of which are inhabited (see the map of Vanuatu at the beginning of this book). It has a population of a little over 280,000 people.[12] It lies about two thousand kilometers east of northern Australia, and its islands form a Y-shape running about nine hundred kilometers from the Torres Islands in the north to Hunter Island in the south. Its nearest neighbors are New Caledonia four hundred kilometers to the southwest, the Solomon Islands eight hundred kilometers to the northwest, and Fiji eight hundred kilometers to the east.[13]

Among those outside of the Pacific region, very little may be known about Vanuatu. As recently as 2010, thirty years after independence, Vanuatu Prime Minister Edward Natapei is quoted as saying that his country is "not widely known globally. People look at the passport and say 'Vanua-Where'?" He went on to relate that he had been held at airport immigration desks in both South Africa and Japan while his passport was validated.[14] Perhaps the reason for this lack of familiarity is that Vanuatu comprises very small populations of people who are scattered across a vast expanse of tiny islands, whose cultures are oral, and whose level of formal (Western)

12. See "Vanuatu Population."

13. Whyte, Vanuatu, 13.

14. Quoted in NZPA, Dominion Post, August 7, 2010, A13. See Taurakoto, Fighting, 58.

education is limited, all of which means that there is little that is published or publicized for the wider world to read or hear.

This is especially so in the field of theology. Even in those publications that focus in detail upon the Third World, there may be no reference at all to the whole region of the South Pacific within which Vanuatu is located. For example, the publication, *Dictionary of Third World Theologies*, a survey of theologies across the Third World, makes no mention at all of the South Pacific; the nearest it gets is a one page article by Anne Patel-Grey on aboriginal Australia.[15]

Culturally the Pacific is divided very roughly between three defined groups of people—the Micronesians ("little islands"),[16] the Polynesians ("many islands")[17] and the Melanesians ("black islands").[18] Broadly speaking, Vanuatu belongs to the last of these groups. Melanesian cultures are notable for the fact that they comprise small and autonomous tribal communities each with its own language, culture and structure, and without direct inter-connections with any neighboring community; in fact inter-tribal relationships were often marked by conflict.[19] Vanuatu has over one hundred different and distinct languages and cultures, and some six hundred dialects. While there is discernible difference between the numerous cultures within Vanuatu, they are marked by the number and strength of their common features that, taken together, mean that they can be described as if they form a cultural classification.

The name "Vanuatu" in local language is best translated "from the beginning and forever, with God we stand strong on our land."[20] But the land was not always "our land." It was visited in May 1606 by the Spanish explorer Ferdinand de Quiros who, with six Franciscan priests and four monks from the order of St John of God on board, thought they had discovered the Great South Land. Claiming it "for God and for Spain," they called it "Terra Australis del Espiritu Santo" ("The Great South Land of the Holy Spirit"). They

15. Fabella and Sugirtharajah, *Dictionary*.

16. This includes Kiribati, Marshall Islands, the Mariana Islands, Guam, the Federal States of Micronesia, Nauru, and Palau.

17. This includes Tonga, Samoa, American Samoa, Tahiti, Tuvalu, Niue, Cook Islands, Tokelau, parts of Fiji, the Maoris of Aotearoa New Zealand, and Hawaii.

18. This includes Papua New Guinea, West Papua, Solomon Islands, New Caledonia, Vanuatu, and parts of Fiji. Melanesians share great cultural affinity with indigenous Australians.

19. For very helpful summaries of the cultural features of Melanesian peoples, see Chowning, *Introduction*; Whiteman, *Introduction*.

20. This translation is given by Ann Karie, the daughter of Chief Tom Tipoloamata, from the village of Itakoma on the island of Tongoa, who first proposed the name. See Karie, "Leadership of Women," 118.

attempted to establish a settlement but encountered hostilities, and after just one month, they left.

In 1768, French explorer Louis Bougainville arrived in the island group, ritually took possession of it, and named it "Grandes Cyclades," correcting what had been recognized as a false claim made by de Quiros. Just six years later, in 1774, James Cook charted the islands and gave them the name "New Hebrides," the name by which it continued to be known throughout its years under subsequent colonial rule.[21]

Through the nineteenth century, increased exploration led to the arrival of traders out of which grew the notorious "blackbirding era," bringing decades of exploitation and cruelty to local island people. Bonnemaison reports that "an estimated total of nearly 40,000 Vanuatans were involved in the labour trade between 1865 and 1906. About one in four never returned from the great journey."[22]

The New Hebrides was colonized by the British and the French. In 1888, under pressure to do something to protect the local people, they formed a Joint Naval Commission to settle disputes and to control the slave trade. In 1906 they officially established joint colonial rule—a "condominium." This co-colonized collection of dispersed islands and peoples was now gathered formally into a nation called The New Hebrides. Under colonial rule, it became structurally divided when the British and French could not agree on the way in which a united colonization ought to work. They created two systems of education, two health services and two structures of judiciary oversight. This complicated matters among this small population of island peoples, who were forced to link up with one or the other of the two contrasting systems of colonial rule.[23] Adding to this structural division was the further complication created by the fact that the Protestant church missionaries came from English-speaking countries and the Roman Catholic missionaries came from France, so that the Christian traditions lined up with the respective colonial authorities.[24]

Missionaries began to appear in the New Hebrides in the first half of the nineteenth century, originally through the London Missionary Society.[25] In 1839 John Williams, after first visiting the New Hebridean island of Tanna where he left three Samoan teachers, landed on the nearby island of

21. Bonnemaison, *Vanuatu*, 13.

22. Bonnemaison, *Vanuatu*, 16.

23. The complications are represented in the title chosen for the publication by the first indigenous Prime Minister of post-colonial Vanuatu. See Lini, *Beyond Pandemonium*.

24. Bonnemaison, *Vanuatu*, 19.

25. This very early period is covered in Miller, *Live (1)*.

Erromango. By circumstance of his arrival, he and one of his companions, James Harris, were clubbed to death.[26] Through the early 1840s further attempts were made to plant the gospel among the islands, but it was not until the arrival of John Geddie from the Presbyterian Church of Nova Scotia, that the first Christian church was founded. Geddie landed on the tiny southern island of Aneityum in July 1848. Like a lot of missionaries of his era, Geddie was influenced by the revival movements of the early nineteenth century, and was a great enthusiast for the spreading of the Christian faith. He remained on Aneityum from 1848 to 1872. During the first nine years of that time he kept a diary of his missionary life and work.[27]

In appreciating one of the main features of the historical context of Vanuatu at the time of independence, it is important to glimpse something of the presuppositions that formed the missionary theology of Geddie and of his contemporaries in mission. These are well illustrated in the following quotation taken from his diary:

> This is truly one of the dark places of the earth, and all the abominations of heathenism are practised without scruple or remorse. Our hearts are sometimes tempted to say, "Can these dry bones live?" But we know that the gospel must be "preached to every creature," that Christ shall have the heathen for his inheritance and the uttermost parts of the earth for his possession, and that all things are possible with God. May the time to favour this dark island soon arrive. (July 29, 1848)[28]

One week later, on the departure of the boat from which they had disembarked, Geddie spoke of the "stern realities of a missionary life" now that they were "left to ourselves on this dark isle of the sea, cut off from civilized and Christian society. (August 6, 1848)"[29] What is pertinent here is that Geddie made these two diary entries upon the first and ninth days respectively after his arrival on the island. As such, they express not what he discovered following a period of observation, experience and enquiry, but rather the theological and cultural presuppositions that he, and the Protestant mission of that era, brought into their mission work. In terms of the particular relationship between the gospel and the indigenous cultures, the diary entries reflect a clear view held by the missionaries: their

26. Miller, *Misi Gete*, 6–7.

27. The publication by Robert Miller contains a fully edited version of the diary kept by Geddie from the day of his arrival on July 29, 1848 until his last entry on December 11, 1857.

28. Miller, *Misi Gete*, 31.

29. Miller, *Misi Gete*, 31.

own Western culture was "civilized and Christian" while the cultures of the recipient local people represented an extreme form of "heathenism" and were dominated by "powers of darkness." To this domination the people gave themselves blindly and willingly. The preaching of the gospel was then necessary to save the souls of the people from "perdition,"[30] to bring the people out of the darkness and into the light. It is notable that, even today, in ordinary street conversation, the expressions "in the time of darkness" and "when the light came," are frequently used to mark the periods before and after the arrival of the missionaries.

For this era, conversion to Christianity was accompanied and measured by the points of disconnection between their own traditional cultures and those of the newly arrived "civilized and Christian society" embodied by the missionaries. While these very early diary entries are not able to do justice to the fullness of Geddie's mission theology, they do represent one clear expression of the framework of theological thought that he brought to the understanding and practice of mission through his time in the New Hebrides.

It should be noted, however, that this does not automatically imply that Geddie and his Protestant missionary colleagues set out to destroy the traditional cultures in Vanuatu. This view is far too sweeping and simplistic. While acknowledging that his diary entries suggest that "Geddie did indeed fit the popular picture of the imperialistic destroyer of traditional culture," my own research on the impact of Geddie's work on the cultures of the people of Aneityum, led me to "some significant qualifications to this conclusion."[31] A somewhat more nuanced perspective on his theology, taken from his diary entries over more than nine years, is indicated in the following:

> Geddie operated with a set of dualisms: God—Satan, Christian—
> heathen, belief—unbelief, light—darkness, salvation—damna-
> tion, with the missionary being represented by the former and
> the people of the islands and their cultures being represented
> by the latter. Thus, for Geddie, the culture within which people
> lived was ruled by Satan and exhibited all forms of darkness
> and abomination; the mission of the church involved a spiritual
> battle with Satan, calling people to the rejection of this heathen
> culture and the acceptance of the biblical culture of Christianity
> which Geddie himself embodied. Geddie disallowed the pos-
> sibility that the gospel may become incarnate within the culture

30. This expression is taken from Geddie's report which he wrote for the Assembly of the Church in Nova Scotia. Miller, *Misi Gete*, 14.

31. Prior, *Relationship*, 170. For a summary of the negative and positive impacts, see 170–77.

of the people; he assumed that his articulation of the gospel was universally valid, supra-cultural and led to uniform outcomes in personal and cultural life. . . . Geddie understood himself as a servant of the people; as such he displayed genuine humility, a sincere love and deep respect for the people, and was keen not to offend them or their customs unnecessarily. Geddie also did his best to involve his converts in aspects of the church's mission and leadership. This approach to his mission work gained the respect and trust of the people.[32]

This modified perspective is shared by Darrell Whiteman. About the impact of Protestant missionaries in Melanesia, he writes, "A popular but inaccurate notion is that one of the major changes introduced by Christian missionaries has been the destruction of traditional culture. This charge is frequently made, but it is seldom based on a solid foundation of research and understanding of how change has been introduced and how Melanesians have responded."[33]

In terms of the missionary theology of Geddie and his Protestant colleagues, the theological content was contained within the creedal summaries of the faith of the church, which were themselves based on and regulated by the Scriptures. Central to this confession was that God was revealed uniquely in the life, death and resurrection of Jesus, the Savior of the world. The message about him was proclaimed in the power of the Holy Spirit, with the purpose of bringing about the conversion of all people from "darkness" to "light." As indicated in the above excerpt from Geddie's diary, such a conversion would display itself in the convert's rejection of their heathen past, obedience to the teachings of Jesus and the embracing of Christian civilization. This Scripture-based message was considered universal, timeless and supra-cultural.

The Scriptures, as the Word of God, constituted the focus of Geddie's theological methodology. The sharing of the Christian message was done primarily through proclamation and teaching based on the Scriptures. In order to achieve this end, the translation of the Scriptures into the languages of the people was considered a priority.[34] This was accompanied by the

---

32. Prior, *Relationship*, 98–100. More detailed information is provided on pages 71–97. See also Prior, *Founding Missionary*, 52–60.

33. Whiteman, *Introduction*, 96.

34. Lamin Sanneh, exploring the impact of mission in Africa, identifies the translation of the Scriptures into the vernacular languages of the people to have been fundamental in enabling the Christian faith, subsequently, to establish its own distinctive roots within the local cultural context. He notes that this was not the motivation behind the missionary action but rather an unexpected result of it. See Sanneh, *Translating*, 157–90.

teaching of people to read, thereby making the written Scriptures accessible to the people in literary form. Important too was that the missionary develop a relationship of trust so that the heathen were then open to respond to the message of salvation, to be saved from damnation, to be baptized, and to become part of the church community.

This content and methodology of Protestant missionary theology provided the clear and strong heritage that shaped the Protestant churches in the New Hebrides as they came through the subsequent decades of colonial control. However, in the latter period of colonialism, especially from the late 1960s, the prospect of national independence among New Hebrideans was to set the scene for profound political and cultural changes. These changes, together with the coinciding international movement of the contextualization of theology, acted as the catalyst towards a more culturally grounded and locally authorized theology. In particular, they provided the momentum for the birth of the "Gospel and Culture in Vanuatu" project.

A PERSONAL EXCURSUS

I arrived into this new cultural, political, and ecclesial climate in January 1983, just over two years following Vanuatu's independence, and found myself—almost unconsciously—swept up into the movement raised by the question, "What is the relationship between the gospel and the local cultures of the people of Vanuatu?" Another way of expressing this same challenge is to put the question, "What does it mean for the church to move from the heritage of a Western missionary theology to a theology that is appropriately contextual?" This was, at the time, already an emerging question in international theological circles and in the wider context of Pacific Island churches.

If I was not already aware, on my arrival, of the changing ecclesial and theological climate in this newly independent nation of Vanuatu, it was not long before I was to find out. At the occasion of my induction into the parish, one of the more senior pastors of the Presbyterian Church, himself among the pioneers of independence and elected into the first independent Government of Vanuatu, gave a speech. "We want you to remember, Randall, that you are here by our invitation, you are to work in the Melanesian Way, and your appointment will be reviewed annually."[35]

In order to respond to the challenge appropriately, I had to learn the language of Bislama, and learn about the cultures of the people, so that my ministry was exercised in a way that was embedded in the context of the church and the people. Over a period of time, I became more and more

35. Sunday, February 13, 1983 in Prior, *Diary 1*.

familiar with the local language and cultures, with the local way of thinking, acting, doing, communicating and living.

Much of this learning, I owe to Pastor Fiama Rakau with whom I worked in partnership from the beginning of my ministry in Vanuatu. From the southern island of Futuna, Rakau had a background of secondary school teaching before going into ministry. Following his local theological studies, he completed a degree in theology at the Pacific Theological College in Suva in 1982. He returned to Vanuatu and took up his first appointment in the parish of Vila in January 1983; we were inducted into ministry at the same time. He was a most astute and thoughtful young man in his early thirties, and deeply formed by, and informed about his own traditional culture. He was like-minded in his commitment to engage actively with the issues of Gospel and Culture. We met every Tuesday morning over a period of three years. We spent the time together preparing the worship for the following Sunday. Our focus was on the Scripture readings and their message, and how that message engaged with the cultural context of the local people. It proved to be a very rich learning process in exploring the relationship between the gospel and Vanuatu cultures—for both of us. As I later recorded in the Preface to the first publication in the "Gospel and Culture" series: "I acknowledge my dear friend and colleague in Vanuatu, Fiama Rakau, who shares a similar passion for issues of Gospel and Culture, and who has taught me so much."[36] Rakau himself writes, "In our meetings to prepare the Scripture readings for the Sunday, each week we had to wrestle with the issue of the Gospel and Culture: how do we apply the Word of God in a changing culture to a people who look both to their culture and to their God for their survival and their livelihood?"[37]

With this growing familiarity with local issues of "Gospel and Culture," I came to realize that all aspects of ministry, as I had understood and conducted them, had to be relearned. Even the gospel itself had to be newly understood in a contextually located way.[38] While superficially and institutionally, the life of the church and its people was recognizable to me, the mode in which these operated was not. Cultural presuppositions and cultural practices defined all things, and there was nothing about the nature of the church and the exercise of ministry that was untouched by these presuppositions and practices. This included leadership, worship, prayer,

36. Prior, *Founding Missionary*, 3.

37. Prior, *Founding Missionary*, viii.

38. This discovery is now recognized to be the norm for missionary experience; witness, for example, the story of Vincent Donovan, for whom not only the practice of ministry but also the understanding of the Christian faith underwent profound change. See Donovan, *Christianity Rediscovered*.

preaching, singing, teaching and learning, rituals of baptism and eucharist, dynamics of meetings, modes of communication, and pastoral ministry. In fulfilling my own role of leadership, I became more and more aware of the need to engage with the local church, its pastors, its leaders, and its people, in the issues of "Gospel and Culture." I found myself not only leading studies on topics that dealt with the encounter between the gospel and the local cultures, but attempting to do this in such a way that the methods of communication were culturally informed. At a much later stage, it became clear to me that, whatever the topic of engagement, the methodology pursued in relation to the topic seemed to be the key to effective contextual communication with local people.

My own journey in "Gospel and Culture" in Vanuatu was given significant energy and opportunity after my departure from Vanuatu. The demands of ministry in Vanuatu, and the challenges of the context, left me with a deep yearning to do some serious reflection on what I had experienced. I spent one year at Selly Oak Colleges in Birmingham, UK, completing the Diploma of Mission Studies. The choice to go to Selly Oak Colleges in Birmingham was influenced by the fact that this was becoming the hub of the "Gospel and Our Culture" (GOC) movement in the United Kingdom. The Colleges were located near the retirement home of Lesslie Newbigin, and in the year that I was in College (1987–88), the GOC movement was at its height, with its administrative base in Selly Oak.[39] Lesslie Newbigin had been the intellectual catalyst for the formal foundation of the movement. He had made a name for himself by "throwing down the gauntlet"[40] to the churches in the (post-Enlightenment) Western world. He challenged their profound cultural captivity, forecast the irretrievable disintegration of the era of Christendom, and questioned the possibility that the Christian church might any longer be able to engage in effective mission within the very society that for so long had assumed itself to be Christian.[41] Beginning with "an invitation to the British Churches to a more forthright missionary encounter with contemporary British culture,"[42] Newbigin raised the more general question, "What would be involved in a missionary encounter between the gospel and this whole way of perceiving, thinking, and living that we call 'modern Western

39. Notably, Newbigin's significant publications on Gospel and Culture became available in 1983, 1986, and 1989. See Newbigin, *Other Side of 1984; Foolishness; Gospel.*

40. Hunsberger, *Newbigin Gauntlet*, 394.

41. See comments about Newbigin's contribution in Gelder and Zscheile, *Missional Church*, 38–39. see also Newbigin, *Can the West Be Converted?*

42. Newbigin, *Foolishness*, iv.

culture'?" The abbreviated and more confronting version of this question became "Can the West be Converted?"[43]

This missiological pursuit defined the climate of my time at Selly Oak Colleges. My own pressing questions and experience in Gospel and Culture, provided by the period of my involvement in Vanuatu, was sufficient reason for me to become immersed in the same pursuit. If I was not already convinced that "Gospel and Culture," and its complementary theme of the "Contextualization of Theology," was evolving as a major issue of Christian mission for the whole world, I left Selly Oak Colleges thoroughly convinced that this was so, and that my own vocation was to be shaped irretrievably by it.

---

43. Newbigin, *Foolishness*, 1; *Can the West Be Converted?*, 2.

1

Tracing the Movement of the Contextualization of Theology

HAVING SET THE INTRODUCTORY framework and foundations of this book, it is important now to trace the international movement of the contextualization of theology. It is this movement that has not only had a remarkable impact on the evolution of Christian theology over the last two generations, but relevant to this book, the struggles involved in this movement have left their own deep imprint on the evolution of theology in the South Pacific.

CONTEXT-FREE WESTERN THEOLOGY

In 1889, the Student Volunteer Movement in the United States adopted the now famous dictum, "the evangelization of the world in this generation,"[1] and at the turn of the century in Western missionary circles, "the mood in both church and state was forward-looking in terms of progress and expansion, with a triumphant expectation that this would be 'the Christian century.'"[2] For some, this was a scientifically calculated expectation. In the year 1900, Norwegian Missionary Society General Secretary, Lars Dahle, made a mathematical prediction, based on the previous one hundred years of statistics, that "by 1990, the entire human race would be won for the Christian faith."[3]

The first international missionary conference was held during this same momentous period, in Edinburgh in 1910. Missiologist Gerald Anderson

1. Robert, "Origin," 148.
2. Anderson, "American Protestants," 101.
3. Bosch, *Transforming Mission*, 6.

describes it as "the milestone event" in Christian mission, which came at a time of high enthusiasm in the missionary endeavor, and the missionary obligation was considered a self-evident axiom to be obeyed, not to be questioned. Edinburgh was primarily concerned with strategy, consultation, and cooperation to complete the task of evangelizing the world; the Great Commission of Christ was the only basis needed for missions.[4]

Two prominent international leaders in Christian mission, Robert Speer and John Mott, spoke at the opening and closing occasions respectively. Speer offered a challenge to all members to anticipate "the immediate conquest of the world," while Mott concluded the assembly with the declaration that "the end of the conference is the beginning of the conquest."[5] This whole era was marked by a particular form of globalization, the purpose of which was to "extend the message of the Christ and His church through the whole world."[6]

It was an era marked also by a specific approach to theology, one that Schreiter has called "theology as sure knowledge"[7], accompanied by an assumption that this form of theology was universal, supra-cultural and context-free. Most especially through the nineteenth and twentieth centuries, it was this form and this assumption that "dominated the theological scene."[8] It became the normative view of theology, so that "when people think of theology, they think of this kind of theology."[9]

Increasingly, commentators on the history of Christian mission and its accompanying Christian theology endorse this viewpoint. David Bosch speaks of the period of missionary expansion through the nineteenth century, leading into the twentieth, as being fanned by the combination of Enlightenment categories and the 18th century revival movements ("awakenings"). It was these that nurtured missionary fervor, first in America, and then in Europe. In particular, he describes the period 1800–1950 as the "era of non-contextualization"[10] in both Protestant and Roman Catholic mission.

---

4. Anderson, "American Protestants," 104.

5. Anderson, "American Protestants," 104.

6. Schreiter, "Contextuation," 80. See the coverage of meetings of the IMC at Whitby in 1947 and at Willingen in 1952 as summarized in Anderson, *American Protestants,* 108–9.

7. Schreiter, *Constructing Local Theologies*, 88.

8. Schreiter, *Constructing Local Theologies*, 88.

9. Schreiter, *Constructing Local Theologies*, 88.

10. Hiebert, "Critical Contextuation," 104. Hiebert refers to the approach taken by Protestant missionaries in India and later in Africa and their assumption that "there is nothing in non-Christian culture on which the Christian missionary can build and, therefore, every aspect of the traditional non-Christian culture had to be destroyed."

In each case, theology (singular) had been defined once and for all and now simply had to be "indigenized" in Third World cultures, without, however, surrendering any of its essence. Western theology had universal validity, not least since it was the dominant theology. The Christian faith was based on eternal, unalterable truth, which had already been stated in its final form, for instance in ecclesiastical confessions and policies.[11]

Bosch records that for "the father of nineteenth century Protestant missiology," Gustav Warneck, Christian mission was founded on both monotheism and the "Great Commission" (Matthew 28:18–20). It operated on four assumptions; first, of the absoluteness and superiority of the Christian religion; secondly, its universal acceptability; thirdly, its superior achievements in mission fields; fourthly, its superior strength over against all other religions.[12]

In accord with Bosch, in his foundational work on "Gospel and Culture," Lesslie Newbigin describes the era of Western missionary expansion in the eighteenth and nineteenth centuries as the era, not of context-free theology, but of "false contextualization."[13] Newbigin considered that during this era, missionaries assumed that their own distinctive cultural approach to theology and the gospel was culture-free, able to be applied to any and every culture, and essentially having the same outward appearance in all cultures. Rightly or wrongly, this, he said, became the heritage and perception of the Third World recipients of much of Western missionary activity through this era.[14]

Another important commentator on this topic is the Jesuit missiologist, Peter Schineller, who notes the growing awareness of the fact that the missionary expansion of the Christian faith, from the Western to the non-Western world, has been accompanied by "the myth of superiority of Western European culture," and the transplanting of Western Christianity into foreign soil, "showing little respect and often disdain, for traditional local cultures."[15]

As illustrated in the diary entries of John Geddie, and affirmed in recent times by indigenous leaders of the church, that same thinking dominated Protestant mission work in the New Hebrides from its beginnings in the nineteenth century. "It is very sad to look back over the history of the church on Tanna and realize that from the beginning in 1839, and

11. Bosch, *Transforming Mission*, 437.

12. Bosch, *Transforming Mission*, 5.

13. Newbigin, *Gospel*, 141.

14. Newbigin, *Gospel*, 141–42.

15. Schineller, *Handbook*, 11.

for a very long time afterwards, the approach of the Western missionaries towards our culture was one of rejection. They operated within and promoted their own culture."[16]

It was the assumptions about the validity and authority of Western culture, with its particular forms of Christianity and Christian theology that led to an uncritical imposition onto cultures and contexts around the world. As a recipient of this imperial approach to mission, widely travelled Japanese theologian Kosuke Koyama comments, "World Christianity has been busy, particularly in the last 150 years, learning Western theology." Koyama then illustrates the domination of Western theology and Western theologians across the Third World by declaring,

> If one wants to be theologically educated, whatever one's ethnic and cultural background, one must study theologies of the West. Hence, Anselm, Aquinas, Luther, Calvin, Schleiermacher, Barth, Niebuhr, and a host of other figures and events in the Western theological world have been diligently studied in Calcutta, Tokyo, Djakarta, Suva, Harare, Freetown, Lima, Sao Paulo, and Buenos Aires.[17]

To become Christian in the non-Western world meant "to be circumcised into Westerners first."[18] For female theologian and South African, Marilyn Naidoo, to do theology in the non-Western world meant to be "fed on a diet of pre-packed theologies, ethical systems and pastoral methods all imported from the West."[19]

Any understanding of the subsequent eruption of contextual theologies through the latter half of the twentieth century requires an appreciation of how keenly felt was this background that led into the first half of the twentieth century. It had been a period of self-confident Western colonial and missionary expansion in partnership with the uncritical imposition of Western theology across the colonized world. It reached its zenith at the turn of the twentieth century, a century that at the 1910 Edinburgh conference, was expected to be "the Christian century."

THE TIDE BEGINS TO TURN

However, far from being "the Christian century," the twentieth century witnessed a remarkable turnaround in the situation of the church and mission.

16. Prior, *Voice of the Local Church*, 17.

17. Koyama, "Theological Education," 91.

18. Tutu, "Whither Theological Education," 269.

19. Naidoo, "Ministerial Training," 349.

The various forces that had come together to produce a triumphalist and expanding Western Christian church, with the associated assumption of a universal context-free Christian theology, began to dissolve. It resulted in a dramatically different environment that, at the start of the twentieth century, could not have been forecast. Such was the nature, pace and impact of these unexpected changes that it was spoken of in terms of "a crisis which affects the entire church, indeed the entire world."[20] The era of Western colonial imperialism and Western ecclesial expansion was being replaced by an era that was marked by the rejection of Western dominance, a mood of post-colonial self-determination, and the reclaiming of indigenous cultural identities. While not all scholars shared this view,[21] already by the middle of the twentieth century it was becoming apparent that the "Vasco da Gama epoch" of Western expansion had come to an end.[22] It was the termination of "nearly sixteen centuries of official Christianity in the Western world."[23]

It is difficult to describe adequately the dramatic nature of this collapse and the profound consequences for the churches in the Western world. To speak of this as "a major transition is to indulge in understatement."[24] In the framework of Bosch's construction of mission history and theology, it constitutes the ending of an old, and the ushering in of a new, "paradigmatic era."[25] The principal manifestations of the changes provide a telling summary of the breadth and depth of this "world crisis." Bosch notes that "the advance of science and technology . . . have made faith in God redundant" so that the Western world is "slowly but steadily being de-Christianised," with vast numbers leaving the church; there is growing awareness of the complicity of the church in colonial "subjugation and exploitation of peoples of color"; the West has now become "a mission-field, in the grip of atheism, secularism, unbelief and superstition"; at the same time, it is now much more pluralistic with people of other faiths whose devotees are "more actively and aggressively missionary than the members of the Christian churches"; the impact of all this is that the few in the West who remain Christian have lost

---

20. Bosch, *Transforming Mission*, 3.

21. Latourette, writing in 1944, affirms the universal content of the Christian faith and is optimistic about its ever-progressive global expansion within and beyond the Western world. See especially the conclusions to his seven volumes in Latourette, *History*, 7:483–505.

22. Anderson, "American Protestants," 108–9. See also Anderson, "Church and Mission."

23. Hall, *End of Christendom*, ix.

24. Hall, *End of Christendom*, 1.

25. What Bosch terms "The Postmodern Paradigm." Bosch, *Transforming Mission*, 357–71.

confidence in their faith. At the same time Western theology has become "suspect in many parts of the world. It is often regarded as irrelevant, speculative, and the product of ivory tower institutions."[26]

While changes in the Western world have been dramatic and redefining, the same has been true in relation to the changes taking place across the Third World, most especially in Asia and Africa. Over forty nations within these two continents gained their political independence through the generation following 1945. This brought also a fundamental change in the dynamics of the relationship between the Western world and the Third World. Bosch declares, "For centuries, Western theology and Western ecclesial ways and practices were normative and undisputed, also in the 'mission fields.' Today the situation is fundamentally different. The younger churches refuse to be dictated to and are putting a high premium on their 'autonomy.'"[27] Desmond Tutu comments out of the African experience,

> The outstanding feature, of course, of the second half of the twentieth century has been the emergence of the Third World as a reality not to be ignored. Africa has participated in this exhilarating movement characterised by the fairly rapid decolonisation of the African Continent through the creation of independent states in which the inhabitants have exercised their inalienable right to political self-determination . . . Africa has exploded into the twentieth century.[28]

In company with the changes sweeping across the Western and Third Worlds, there has a remarkable shift in the statistical makeup of the global Christian world. It is now widely acknowledged that numerically, the global center of the Christian faith lies no longer in the North (i.e., Europe and America) but in the South (in Africa, Asia, Latin America and the Pacific), and most particularly in Africa.[29] Gambian missiologist, Lamin Sanneh, documents the fact that between 1900 and 2005, the numbers of Christians in Africa grew from nine million to over 390 million—measuring now around 50 percent of the African population.[30] Further figures provided by the Centre for the Study of Global Christianity indicate that in 1910, 66 percent of all Christians lived in Europe and 2 percent in Africa, while a century later, in 2010, 25.6 percent of Christians lived in Europe and 22 percent in Africa. In the same period of one hundred years, the percentage of all Christians in the

26. Bosch, *Transforming Mission*, 3–4.
27. Bosch, *Transforming Mission*, 4.
28. Tutu, "Whither Theological Education," 268.
29. Robert, *Christian Mission*; Sanneh, *Disciples of All Nations*.
30. Sanneh, *Disciples of All Nations*, xx.

North has decreased from 80 percent to 40 percent, with the corresponding change in the South up from 20 to 60 percent.[31]

The sheer weight of these numbers illustrates the dramatic nature of the shift in the Christian world, and the changing balance in ecclesial vitality, resources, and decision-making. Schreiter notes that "the dramatic growth of the Christian community in Latin America, Africa, Asia, and Oceania during the twentieth century was already evident at the Second Vatican Council where, for the first time, a significant proportion of the world's Roman Catholic Bishops were coming from outside the North Atlantic community."[32]

All of this forms part of the evidence to support the view that what has been happening, in this past century of church history, constitutes a cosmic shift, away from one era, into a very different one. It is as if "the world itself is in revolution."[33] It has created a situation where the notion of a single context-free, universal theology is being permanently dislodged, and replaced by a diversity of what are being called "contextual theologies," evolving from the notion that all theology is contextual. It is important to trace this evolution in more detail before exploring its particular impact in the South Pacific.

MOVING TOWARDS AN AGENDA OF CONTEXTUALIZATION

The changing global circumstances in the first half of the twentieth century created the environment for shaking the foundations of what had assumed the status of a universal and supra-cultural Christian theology. In particular theological leaders across the Third World were awakened to the importance of taking seriously their own unique situations. "The shift in perspective, concentrating on the role that circumstances play in shaping one's response to the gospel, first became evident in regions where Christianity was relatively new. It started coming to the world's attention in the 1950s in parts of Africa and Asia."[34] It led to a situation where "there must be a radical decolonisation in cultural and spiritual matters as there has been in

---

31. Johnson and Ross, *Atlas*. Updates to 2010 were provided at the Edinburgh conference and documented, for example, in Werner, "Theological Education," 5.

32. Schreiter, *Constructing Local Theologies*, xi. The same was also becoming evident in meetings of the IMC in 1938, 1947, and 1952. See also Schreiter, "Mission and Church."

33. Coe, "Theological Education," 6.

34. Schreiter, *Constructing Local Theologies*, 1.

the political."[35] This African call from Tutu was matched by the Asian voice of Koyama, for whom, across the whole of Asia, awareness was being raised that the "theology of the West should not be transplanted wholesale to the East. The Christian faith should be presented in relation to the totality of questions raised by the local situation, and it should not be assumed that certain questions are relevant to all times and situations."[36]

Of outstanding relevance was the pressing demand upon the church to confront the fast-developing issues of oppression and injustice that were a daily threat to people's lives in so many of these regions of the world. "The burning question for Christians must be: What is Christian ministry in terms of movements against oppression, or struggles for full, human development?"[37] In reference to the political upheavals across Asia, Shoki Coe (using his Taiwanese name Chang Hui Hwang) writes,

> If there is one area which is exerting a violent pressure in the lands of new nations and upon the younger churches, it is the area of rapid social change. . . . To call it a rapid social change seems almost too mild a term. . . . It is not a matter of the church confronting rapid social change. The church is being confronted.[38]

For Oduyoye in Ghana, these challenging social concerns were not merely social or political in character; they were essentially theological at root. As such they demanded a theological response, one that takes up "resistance against evil and death" in a situation where "blacks, women, and the poor have discovered that the oppressive forces that seek to control their lives, whether cultural or ecclesiastical, are demonic and must be exorcised."[39]

Inevitably, this rapidly changing mood across the Third World began to have its impact also upon the mission-inherited institutions of theological education, the official centers of theological pursuit. "The key question has become: How can Third World theological education discover and develop forms of theological training and ministry authentic to particular cultural contexts within Asia, Africa and Latin America?"[40] South African

35. Tutu, "Whither Theological Education," 271.

36. Koyama, "Theological Education," 93. Here Koyama is reporting on a statement from the Conference on Theological Education in Southeast Asia, held in Bangkok in 1956.

37. TEF, "Theological Curriculum," 143.

38. Hwang, "Rethinking," 31.

39. Oduyoye, "Contextuation," 119.

40. Bergquist, "Theological Education Fund," 246.

theologian Marilyn Naidoo comments, with a hint of cynicism, that "it is entirely possible that Christianity in the West may have overemphasised formal education because it yields curricula insensitive to contextual needs of Africa, curricula that produce decontextualized thinkers and theologians." She laments the fact that "the curriculum in African theological institutions does not include more relevant courses," referring specifically to "socio-economic development, African biblical and cultural hermeneutics, gender and theology, peace building and ecumenical studies."[41] Tutu echoes the same sentiments in pleading for a locally grounded theological education. Only if theological education addresses the local context can the outcome be "a theology that is authentically African" because "we shall be compelled to give expression to the deep things of our faith not in alien terms and thought forms but in ones that are truly African."[42]

The uncritical adoption of Western theology had also led to perplexing problems of elitism in the local churches. Local theological institutions were producing people for whom "ordination was the gateway to a cadre of the elite whose chief characteristic was an authoritarian attitude."[43] Western structures of theological education "succeeded in isolating the discipline for elitist study that was not seen as relevant except to give preachers occasion for showing off before their captive audiences."[44]

The growing disaffection included not only the curriculum content, but also the very structures of theological institutions and their pedagogy, one key aspect of which was the relationship between classroom learning and the practice of ministry. The lack of integration between "theory and practice" and between "academic and practical" was felt to be anachronistic, creating "an apparently unbridgeable dichotomy between what happens in the lecture room and what happens outside it."[45] It prompted Tutu to declare, "What a topsy-turvy set of values we seem to have! We set so much store by classroom education that we fail to prepare our students properly for what will after all be their major tasks—practical pastoral work. We have idolized academic performance and forgotten that pragmatic criteria are also standards of excellence."[46]

Speaking out of the very different situation of Latin America during a period that was giving birth to theologies of liberation, Aharon Sapsezian

41. Naidoo, "Ministerial Training," 359.

42. Tutu, "Whither Theological Education," 272.

43. Tutu, "Whither Theological Education," 270.

44. Oduyoye, "Contextuation," 113.

45. Tutu, "Whither Theological Education," 270–71.

46. Tutu, "Whither Theological Education," 270–71.

discerns that what was needed for theology to recover its true purpose in that environment was nothing less than "the liberation of theology." Aware of the profound influence across Latin America, through the 1960s, of Paulo Freire's work in the field of education,[47] he writes of a growing awareness that "without a liberation of theology there could not be a theology of liberation."[48] What was at stake was the authenticity of the Christian church, which "could hardly be of service to the promotion of man's emancipation, unless a fundamental change in theological outlook took place." There was a mood of "dissatisfaction regarding scholastic theology, the theology that had an elaborate and balanced answer to every human problem, produced by experts and perpetrated in the institutional churches."[49]

There was one further catalyst in the growing desire to break free from a dominant Western theological and ecclesial agenda, and to focus attention onto the local context. It was the emergence in the Third World of forms of local Christian community life that were alien in style to those in the Western world. These were being treated with condescension or disdain by Western mission churches. The impression was given that churches in the Western world simply could not recognized the validity of anything outside of their own cultural frame of normality. Such was the extent of this problem that Schreiter identifies it as one of the three primary concerns that prompted churches across the Third World to begin to turn their backs on the Western missionary churches.[50] He describes it as "an attitude that was perceived by the local people to be one of paternalism with no real interest in understanding or appreciating their local context."[51] This experience was well illustrated in the extra-mission emergence of the independent churches of Africa. Oduyoye notes,

> The earlier manifestations of these were "break-aways" from Western churches in Africa. The late nineteenth century versions were the result of racism and ethnocentrism of the missions of the period that would not see anything good in Africa. The mission theologies simply ignored them, or else labelled them syncretistic and not worthy of the name Christian.[52]

47. Freire's best known work was published in Portuguese in 1968, first made available in English in 1970. See Freire, *Pedagogy*. See also Freire, *Education*.

48. Sapsezian, "Theology of Liberation," 256.

49. Sapsezian, "Theology of Liberation," 256.

50. Schreiter, *Constructing Local Theologies*, 2–3.

51. Schreiter, *Constructing Local Theologies*, 3.

52. Oduyoye, "Contextuation as a Dynamic," 117.

In a summary of the situation, Bergquist identifies what he refers to as the "five crises" of theological education in the Third World during this time: i) a failure to engage adequately with "the radically politicised situations" of the Third World; ii) an inappropriate ("unwholesomely elitist") pattern of ministry; iii) an unsuitable pedagogy (which "equated excellence with Western standards of academic theology"); iv) a heavy financial dependence on the churches in the West ("propping up the status quo); v) an inauthentic theology (largely uncritical acceptance of "North Atlantic Theology" as if this theology is universal).[53]

The combination of these various concerns across vast regions of the Third World fanned the flames for the development of an approach to theology that was embedded in the uniqueness of local situations and that was able to equip the local churches to engage more appropriately with those situations. The term that would soon be adopted to satisfy this demand, and to describe this theology, was to be the word "contextualization."

ADOPTING THE FORMAL LANGUAGE
OF CONTEXTUALIZATION

As a way of reflecting upon the actual adoption and promotion of the new language of contextualization, I will offer comment on four particular contributions, each of which has significance in its own way. The first two relate directly to the emergence of the specific language of "contextualization" within the Third World, and for that reason are given lengthier attention; the second two offer a particular contribution and perspective from the Western world.

Shoki Coe[54]

The official adoption and explanation of the language of "contextualization" are largely attributed to one individual, Shoki Coe. On the missiological legacy of Coe, Ray Wheeler comments,

> When he stepped up to the podium at a 1972 World Council of Churches consultation to present his paper on contextualization, he roiled the pond of missiological thinking. How did this man of small frame, athletic build, and a deep sense of destiny

---

53. Bergquist, "TEF and the Uncertain Future," 250.

54. An account of the development of the language of contextualization and the role of Shoki Coe are documented in the account given in Lienemann-Perrin, *Training.* See also Wheeler, "Legacy."

come to conceptualize a wave that continues to reverberate through mission circles well beyond his death in 1988?[55]

While it is too much to claim that Coe bears singular credit for the formal adoption of this word into the language for theology,[56] certainly there is evidence to endorse the assertion that he was "one of those responsible for the coining of the term."[57] His own circumstances of personal life and ministry vocation meant that the notion of "context" had come to have personal relevance before he gave it more prominent public expression as a vital element in the approach to theology.

Coe was born in Taiwan in 1914 and given the name Chang Hui Hwang; he died in England in 1988. From 1934–37 he studied philosophy at Tokyo Imperial University, he spent the ten years until 1947 in England, pursuing theological studies in Birmingham and then in Cambridge before teaching within the School of Oriental Studies in London University. He returned to Taiwan in 1947, following the turbulent years of the war, and after a short period of teaching at a boys' school, he was appointed by the Presbyterian Church of Taiwan as Principal of the newly re-opened Tainan Theological College, a position he held from 1949 until 1965.[58]

The fundamental importance of context for theology came to Coe after leaving his homeland of Taiwan in 1937, when "the Asia I travelled through was still in a colonial context," returning ten years later, when Taiwan was in a state of political upheaval, and when across Asia, "new independent nations were coming into being, one after another."[59] After his unexpected appointment as Principal of the Tainan Theological College, he suddenly found himself faced with the challenge of providing theological leadership in a post-war environment of socio-political unrest, the struggle for national independence, and the search for an authentic Christian identity.[60]

---

55. Wheeler, "Legacy of Shoki Coe," 77.

56. Ross Kinsler, a prominent contributor in the work of the Theological Education Fund and its successor bodies, attributes the introduction of the term "contextualization," in 1972, to Coe's colleague, Aharon Sapsezian, from whom "it spread rapidly throughout ecumenical and evangelical circles." See Kinsler, "Relevance and Importance," 2.

57. Lienemann-Perrin, *Training* 63.

58. Wheeler, "Legacy," 77–79. Coe's advocacy for the independence of Taiwan led finally to his exile to England.

59. Coe, "In Search of Renewal," 233–34.

60. The socio-political upheaval over the years from 1895 through to the 1950s is well summarized in Lienemann-Perrin, *Training*, 36–43. For the way this impacted personally on Coe, see Wheeler, "Legacy," 77–78.

Beginning as he only knew how at the time, he set the goal of "upgrading the school from more or less Bible-school level to something comparable to what I had experienced in the West."[61] In other words, he applied Western parameters for theology and theological education into his own local context. While this initial goal brought some significant outcomes,[62] it was radically redefined over his years as principal, subsequently setting him on a journey towards the notion of contextualization. This happened in part through his growing awareness of the distinctive challenges facing the churches in post-colonial Taiwan. But in partnership with this, and more important, was Coe's emerging involvement with the Theological Education Fund (TEF) of the International Missionary Council (IMC). It is this influential ecumenical organization, of which he was later to become Director, to which Coe himself attributes the formal adoption and explanation of the interconnected terms "contextuality" and "contextualization." In fact, it is not too much to claim that the influence of Coe on the TEF, and reciprocally, the influence of the TEF on Coe, combined to bring about this historic outcome. The way in which this happened needs some brief description as it came to define the parameters of this new terminology.

The work of the TEF over the twenty years from 1957–77 was separated into three separate "Mandate" periods, the first from 1958–65, the second from 1965–70, the third from 1970–77. A major review was conducted between each stage. During the first period, Coe's own college in Taiwan was a major beneficiary of financial support. It was through this contact that Coe himself was now coming into direct contact with others around the Third World who were engaged in issues comparable to those being faced in Taiwan. As a result, his own horizons were expanding.[63]

While still principal, Coe was invited to be a team member for the review of the First Mandate period. In fact, he was given the key responsibility for working out the theological outlines for the next period. At the request of the advisory group, he wrote a paper which was later published.[64] The evaluation process was thorough, involving widespread consultations and discussions over a two-year period from 1961–63.[65] This undoubtedly raised his profile and deepened his involvement with theological educators across the Third World, as well as demanding of him deeper reflection about

61. Coe, "In Search of Renewal," 234.

62. Coe, "In Search of Renewal," 235.

63. Hwang, "Rethinking," 7.

64. Hwang, "Rethinking," 7–24.

65. Lienemann-Perrin, noting the importance of this period in reshaping the directions of the TEF, devotes forty pages to the evaluation. See Lienemann-Perrin, *Training*, 82–122.

the theological challenges being faced in the Third World. The conclusion to the review established "how strongly people in ecumenical circles were still oriented to the Western form of academic ministerial training."[66] The ongoing creation of a "theological elite" raised serious challenges for the local churches, faced with their own socio-economic contexts of poverty, injustice and oppression.[67] Coe comments that, "Many of us in Asia were becoming increasingly uneasy and restless."[68]

As a result, the Second Mandate period of the TEF, which was now influenced by Coe's theological work, took greater account of the socio-political and cultural contexts of the recipient churches, and their need for a more genuinely indigenous theological education.[69] The focus of theological education was now to be directed towards the challenge of equipping the church and its ministry to witness to the *Missio Dei* in their own distinctive socio-political and cultural contexts.[70] The urgent task of the church was "to be a community of the first fruits, participating in the rigorous task of nation building."[71]

The notion of excellence in theological education was now re-focused, from academic criteria to a formational student-centered engagement with local context. This was accompanied also by a shift in the understanding of theology itself, its content and its methodology. Lienemann-Perrin notes that across Asia, "theologians testify increasingly to their turning away from North Atlantic academic theology because they themselves replace academic theology with theological action."[72] Referring to a range of theological voices at the time, she notes the appearance of various terminologies to describe this fundamental shift. "What some call 'theology in action,' others call 'doing theology,' 'experimental theology' or 'primary theology.'"[73]

A turning point was coming. Coe acknowledges, "In these years of search for renewal, I had become more and more convinced that theological education, for better or for worse, occurs invariably as interaction between text and context, and out of this interaction the form is shaped."[74] Coe speaks

---

66. Lienemann-Perrin, *Training*, 122.

67. Lienemann-Perrin, *Training*, 126.

68. Coe, "In Search of Renewal," 235.

69. Lienemann-Perrin, *Training*, 114.

70. Coe, "In Search of Renewal," 236.

71. Coe, "In Search of Renewal," 236.

72. Lienemann-Perrin, *Training*, 166.

73. Lienemann-Perrin, *Training*, 166.

74. Coe, "In Search of Renewal," 237. In 1966, he gave the keynote address on theological education to the inaugural meeting of the North East Asia Association of Theological Schools. It was later published as Coe, "Text and Context."

of the notion of a "double wrestle" to explain this further, "wrestling with the Text from which all texts are derived and to which they point, in order to be faithful to it in the context; and wrestling with the context in which the reality of the Text is at work, in order to be relevant to it. This 'double wrestle' may involve what I call 'textual-cum-contextual criticism.'"[75]

The question was how to address and resolve this wrestling. This question was not Coe's alone. The then Director of the TEF, Dr. James Hopewell, was himself critical of the failures of this second period to engage adequately with the question of what constitutes a relevant form of ministry and ministry training in the Third World.[76] By the end of the Second Mandate in 1970 and during the period of review leading into the next period, the quest became the primary focus for the TEF.

It was at this particular stage that the language of contextualization became formally and publicly adopted. In Coe's own words, "It was in struggling with this question during the study period required by the Third Mandate that we came upon the two words *contextuality* and *contextualization* as the way towards reform in theological education."[77] One could also add, "and as the way towards reform in theology," for this was its corresponding agenda; the approach to theological education and the approach to theology were fundamentally interwoven. Significantly, in relation to the mutual influences of Coe and the TEF in the adoption of the two words, Coe comments, "I feel that in a way they were the culmination of a long process of historical development, both in the TEF itself, and, speaking for myself, in the personal pilgrimage as a theological educator from Asia."[78]

Coe was careful to explain the intention of these new terms, particularly to distinguish them from the terminology previously used by the TEF until that time, namely "indigenization." For Coe, the value of the word "indigenization" was that it took seriously the cultural realities of the people, but it was inclined to be past-oriented, not giving adequate recognition to the radical changes impacting on these traditional cultural realities, especially since 1945. "So in using the word *contextualization,* we try to convey all that is implied in the familiar term *indigenization,* yet seek to press beyond for a more dynamic concept which is open to change and which is also future-oriented."[79]

75. Coe, "In Search of Renewal," 238.

76. See Lienemann-Perrin, *Training,* 137–38.

77. Coe, "In Search of Renewal," 239.

78. Coe, "In Search of Renewal," 240.

79. Coe, "In Search of Renewal," 241.

By way of further explanation, Coe was aware of the need to address particular challenges now emerging from the theologians of the West. The first of these was that the "contextualization of theology" would lead to theology becoming "chameleon theology, changing according to the contexts."[80] In response to the challenge, Coe explained that the word "contextuality" is to be understood not in terms of privileging the context over the text, but on the contrary, it brings the context under the scrutiny of the text. It requires "assessing the peculiarity of the context in the light of the mission of the church as it is called to participate in the *Missio Dei*."[81]

Understood in this way "authentic contextuality leads to contextualization," and "indicates a new way of theologizing" that integrates both words and actions. As such, for Coe, it overcomes the dangers inherent in the Western dichotomies of theory and practice, action and reflection, the classroom and the street. Notably, because this theology involves "an ongoing process, fitting for a pilgrim people," the terminology used is carefully chosen; it is deliberately not "contextual theology" nor "contextualized theology" but "contextualizing theology."[82]

The further challenge from Western theologians was that such a contextualizing approach to theology might be seen to be undermining the catholicity of the gospel, dissecting theology into a myriad of idiosyncratic, fragmented contextual theologies, unaccountable beyond themselves. In response, Coe makes reference to the event of the incarnation of the Word "as the divine form of contextualization," a deeply rooted and particular contextuality through which the very catholicity of the gospel is manifest.[83] There can be no such thing as a "utopian theology," free of any specific context. Therefore, he asserts that not only is contextualization a missiological necessity, but so also is it a theological necessity. The theological task, he says, "should be through our responsive contextualization, taking our concrete, local contexts seriously."[84] The nature of a genuine catholicity, "could not be a colorless uniformity, but must be a rich fullness of truth and grace, which unfolds and manifests itself as we take the diversified contexts in time and space, where we are set, and respond faithfully as the Incarnate Word did on our behalf, once and for all."[85].

80. Coe, "In Search of Renewal," 241.

81. Coe, "In Search of Renewal," 241.

82. Coe, "In Search of Renewal," 242.

83. Coe, "In Search of Renewal," 242.

84. Coe, "In Search of Renewal," 242.

85. Coe, "In Search of Renewal," 242–43.

At this point, it is worth noting that somewhat ironically, it was the broadening of the agenda of contextualization "beyond indigenisation," that was later to lead, in the South Pacific at least, to the neglect of the essential role played by "cultural realities" in the contextualization process. As will become clear, this neglect has greatly impaired the development of effective contextualization in the South Pacific. The cultural realities remain an essential ingredient in the ongoing process of contextualization, alongside the socio-political or other issues that define the context.[86]

Two Definitive Publications of the TEF

Subsequent to Coe's passionate advocacy, the notion of contextualization came to be "the key concept of the Third TEF Mandate."[87] Through the TEF, it was formally promoted across the Third World, and beyond, as the most authentic approach to both theological education and to the theological task.

Appointed in 1970 as the General Director of the TEF, and now with responsibility for the implementation of The Third Mandate from 1970–77, Coe, with the TEF staff, began to disseminate the foundational ideas that were to inform the next era. Together they were responsible for producing two defining publications by the TEF: "Mission in Context" and "Learning in Context." These two publications were directed to "the Two-Thirds World" churches. They were targeted at re-shaping the processes of theology and the nature of theological education in emerging non-Western communities, urging them to take seriously their own context in the process of developing local leaders for their churches. It was through these two publications that the notion of the contextualization of theology spread rapidly, and subsequently became normative across the Third World.

The 1972 publication, "Mission in Context," announced to all that "contextualization" was now to be the "central issue" that needed to be addressed in theological education in the Third World.[88] The document then describes what it calls "four marks" of responsible contextualization: missiological contextualization (with the aim of renewal and reform of the local churches and engagement with particular local issues of development and justice), structural contextualization (appropriate to the cultural, social, economic and political situation), theological contextualization (doing theology in such a way that it relates the gospel to urgent issues both within and beyond the cultural context), and pedagogical contextualization (forms of theologi-

---

86. See chapters 3 and 4 for issues of contextualization in the South Pacific.

87. Lienemann-Perrin, *Training*, 174.

88. TEF, *Ministry in Context*, 31.

cal education that avoid the dangers of elitism and authoritarianism, that merge the academic and practical, and that display the educational process as liberating and creative).[89]

These "four marks" provide a definitive summary of what was envisaged by the notion of contextualization in terms of both theological education and the overall theological process. It seems clear in this four-pronged description that its purpose was two-fold: to address the broad range of dilemmas inherited from the era of Western ecclesial and theological colonialism, and to ground the theological task of the church within the local context. The "missiological" dimension ensures that the goal of theology is to equip the local church community for mission, thus overcoming the dilemma created by the disjunction between theology and local church. The "structural" dimension seeks to address the sense of alienation between the "culture," mirrored in the institutions of theological education, and the situation experienced by the local people. Among these would be the problems associated with theology's association with a "privileged elite" in situations marked by profound poverty and oppression. The "theological" dimension addresses the failure of theology to be relevant to the major issues affecting the people, and unable to reflect upon them or speak into them. The "pedagogical" dimension indicates that the theological task demands a learning methodology that integrates classroom learning and street life, overcoming the dilemma of producing a-contextual church leaders who pursue theological pathways that are alien to context and that distance theology from life.

Because of the critical importance of the "pedagogical dimension" of contextualization within the South Pacific, and the way this impacts upon the methodology of theology, it is worth noting that, in this initial TEF statement, there is no suggestion that the pedagogy is in any way to be shaped by the modes of learning unique to the cultures of those who are in the community of learning. Contextual methodology seems focused on the integration of theological learning and the socio-political dimensions of the context, the integration of theory and practice. It ignores or overlooks the critical role of culture-specific modes of learning. It is important therefore to explore further how this first TEF staff paper attends to the particular question of the methodology of the theological task.

Only one chapter, "Theological Curriculum and Teaching Methodology," is given to the topic of methodology in this first publication. It acknowledges that "the need for improved teaching methods and pedagogical approaches is widely felt throughout the world."[90] Promisingly, the paper asks,

---

89. TEF, *Ministry in Context*, 31.
90. TEF, *Ministry in Context*, 77.

"Where and how does one do theology?" Critical of the Western approach that prioritizes the classroom lecture as the primary pedagogical method, the paper announces that the TEF will be offering its resources in support of those projects "of pedagogical significance." By this it means those centers that address "ways of developing better methods of teaching and communication," and that explore "the deeper pedagogical issues now at stake in theological education."[91] These deeper issues include giving attention to "the teacher/learner relationship, an orientation of education more clearly toward liberation and mission, and an understanding of education as a dialogical process in response to the nature of the gospel itself as a Word addressed to people in their particular socio-cultural situations."[92]

In this way, the paper illuminates the importance of contextualization in the pedagogy of the learning of theology. In particular, in addressing the perplexing dilemma of "elitism," it asserts that a genuine contextualization of theology "involves a stance of commitment toward the integrity of the learner and his creative possibilities within his own situation, no matter how unschooled or non-academic he might be."[93]

While this and a number of other issues are addressed in the paper, it is significant that here too no deliberate attention is given to the question of culturally contextual modes of learning. For example, there seems to be no apparent awareness of the important distinction between modes of learning appropriate to primary literate cultures (for example Western cultures) and those appropriate to primary oral cultures (for example tribal African cultures). It will be shown later that this distinction is a fundamental element for the contextualization of theology in the South Pacific.

The urgency of a contextual learning methodology for the theological task in the Third Word was represented more obviously in the second of the two formative publications of the TEF, "Learning in Context." The publication's subtitle, "Innovative Patterns of Theological Education," was the theme that was also chosen for the 1973 annual meeting of the TEF Committee. It includes six case studies in theological education, each of which addresses the challenges of a contextual methodology.

The models offered from the six selected contexts come from both the Western world (the United Kingdom, the United States and Germany) and the Third World (Asia, Latin America and the South Pacific). What they have in common is recognition of the inherited problems created by a preoccupation in theological education institutions with academic studies in isolation

91. TEF, *Ministry in Context*, 78.
92. TEF, *Ministry in Context*, 78.
93. TEF, *Ministry in Context*, 79.

from the context of church life and ministry. Predictably, therefore, the peda-gogical focus is either on explorations of a revised curriculum or on initiatives that seek to integrate theory and practice, classroom and context.

Notably, as for the single paper in the earlier publication, there is little specific attention given to distinctive elements of learning that might be de-termined by cultural factors. In particular, the distinction between suitable methodologies in oral cultures compared with those appropriate to literate cultures is not addressed.

The most evocative case study and partial exception to this observation are offered by Ross Kinsler. While working as a missionary in Guatemala, Kinsler was instrumental in setting up the first experiment in Theological Education by Extension (TEE). This became important as a model that was later taken up with enthusiasm in many other parts of the world.[94] Like many people in Latin America at the time, Kinsler was influenced by the educational philosophy of Paulo Freire. He came to the view that the prac-ticed methodology of education in the school system reinforces "a pattern of oppression all the way from kindergarten through university."[95] He was persuaded by Freire's "radical critique" of such an education system and Freire's methodology of "conscientisation."[96]

Through this new "conscientisation" lens, Kinsler viewed with serious concern the common approach to theological education as it existed across the Third World. He observes that teaching staff have been "scholars beyond criticism" and "purveyors of sacred truths," "unencumbered with method-ological concerns." The curriculum, requiring the completion of a number of courses of "pre-packaged information," is imposed on the student body primarily through lectures. He sees this as a methodology that is domesti-cating and irrelevant.[97]

According to Kinsler, the innovations of a methodology of conscienti-sation produce encouraging outcomes. The result is "a high level of motiva-tion," and a focus, not on the student's need "to memorise notes," but "to get on with the job."[98] In this way, explains Kinsler, theological study contributes to "the basic formation of Christian leaders"; it helps the students "to perfect their gifts and be recognised for what they are and for what they do."[99]

94. Kinsler, "Extension," 27–39.

95. Kinsler, "Extension," 35.

96. Kinsler, "Extension," 36–7.

97. Kinsler, "Extension," 37.

98. Kinsler, "Extension," 38.

99. Kinsler, "Extension," 39.

The differences in methodology that seem evident in TEE are that "the students take only as many courses as they want, and they can choose the ones they want," that the learning process is geographically dispersed into local situations, that study of the course material is integrated with "living issues," and that "teachers and students meet as colleagues in the work of the church, sharing content and experience and learning together."[100] In these ways, the TEE approach offers valuable ways of tackling some of the core problems of the theological task in the context of the Third World.

However, there seem to be two important limitations in the TEE methodology as explained by Kinsler. First, he seems to assume a form of learning that remains literacy-based, or at least requires a level of literacy competence and academic capability. There is no specific attention given to the importance of an oral-based methodology, despite the fact that he is in a context where "the most important learning processes occur in oral teaching."[101] It may well be that, in practice, the structures of TEE do allow scope for oral-based learning. This may explain why the program extended "with astonishing speed in Latin America, Asia and Africa,"[102] where oral-based learning is preferred to literacy-based learning. However, the failure to pay deliberate attention to the importance of this, means that the alternative methodology offered by TEE remains inadequate.

What also seems absent in Kinsler's explanation is any recognition that the local communities of the church are communities of theology. His focus remains on those who are designated to be theological leaders. In this sense too, the TEE process appears to give inadequate attention to one of the fundamental dilemmas of the churches of the Third World, namely the separation of the actual theological task from the life of the local church community.

The final section of this publication from the TEF contains two working papers prepared by the TEF staff. It is the first of these where some attention is given to the issues of methodology in theological education.[103] However, there is again little recognition given to the issues of a methodology that might be culturally relevant. In fact, at one point, the paper seems to maintain certain cultural presuppositions of the West, namely the individual's capacity to think critically. It asserts that "what is often lacking is the emphasis to develop the ability for critical thinking, to learn to analyse and interpret,

---

100. Kinsler, "Extension," 38.

101. Lienemann-Perrin, *Training*, 197.

102. Lienemann-Perrin, *Training*, 197.

103. TEF, "Theological Curriculum."

to relate and apply."[104] As was the case with Kinsler's approach in TEE, there is no recognition of the distinction between oral and literate communities, and how this may impact on "theological learning."

Overall, however, the energetic attention given by the TEF to the critical importance of contextualization for the theological task is undoubted. Indeed, as a result of the work of the TEF, "contextualization" was formally recognized as the prescriptive word for every aspect of the theological and missiological task of Third World churches. Lienemann-Perrin, in her retrospective account of the history and impact of the TEF, asserts that it was through the period of the Third Mandate of the TEF from 1970 until 1977, under the leadership of Shoki Coe, that "the term 'contextualization' came to be used as a common theological expression in the Younger Churches."[105]

James Burtness and Paul Lehmann—Two Voices from the West

At the same time as the formal adoption of this terminology was developing in the Third World, and perhaps as a corollary of those developments, there was, appearing on the Western cultural and academic agenda, a growing awareness of the importance of "context" as a key element in diverse academic disciplines, including theology.[106] James Burtness, Professor of Systematic Theology at Luther Theological Seminary in Minneapolis, writing about the cultural situation in the United States in the early 1970s, notes, "One of the big words of our time is 'context' . . . this word 'context' so gathers up various themes and attitudes of our time that if the word did not exist it would have to be invented."[107] He suggests that this focus on context results from fundamental shifts in the Western world that have accompanied the post-Enlightenment era. "It points to the demise of absolutes and the embracing of relativities, whether in physics or theology or politics. . . . 'Context' is a word that fits naturally with such phrases as 'theory of relativity,' 'scientific method,' 'situation ethics,' 'statistical probabilities.' It is a very modern word and a very modern emphasis."[108] In this

104. TEF, "Theological Curriculum," 150.

105. Lienemann-Perrin, *Training*, 176.

106. Recognition of the important role of context was not new in Western thought. Scholars such as Adolf von Harnack, Friedrich Schleiermacher, and Albrecht Ritschl are among important contributors to changing theological approaches to contextual issues of their time. Much later, Bultmann's schema for "demythologizing" and Tillich's "correlation" approach constitute further attempts to take account of the importance of context as a key element of theologizing. The exploration here is focused on application of the specific language of contexualization to the theological task.

107. Burtness, "Innovation," 9.

108. Burtness, "Innovation," 10.

sense, Burtness acknowledges the lengthy and complex historical processes that have given rise to the situation in the Western world where "context" is now such a "big word."

For Burtness, "an emphasis on 'context' insists that there is no such thing as a naked text, that there is always something 'with' the text."[109] Because what goes "with the text" consists of a wide range of possible variables, there is always a task of identifying and arranging any description of the "context." "The setting of a text in context (the contextualization of the text) always requires a decision," says Burtness.[110] When it comes to the learning of theology, he continues, "Theological Education has to do with equipping Christians to make appropriate (to say 'correct' or 'true' would ignore precisely that relativity upon which 'context' insists) decisions about the text and the context of the Christian commitment."[111] It is notable that as a systematic theologian in the Western world, Burtness credits the TEF with pioneering and promoting the notion of the contextualization of theology. "Thus one can only applaud the TEF for seizing the word 'context' to describe its Third Mandate and for bringing to a wide audience the notion of contextualization."[112] However, in the way in which Burtness makes use of the term "context," it embraces a very much wider network of potential meanings than those that shaped the approach of the TEF. For Burtness too, there is no attention given to the culture-specific modes of learning that may be important in the overall theological task of contextualization.

Another theologian in the Western world, who, as early as the 1960s, was beginning to give serious attention to the notion of "context" for theology, was Paul Lehmann, Professor of Systematic Theology at Union Theological Seminary in New York. The fact that Lehmann was writing as an academic theologian within the Western cultural world, and within the world of formal theological education, makes his 1966 essay, "On Doing Theology: A Contextual Possibility," particularly significant.

Invited to contribute to a publication with the title, "Prospect for Theology," Lehmann explores the challenges involved in the task of "doing theology," at what he recognizes to be a turbulent time in the theological world. It is a time marked by "a conspicuous lack of consensus" about the methodology of theology.[113] In his proposal about what it means to "do theology," Lehmann brings together two basic elements. The first is the fact that God continues to act formatively and concretely in contemporary human life (that is, within particular contexts). The second is that the purpose of theology is

109. Burtness, "Innovation," 10.
110. Burtness, "Innovation," 10.
111. Burtness, "Innovation," 10.
112. Burtness, "Innovation," 10.
113. Lehmann, "On Doing Theology," 122.

to respond to, and to describe, this reality. This leads him to the "prospect for theology" being "contextual." He writes, "The method by which theology exhibits both its specific content and its positivistic occasion and significance is contextual. As a theological method, contextualism may be said to be that way of doing theology which seeks to explore and exhibit the dialectical relation between the content and the setting of theology."[114]

It is pertinent that Lehmann's attention is focused on the method of doing systematic theology within the Western world. He calls for a theology that overcomes both the inherited "abstract intellectualism of scholasticism," and the risk of "anthropomorphising theology." Lehmann's prophetic plea is for a "contextual method" that breaks away from the "unfruitful dichotomies," for example, between theology and culture, faith and ethics, that plague the theological task.[115] In this sense, Lehmann addresses one of the major dilemmas facing the church of his time, the separation of "academic" and "practical." His proposed method "concentrates attention upon the dynamic and dialectical relation between the phenomenological and the referential aspects of the theological tasks."[116] The "phenomenological" refers to the "empirical reality of the Christian community" as it lives out of the past and open to the future, while the "referential" refers to the heritage of theological tradition represented in confessional, liturgical and doctrinal language.[117]

In proposing this methodology, Lehmann forecasts a theology that will integrate present experience with tradition. Further, it will relocate theology and the theological task within the ongoing life of the Christian community. "The promise of such a contextual theology may be that as it seeks to be faithful to its confessional, dialogical and catalytic character, it may become the bearer in our human situation today of the answer to man's profoundest need and question . . . to express his genuine humanity."[118]

Like Burtness, Lehmann also provides broad scope for the parameters that may be applied to the word "context." This would need to be defined more precisely in any particular "contextualism" of theology. Nevertheless his contribution, coming as early as the middle of the 1960s, gives to him something of a pioneering role in the development of the language of theology as contextual. In his impressive survey, Paul Matheny remarks that it was Lehmann who "helped to catalyse the discussion in the academy at about the same time as the proposal of the TEF and Shoki Coe," and "may

114. Lehmann, "On Doing Theology," 131.
115. Lehmann, "On Doing Theology," 133.
116. Lehmann, "On Doing Theology," 133.
117. Lehmann, "On Doing Theology," 134.
118. Lehmann, "On Doing Theology," 136.

have been one of the most influential theologians to address the concretisation of theology."[119]

However, as noted in relation to the other contributors to the notion of contextualization, there is no attention given by Lehmann to any culture-specific elements of the methodology.

IS ALL THEOLOGY CONTEXTUAL?

The dramatic changes taking place through the twentieth century, and the impact of these changes on the understanding and practice of theology, have led to the burgeoning of contextual theologies around the world, and to the increasingly widespread recognition that theology has always been, and will always be, contextual. As Bevans comments, "A study of the history of theology will reveal that every authentic theology has been very much rooted in a particular context in some implicit or real way."[120] By the time he writes his book on "Models of Contextual Theology" in 2002, such is the increasing acceptance of the contextuality of theology that he begins, "There is no such thing as 'theology'; there is only contextual theology. The contextualization of theology—the attempt to understand Christian faith in terms of a particular context—is really a theological imperative. As we have come to understand theology today, it is a process that is part of the very nature of theology itself."[121]

For some scholars, that "all theology is contextual" seems now to be so widely acknowledged that the claim is described as a cliché.[122] However, this is overstating the case. We remain in a period of transition from one paradigmatic era to the next. Certainly, one of the most significant features of this transition is the way in which Christian theology is to be understood and the way in which the theological task is to be engaged. As the previous era had been marked by a theology that claimed universal and context-free validity, so the emerging era is witnessing the birth of a plurality of particular theologies for which the context is understood to be integral in prescribing that theology. Equally, while the previous era had been marked by a theology whose content was defined by objective information and doctrinal confession ("theology as sure knowledge"), so the emerging era is witnessing the notion of theology whose content must be far more integrated with context, and including a commitment to action and social change.

---

119. Matheny, *Contextual Theology*, 64.

120. Bevans, *Models*, 7.

121. Bevans, *Models*, 3.

122. Havea, "Cons of Contextuality," 40.

In that sense, there is newness about the recent emergence of the phenomenon of contextual theology. "Contextual theology understands theology in a new way,"[123] writes Bevans, who adds, "We are not just adding context as a third element (to Scripture and tradition), *we are changing the whole equation*" (his emphasis).[124]

Doubtless, a significant progression is taking place, with one eventual consequence that all theology will come to be understood as forms of contextualization, and all theologians will acknowledge themselves to be theologians in context. While this process continues, the tensions between the previous and the emerging eras remain. These tensions find their greatest expression in the actual methodology of theology, and in the way in which "cultural realities" prescribe the contextual task. It is this tension that has been and remains the most challenging issue for the contextualization of theology in the South Pacific.

The above account of the contextualization of theology, its evolution through the twentieth century, and the issues that it seeks to address, all form the backdrop to the emerging theology within the particular context of the South Pacific. As remarked, what is significant in the developments that have taken place, is the apparent omission of the way in which culture-specific parameters shape the content and the methodology of contextualization. This is represented, for example, in the lack of attention given to the important distinctions between oral cultures and literate cultures. The overall impression is that the notion of "contextualization," rather than embracing also the ideas previously included in the notion of "indigenization" (as intended by the TEF), has re-directed the primary attention of theology to social and political challenges, especially in the Third World. While there is every reason to engage with these contextual challenges, culturally distinctive elements of context seem to have been suppressed.

In the South Pacific it is these latter elements that hold the key to a more effective contextualization of theology, irrespective of what else may be defined as that context. In other words, to be effective, the contextualization of theology in relation to socio-political issues cannot overlook the culturally distinctive features that define the very peoples involved in that theological task. The contextualization experiment represented by the "Gospel and Culture in Vanuatu" project is an attempt to respond directly to the challenges and questions posed by the distinctive parameters of the cultures of the South Pacific. Before looking more closely at this particular case study, it is important to explore the ways in which the broad global movement of contextualization has taken root within the South Pacific, and how this has influenced the indigenous approach to the contextualization of theology.

123. Bevans, *Models*, 5.
124. Bevans, *Models*, 5.

2

The Contextualization of Theology within the South Pacific

THE BEGINNINGS

IN IDENTIFYING THE FIRST indications of contextualizing theology within the South Pacific, Dr. Sione 'A. Havea, the man sometimes referred to as "the father of contextualization in the Pacific,"[1] brings to mind a particular event in 1976, which for him marks "perhaps a starting point which led our thoughts to go beyond the Pacific Christ as a picture to Pacific Theology as a theme."[2] He writes,

> My thoughts go back to January 1976 at Port Moresby when the then Governor General, Sir John Guise, challenged the Pacific Conference of Churches Third Assembly with the question whether the time had come that we look to a Pacific Christ: instead of a figure with white face and firm lips with blue eyes, that we start to visualize a figure with brown eyes and fussy-wuzzy hair.[3]

Havea considered the 1986 consultation on the topic "Pacific Theology," the first of its kind, as an important step in the process of responding to that call made a decade earlier. It was the occasion on which he reiterated the same call, "pressing upon all theologians of the Pacific to take up seriously this moving towards a Pacific theology."[4]

1. Palu, "On Pacific Theology," 33. See also Palu, "Dr. Sione 'Amanaki Havea."
2. See Havea, "Foreword," 7.
3. Havea, "Foreword," 7.
4. Havea, "Foreword," 7.

Indigenous Kiribati historian Kambati Uriam advocates for an earlier origin for the contextualizing of theology. Uriam's voice is authoritative within the South Pacific. After some years of teaching in theological institutions including as Assistant Principal at the Pacific Theological College, he became a lecturer in History at the University of the South Pacific. His doctoral thesis is unique in the material it covers.[5] He surveys theological education in the period which includes the earlier stages of the contextualization of theology, and so his work is relevant. Importantly, he is one of very few local voices to offer such an informed historical perspective. Although he identifies the Assembly of the Pacific Conference of Churches held in Tonga in 1981 as a "watershed" in the search for a theology within the South Pacific,[6] he dates the beginnings of that search back to the 1960s. For him, the 1961 gathering of Pacific churches and missions in Samoa, followed up immediately by the consultation on "Theological Education in the Pacific" held in Fiji, already show clear evidence of the desire to localize theological education and to encourage local theological leadership. The establishment of the Pacific Theological College and the Pacific Conference of Churches through this period is a decisive symbolic move away from colonial influence, and towards the contextualizing of theology in the South Pacific. "The hope is that this College will not only provide careful and exact training in Biblical and Theological studies, but that the type of training will be such as to make these studies deeply relevant to the changing social conditions of the Pacific world."[7]

Bringing both Havea and Uriam together, it is safe to suggest that, in the South Pacific, the 1960s were significant years in providing the momentum for what, in following decades, emerged as a focused agenda for the contextualizing of theology. It was on the back of the 1960s that "the end of the 1970s and especially in the 1980s saw a growing proliferation of Island theologies."[8]

What was it about the 1960s that gave birth to the conscious contextualizing of theology in the South Pacific? What were the key factors that led to this emergence and stimulated the subsequent proliferation of Island theologies? These fundamental questions need to be explored further if we are to understand the directions taken in the contextualizing of theology within this particular region of the world.

5. Uriam, "Theology and Practice." A significant portion of his thesis was edited and published in 2005. See Uriam, "Doing Theology," 287–311.

6. Uriam, "Theology and Practice," 135.

7. TEF, "Theological Education," 15

8. Uriam, "Theology and Practice." See the opening page of his thesis preceding the contents.

SIX CATALYSTS FOR CONTEXTUALIZATION WITHIN THE SOUTH PACIFIC

1. Globalization and the "New Pacific"

The movement to contextualize theology within the South Pacific did not occur in isolation from what was already happening in the global context. Indeed, this impetus in the South Pacific could not have occurred apart from the powerful wave of contextualization that, through the period from 1945, was impacting upon the Third World countries of Asia, Africa and Latin America, and correspondingly, upon the Western world. The South Pacific was not immune from its impact.

Reflecting something of this, Uriam claims that it was the Second World War that was the key event in initiating a global disturbance that subsequently set the region of the South Pacific on its own pathway to change.[9] He explains that this was the period when warfare, human suffering, and threats to the survival of the world, prompted questions and doubts about the Western world view, about the Western model of Christendom, and about the theological heritage of the missionary era:

> Following the Second World War, how could one continue to think in terms of power and glory as demanded by the "Christendom mould," now that we know that power could be destructive to our world; and how could one continue to think in terms of expansion and growth when many people are getting swallowed up by the greed of others; perhaps, there is a better theological position to look at reality and life than from the vantage point of the "Christian kingdom."[10]

It should not be forgotten too that many island nations of the South Pacific were caught up in the events of this war, prompting the local islanders to become more alert to the way in which major events, from beyond their region, impacted upon their own remote, dispersed and sparsely populated island communities. The United States used the islands of the New Hebrides as a war base against the Japanese, and a New Hebrides Defence Force was established. Miller comments, "The advent of World War II threw everything into confusion . . . the thunder clap of war on their doorstep, the sight of planes overhead, the massive troop movements."[11]

The particular and dramatic developments that took place in Africa, Asia and Latin America through the middle years of the twentieth century

9. Uriam, "Theology and Practice," 23.

10. Uriam, "Theology and Practice," 50.

11. Miller, *Live*, 6:206.

are then parallelled in the experience and agenda of the South Pacific nations and churches: a changing socio-political context, a re-claiming of local identity, a growing critique of the hitherto assumed supremacy of Western theology and Western culture, and the redefinition of the nature and purpose of theology.

The most comprehensive evidence of the impact of this is provided in the voluminous 2006 publication, edited by Manfred Ernst, who was then one of the Faculty members of the Pacific Theological College.[12] The material contained in this substantial work is the result of five years of research across the Pacific Islands. Its primary focus is on the way the global changes that have taken place through the twentieth century, have profoundly "reshaped Christianity in the Pacific Islands."[13] While noting that the nineteenth century arrival of the Christian faith in the Pacific was itself fused with one particularly powerful form of cultural and socio-political globalization,[14] the force of the book is to indicate that the latest wave of globalization, that which has been a mark of the era following the Second World War, has profoundly redefined the whole of the Pacific context, and not least its religious profile. It "has led to an ongoing reshaping of the religious landscape in the different Pacific Island nations; the changes in religious affiliation have also led to an unprecedented diversity of Christian denominations in the region."[15] At the same time, there has been an emerging influx of religious groups representing faiths other than Christian. This change in religious profile has gone hand in hand with the rapid development of urbanization, the conquest of the Pacific by a capitalist market economy, and a technological and communications revolution bringing world-views and lifestyles, not hitherto known, into the region.[16] The outcome has been so far-reaching that it has forged what might be described as "a new Pacific."[17]

As a result, the traditional churches have found themselves seriously challenged, even if they remain prone to continue to live by certain "myths" of

---

12. Over 860 pages with a thoroughly documented bibliography and index. Ernst, *Globalization*.

13. Ernst, *Globalization*. See my own review of the book in Prior, Review of *Globalization*, 104–5.

14. Ernst, *Globalization*, 3, esp. 694.

15. Ernst, *Globalization*, 4.

16. Ernst, *Globalization*, 49.

17. Uriam, "Theology and Practice." Note the full title of Uriam's thesis. For a detailed description, see esp. Uriam, "Theology and Practice," 1–21.

their own success and influence.[18] They have been compelled to re-think the nature and content of both theological education and theology.[19]

For Uriam, the actual development towards the contextualization of theology in the South Pacific was, more than anything else, a necessary product of these changes and challenges that came to the Pacific from exterior influence. In the introductory page to his dissertation, he writes about the period from 1947–97, "The agenda for action for most Churches was drawn up for them by secular society. . . . For the churches to be truly relevant in the Islands many Church leaders and theologians found it necessary to contextualize their faith."[20]

Given what is said below about other significant catalysts, this claim is overstated, but certainly these global changes played an integral part in helping to establish the early momentum for the contextualizing task. Uriam notes the agenda of the Fourth General Assembly of the Pacific Conference of Churches, held in Tonga in 1981, an agenda that included such issues as nuclear testing, militarism, colonialism and decolonization, international trade, powerlessness, women's rights, racial discrimination, sectarianism, the impact of other faiths, education, and challenges to family life. In response, he rightly comments, "It is obvious from this list that the agenda was written by the 'world'; the Church was no longer in total control. Either she follows the agenda written for her and adapts herself to the changing times, or she remains within her 'walls' and becomes obsolete."[21]

2. The Global Ecumenical Movement

In a formal sense, the modern ecumenical movement had its origins in the 1910 World Missionary Conference, held in Edinburgh.[22] It was this conference that paved the way, over subsequent decades, for a profound re-shaping of relationships between churches across the world, and, importantly, for Christians in the South Pacific.[23] It opened doors of opportunity for exposure to previously unreachable parts of the Christian world, and to previously unknown horizons of the Christian faith. The influence

18. As asserted by Rev. Dr. Feleterika Nokise, Principal of the Pacific Theological College, who writes the Foreword in Ernst, *Globalization*, v.

19. Ernst, *Globalization*, 749–51.

20. Uriam, "Theology and Practice." See his statement immediately preceding the contents page.

21. Uriam, "Theology and Practice," 18.

22. For a full account of the conference and its significance, see Stanley, *World Missionary Conference*.

23. Uriam, "Theology and Practice," 65.

of this movement in stimulating the contextualization of theology took three forms. Each of these contributions warrant attention in relation to the impact they made.

First, the global ecumenical movement facilitated the exposure of Pacific Islanders to the church and to the world beyond the Pacific. This inspired them to broaden their theological horizons and deepen their theological insight:

> Through their travels, contacts, and involvement in International Christian organisations, many of the Pacific Church leaders were exposed to new ways of witnessing the gospel, more than just conversion of non-believers to the Christian faith, and many became interested also in finding ways of presenting the gospel anew with a new understanding of it within their own Island context.[24]

Through such exposure and opportunity, it was the ecumenical movement that provided "the main impetus which led the Pacific Island churches to move away from an inherited 'Christendom' model of faith and theology, to one by which the Pacific Island churches could respond to and address the growing challenges facing the Pacific."[25]

Secondly, it was the support and encouragement of the global ecumenical movement that led to the birth of the Pacific Conference of Churches as an ecumenical organization across the South Pacific. At its meeting in 1938, the International Missionary Council (IMC) proposed that a mission organization within the Pacific be established. Any follow up of this proposal was postponed by the outbreak of war. Some years after the war, representatives of the London Missionary Society (LMS) and the Methodist Missionary Society called for the formation of a regional organization of churches in the Pacific. At the instigation of the General Secretary of the LMS, letters were sent in 1957 to the mission boards of churches across the Pacific to seek their interest in and support for a gathering of churches. Such support was forthcoming from a majority of those churches.

In February 1959, following the feedback provided by Pacific churches, the IMC was asked by the churches and missions around the Pacific to organize a conference for those working in the Pacific region. Arrangements were put into place by the then General Secretary of the IMC, Lesslie Newbigin, who visited Fiji with the specific purpose of planning the inaugural gathering. The fruit of this was an historic meeting convened by the IMC, and held at the Malua Theological College in Samoa, from

24. Uriam, "Theology and Practice," 136.
25. Uriam, "Theology and Practice," 78.

April 22 to May 4, 1961. It was to lead to "an ecumenical explosion" that "shook the churches of the Pacific."[26]

An account of the formal commitment to create the PCC is found in the more detailed report of that 1961 gathering.[27] It was attended by the major traditions of the churches around the Pacific Islands—Methodists, Congregationalists, Presbyterians, Anglicans, and Lutherans—and at the end of the two-week gathering, the churches made a pledge to keep in touch with one another. This was a significant step towards achieving an ecumenical consciousness and church cooperation that embraced the vast spaces and countless island communities of the South Pacific.

A further meeting of Pacific Churches and Missions was held in Lifou in New Caledonia from May 25 to June 7, 1966. This was the meeting that, in unanimously supporting a drafted constitution, gave birth to the official formation of the PCC, the body that has since been "the chief ecumenical agency in the Pacific."[28]

The fact of the creation of the PCC, and its significance for the development of a theology within the South Pacific cannot be overstated. The most immediate access for Pacific Islanders to the global ecumenical movement, and to the issues confronting churches around the world, came specifically through the Pacific Conference of Churches (PCC). From that time on, ecumenical representatives from the global church came to the Pacific to attend PCC meetings, and the PCC was formally invited to send local delegates to various ecumenical gatherings in other parts of the world. This mutuality of exposure was formative. It stimulated Pacific Island leaders to appreciate, in ways not previously available to them, the emerging and dramatic changes to the theological scene in other parts of the world. It energized them to begin to explore their own theological ideas more deliberately, and they began to make their own contribution to the international theological scene.[29] The impact of these experiences in contributing to the contextualization of theology was immeasurable, particularly as they came in a period that coincided with other events that were under way within the South Pacific, and which were impacting upon the local identity of the people.

The PCC also provided the structure by which the great cultural diversity of Pacific Island people, spread thinly in numbers and separated across a vast and often treacherous ocean of islands, could come together in one place for a common cause. Until its establishment, the members

---

26. Forman, *Voice*, 1.

27. Pacific Conference of Churches, "Beyond the Reef."

28. Forman, "Finding," 115.

29. Gardner, "Praying for Independence."

of the Pacific Island churches were largely isolated, not only from the rest of the world, but also from each other.[30]. Now they had a forum to gather together in one place, to address issues of common interest and be supported in facing common challenges. At each of its subsequent gatherings, the PCC has in particular been occupied with, and given serious attention to, matters of theological substance addressing their own particular region of the world. A summary of PCC meetings and their themes over the years from its founding offers a formative guide: 1966 Lifou, New Caledonia (Founding of the PCC); 1971 Davuilevu (Fiji), Theme: God's Purpose for His People; 1976 Port Moresby (Papua New Guinea), Theme: God's Mission in the Changing Pacific Society; 1981 Nuku'alofa (Tonga), Theme: Confessing Jesus Christ in the Pacific; 1986 Western Samoa, Theme: Challenges of the Eighties and the Mission of the Church; 1991 Vanuatu, Theme: Proclaiming a Living Hope—Born into a Living Hope; 1997 Tahiti (French Polynesia), Theme: Reaffirming God, the Hope of Fenua; 2002 Raratonga (Cook Islands), Theme: Holy Spirit, Weave us Together in Your Peace; 2007 Pago Pago (American Samoa), Theme: Atua, Empower Us to be Liberating Communities; 2013 Honiara, Solomon Islands, Theme: Do Justice, Love Mercy and Walk Humbly with Our God. (Micah 6:8).

Thus, the PCC has been a key driver in providing opportunities for the contextualizing of theology in the South Pacific. It was the PCC meeting in Port Moresby in 1976, for example, where one of the first calls was made for a Pacific theology, and it was the PCC meeting of 1981 in Tonga that has the status of being "perhaps the most important conference for the life and the theological thinking of the Island Christians."[31] It was this meeting that "spelt out what is required and how it should be done."[32]

In addition, it is the PCC that has initiated a number of key consultations, specifically on the topics of Pacific Theology and Theological Education within the Pacific, for example, in 1986 (Papua New Guinea), 1987 (Fiji), 1994 (Fiji), 1996 (Fiji), 2001 (Fiji), 2002 (Tonga), 2003 (New Caledonia), 2004 (Solomon Islands). Each of them has played a significant role in the contextualizing of theology in the South Pacific.

The contribution of the global ecumenical movement in facilitating the development of a Pacific theology came in a third way, namely in directing its own resources towards the growth of local theology. It was the ecumenical movement that provided the funding for the establishment of the Pacific Journal of Theology; the journal came into production as early as 1961 and

---

30. Forman, *Voice*, 1.

31. Uriam, "Theology and Practice," 72.

32. Uriam, "Theology and Practice," 134

provided a regular forum for theological engagement within the South Pacific. It was also the ecumenical movement that initiated and sponsored the first serious discussion on the possibility of a contextual theology for the South Pacific; through the Theological Education Fund of the International Missionary Council, the consultation took place in May 1961, in Suva. It was the first of a series of such sponsored consultations in the region.[33]

In addition, The World Council of Churches in 1983 resourced an international gathering, devoted to the issues of "Gospel and Culture," which several members of the Pacific were funded to attend. This was followed up in October 1986, when the Program on Theological Education (PTE) of the World Council of Churches convened a high-level consultation in Geneva on theological education in the Pacific; its primary concern was with the upgrading of the Pacific Theological College in Suva, but there was discussion about the importance of a vision for theological education across the entire region.[34] The PTE also sponsored a consultation on Gospel and Culture in the Pacific, held in Suva, Fiji, in July 1987. Later, the Ecumenical Association of Third World Theologians (EATWOT) supported the creation of a "Pacific Chapter" that was established in 1994, and became a further venue for theological engagement among Pacific Islanders.

All of these global ecumenical initiatives individually promoted the contextualizing of theology in the South Pacific, and together, over a period of time, harnessed a momentum among Pacific Churches and their leaders, to pursue a home-grown theology. It may be too much to claim in isolation, as Uriam does, that "it was the ecumenical movement that made possible serious theological reflection by Islanders,"[35] but the contribution it made was immeasurable.

3. The Independence of the Churches

Charles Forman identifies the combination of the achievement of political independence from colonial powers, together with the achievement of ecclesial independence from foreign mission-based churches, as the two main factors in the emergence of a localized Pacific theology. In noting the "great variety of changes in island life" in the Pacific, during and after the 1960s, he asserts, "The most obvious change has been the transition from colonial status to independence in most island countries . . . independent churches in independent countries have given an impetus to independent thinking."[36]

33. TEF, "Theological Education."
34. See Snijders, "Religious Studies at Tertiary Level," 9.
35. Uriam, "Theology and Practice," 64.
36. Forman, "Finding," 115.

These combined changes in the power structures of both church and politics not only gave permission for indigenous voices to speak up for themselves, but also created the need and expectation that this would be so. In the editorial of the first volume of the newly launched Melanesian Journal of Theology in 1985, John D'Arcy May comments,

> The full responsibility—and loneliness—of national independence and church autonomy is beginning to dawn on Melanesians, just as the problems confronting them from within and without become daunting. Expatriate experts cannot provide answers to the questions Melanesian Christians are asking deep in their hearts as they face these challenges. Only Melanesians can formulate these questions; only they can identify those elements in scripture and their various traditions which contribute towards answering them.[37]

However, it is wise to draw a distinction between ecclesial independence and political independence in terms of their respective impacts on the contextualizing of theology. In most cases, the independence of the churches preceded the political independence of the nations by some years. For example, in the case of the Presbyterian Church in the New Hebrides, ecclesial independence came in 1948, while political independence was achieved in 1980, a separation of more than thirty years. Uriam observes that "before the end of the 1970s all churches in the South Pacific had become autonomous local churches with indigenous leadership."[38] While most nations had achieved political independence by the end of the 1980s, the struggle still continues, most notably in Tahiti, New Caledonia and West Papua.

Certainly the structural independence of the churches has been an important element in the movement towards the localizing of theology, not least in providing the framework for the indigenous people to step up into roles of ecclesial leadership. Although the indigenization of church leadership was on the agenda from the early period of mission history,[39] it was only the arrival of the formal declaration of the structural independence of the churches that constituted a significant new step in the recognition and role of indigenous leadership. With ecclesial independence, there was a real sense in which the opportunities and responsibilities for the emerging shape of the local church now belonged in the hands of the local people. As such it provided a stimulus to the further development

---

37. May, "Editorial," 3.

38. Uriam, "Theology and Practice," 12.

39. Uriam, "Theology and Practice," 11.

of indigenous leadership, and, importantly, a catalyst for the movement towards indigenization of the Christian faith.

> The emergence of . . . local leadership in the young Churches boosted the growing confidence as well; that now not only could they run the Church but they could make the Church become a truly indigenous institution as well, by thinking about their faith within their own culture and Island context . . . Local church leaders encouraged younger leaders to explore new ways of understanding their Christian faith and make contributions to theological discussions and issues facing the Church, not only in the islands but in the wider context and world in general.[40]

Although foreign missionaries continued to have a measurable influence on the life of these newly independent churches, they played a more modified role. The formal role of leadership was no longer in their hands in the same way, and their own home churches were no longer the bodies to which the independent churches were accountable. The home churches were to become no more than (but no less than) partner churches. However, it was not really until the achievement of political independence that indigenous church leaders had the scope and the permission to offer genuine theological leadership.[41]

4. The Political Independence of the Island Nations

It is of interest that where the achievement of the independence of the church preceded the achievement of political independence, church leaders became, in many cases, the pioneers of their nation's political independence. It may well be that the confidence and freedom engendered to local church leaders, through the granting of church independence, empowered them then to lead the movement of their own people towards national independence. This was the experience in the New Hebrides. "Since 1948, the people have been learning, through self-government within the life of the church, how to approach the question of self-government within the life of the nation. The first experience was the preparation for the second."[42] Anglican priest Father Walter Lini, who was to become Vanuatu's first elected Prime Minister, and Pastor Fred Timakata of the Presbyterian Church, who was to become the elected deputy Prime Minister, were among a significant band of

40. Uriam, "Theology and Practice," 136.

41. For an examination of the interconnection in Vanuatu between the independence of the Presbyterian Church in 1948 and political independence in 1980, see Gardner, "Praying for Independence."

42. Miller, *Live*, 1:125.

indigenous church leaders who together pioneered the movement towards political independence for the New Hebrides. This political involvement of the church leaders prompted its own theological works. By way of illustration, both Lini and Timakata published theological papers on the topic of the relationship between church and politics, defending the importance of church leaders taking up roles of political leadership.[43]

While the independence of the churches placed leadership of the church within the hands of local people, it was the eventual achievement of political independence that did much more to liberate the Pacific Island nations from the physical, emotional and cultural shackles of colonial rule. Political independence authorized Pacific Islanders to re-assert their own cultural identities and traditions in a way that had not been possible since the initial arrival of missionaries, traders and colonial rulers in the nineteenth century. Wherever and whenever political independence came, it gave rise to a renewed pride in the traditional culture of the newly independent peoples, and led to a renaissance of traditional customs and practices. Russell Chandran, an Indian theologian, who edited the report on the 1987 consultation on *Gospel and Culture in Fiji*, notes, "Political independence of the island nations has been followed by the growth of nationalism and reaffirmation of the values of the Pacific Island cultures and the quest for a Pacific identity. The Gospel-Culture relationship is integrally related to this quest for Pacific identity and Pacific theology."[44] This post-colonial appreciation of a "renewed emphasis on the traditions and customs of local people" was strongly affirmed by the younger generation of indigenous church leaders in the case study that forms the focus of chapter 5.[45]

5. Localized Theological Education

As had happened previously in parts of Asia and Africa, so also in the South Pacific, the localizing of theological education played a very important role in providing momentum to the task of contextualizing theology.[46] From the early missionary period, institutions of general education, that in some cases included a form of theological education, were established across the South Pacific. Apart from education in literacy, particular attention was given to instruction in the Christian faith and knowledge of the Scriptures, with the purpose of recruiting local people to support the missionary task. Even if they

43. Timakata, "Political Ethics in Vanuatu"; Lini, "Should the Church?"; "Christians in Politics."

44. Chandran, *Cross and the Tanoa*, v.

45. See for example, Prior, *Voice of the Local Church,* 18.

46. Forman, "Finding," 115.

did equip local people for certain leadership roles, the early establishment of these institutions did not encourage or enhance the development of a Pacific theology. The content of any theological education that did occur, was shaped by the colonial mission agenda, with a focus on biblical stories and teachings, and a rejection of the place of stories and customs from local tribal tradition. It was the view of the missionaries, and of those early generation local Islanders who were converted to the Christian faith, that traditional stories, ideas and customs "were found to be in disagreement or abominable to the 'Christian way' and 'Christian thinking,' things that have no real place now in the present, in the new Christian environment."[47]

Particularly in the first half of the twentieth century, where theological education was provided, the focus was on the need, not only to expand the missionary faith, but also to maintain and expand the structures of the Christian mission. Only limited time was given to theological studies. The fact that the students were self-supporting also meant that time was needed for domestic requirements and food production. "Life in the theological colleges before the Second World War involved a lot of manual labor. . . . More time in the classrooms was given to the teaching of carpentry skills or agricultural techniques than lessons in theology or biblical studies."[48]

After the Second World War, the situation began to change. Responding to a global mood across the churches for a relevant local ministry to address a changing world, the churches in the island nations consciously began to tackle the need for a form of theological education that provided church leaders whose ministry would be capable of engaging the conditions of the Pacific. Uriam records, "A well educated, a better trained, and a well-informed ministry was called for by the people."[49]

From the 1960s a quiet revolution took place in theological education in the South Pacific.[50] Greater attention was given to the standards of theological education, increased funding support enabled students to devote more of their time to theological study, and, most strategically, in 1966 the Pacific Theological College in Suva was established. As observed, the actual origins of the Pacific Theological College came five years earlier, when the Theological Education Fund of the International Missionary Council sponsored a consultation in Suva, Fiji, on "Theological Education in the Pacific."[51] This consultation followed on from the meeting of Pa-

47. Uriam, "Theology and Practice," 45.
48. Uriam, "Theology and Practice," 54.
49. Uriam, "Theology and Practice," 55.
50. Forman, "Theological Education," 151–67
51. TEF, "Theological Education."

cific Churches and Missions in Samoa during the previous two weeks. At this prior event, the delegates in Samoa had considered a report from the Commission on Ministry, a section of which dealt with the issue of "Training for Ministry."[52] The Commission report recommended,

i. cooperation of the churches in the establishment of a central federated theological school to which selected graduates from our present schools can proceed for further training, provided that (a) a higher academic level is established, and (b) it offers the training relevant to the needs of the Pacific Churches.

ii. the churches do all within their power to raise the standard or training in the existing denominational colleges.[53]

Discussion among the delegates in Samoa was strongly affirmative. It "revealed a unanimous desire to raise the standard of theological training in all parts of the Pacific area."[54] The meeting resolved to pass on to the subsequent consultation in Fiji, a recommendation for "the establishment of a Central Theological College in the Pacific area."[55] When it came then to discussion in Fiji, "various issues were discussed: quality and standards of training, current quality of leadership, staffing levels at Colleges, indigenous staffing of Colleges, payment to pastors, recruitment to the ministry, language used in teaching, library resources, books, vernacular texts, financial difficulties, role of the 'mother church.'"[56] In the end, the establishment of a Central Theological College was supported. It was seen as an important step in "bridging the isolation across the Pacific and providing opportunity for a cooperative and communal approach to theological education, pooling resources for theological education, enabling people to train within their own cultural environment, and having a curriculum which was related to the special context of the Pacific."[57]

The growing challenges facing the Pacific Island churches and communities were recognized by the consultation, and the creation of their own regional theological college was considered an important step in addressing these. "The hope is that this College will not only provide careful and exact training in Biblical and Theological studies, but that the type of training

---

52. "Beyond the Reef," 45–46.
53. "Beyond the Reef," 46.
54. "Beyond the Reef," 46.
55. "Beyond the Reef," 46.
56. TEF, "Theological Education," 14.
57. TEF, "Theological Education," 15.

will be such as to make these studies deeply relevant to the changing social conditions of the Pacific world."[58]

At the same consultation, attention was also given to the possibility of a survey of theological education across the Pacific, including Australia and New Zealand. Lesslie Newbigin reported on similar surveys that had been completed in India, Africa, Madagascar, Latin America and the Caribbean, with one to be carried out in the near future in the Near East. It was felt that because of "increasing urbanisation," "the new paganism," and a rapid increase in the number of "better educated young people,"[59] theological education would quickly fall behind in meeting the changing needs of the churches in the region. However, the proposal to carry out a survey of theological education across the South Pacific, together with the recommendation to convene further workshops on theological education, were not approved, due to the high funding costs involved in implementing these in a region that was distinctive for its vastness and the difficulties of communication.

It was notable that, at this stage, there was not yet a call for a Pacific theology. The mood was more one of improving the quality of theological education among local church leaders, and providing an indigenous ministry that engaged more effectively with the contemporary issues and challenges. Predictably, however, such a deliberate approach in theological education would inevitably stimulate the development of a localized theology within the context of the South Pacific. Forman notes,

> It was the first degree-granting institution in the South Pacific Islands and received the top students from the churches of most of the island countries. Its purpose was to train theological teachers and church administrators, rather than local pastors. It also had a further goal, as stated in its original statement of purpose: "to make available to the world the distinctive theological insights which God has given to Pacific Christians." In other words, its establishment implied the creation of a Pacific theology, and from the beginning it took this intention seriously.[60]

From its establishment, the Pacific Theological College came to serve as the focal point for theological education across the churches of the South Pacific. It was normal practice for the better student graduates from local island colleges to attend the Pacific Theological College for higher education. Many of these students subsequently became key leaders and teachers within their

58. TEF, "Theological Education," 15.
59. TEF, "Theological Education," 35–37.
60. Forman, "Finding," 115.

own island churches and colleges, and thereby exercised their own influence on the localization of theology and theological education. Forman's own surveys, in 1968 and 1984, of sixteen Protestant theological colleges in the South Pacific, indicated a dramatic change in the leadership of those colleges over that period. In the former survey, all principals were Europeans, while in the latter survey, all principals were Islanders. He attributed that change to the influence of the Pacific Theological College.[61]

Uriam comes to the same conclusion as to the significance of the Pacific Theological College. In reflecting on its impact, he writes, "The Pacific Theological College continued to play a significant role in the development of theological thinking of Islanders: it continued to provide leaders and lecturers for many of the Churches and local theological colleges."[62] These other local theological colleges were also impacted upon by the call for a more relevant local church leadership and the need to reform theological education. As a result, they were beginning to produce their own generation of local theologians. "Towards the end of the 1980s, many theological colleges were already producing confident theological thinkers and leaders in the individual Churches throughout the Pacific."[63] In a retrospective of the PTC at the end of its first fifty years, the incumbent principal speaks eloquently of "achievement of much success," referring to "over 800 graduates," many of whom have exercised significant leadership in their churches and their island nations.[64]

However, another outcome of the development of the PTC is relevant. While in some important respects it was clearly a great stimulus to the localization of theology, perhaps unknowingly, the PTC has served to perpetrate a view that theology belongs to the field of advanced academic learning,[65] to be performed by those few literate individuals who are able to read difficult books by foreigners from the West, and whose theological education may actually serve to distance them from their home communities and cultures. In the fifty-year retrospective of the PTC, it is of note that the primary measure of the College's success is in "the emergence of Pacific church scholars over the last twenty years" who have engaged with its "high academic standards." There is no mention at all of the significant reality that marks all Pacific cultures, namely their primary oral character. In that sense, as will become clearer through this book, the contextualizing

61. Forman, "Finding," 115.

62. Uriam, "Theology and Practice," 70.

63. Uriam, "Theology and Practice," 70.

64. Nokise and Szesnat, *Oceanic Voyages*, 58.

65. Nokise and Szesnat, *Oceanic Voyages*, 58.

of theology in the South Pacific has perhaps been compromised by the very establishment of the institution that was designed to promote it. The same inner contradictions observed in the Asian and African experience appeared also in the South Pacific. Something of this is reflected in the following observation: "Certainly the College looked impressive, and it raised the level of theological education in the Pacific, but it was more of a Western university in the Islands. 'They impress us with their knowledge, but they confuse us and even destroy our faith' were some of the comments by the people in the Islands."[66]

Despite the impressive numbers of graduates of academic learning, even so the newly acquired capacities of the graduates did not create a flow of literate theologians. Prominent Roman Catholic missionary, Father Cyril Halley, was editor of the Journal of the South Pacific Association of Mission Studies for a number of years. Upon relinquishing that role in 2005, he lamented, "The most difficult task for the editorial board was to obtain material from South Pacific Islanders . . . while we were able to get people to write about the South Pacific, we failed in our aim to get people from the South Pacific to write."[67]

Halley highlights a symptom of a deeper issue, namely that the cultures of the South Pacific are not literate cultures but oral cultures. The difficulty he found in obtaining material for the journal touches on some of the core issues of the contextualization of theology within such cultures. Predictably, these same struggles were experienced by the main theological journals that were launched within the South Pacific, to which publications we now turn.

6. Publications on Local Theology

There is no doubt that the establishment of local journals of theology around the South Pacific acted as a significant stimulus for the contextualizing of theology within the South Pacific. The journals provided a means by which local people could express their views, and a stimulus for them to do so. They served to forge something of a Pacific-wide theological community, and to enable the voices of Pacific Islanders to be heard, within and beyond the Pacific region.

The Pacific Journal of Theology has probably been the most formative journal of theology in the South Pacific. Its birth as a journal resulted from the 1961 consultation that approved the establishment of the Pacific Theological

---

66. Uriam, "Theology and Practice," 66.

67. Spoken at the national Missiology Conference on "Reimagining God in Australian Cultures" held at Whitley College, Parkville, Victoria, Australia on September 30, 2005.

College. "We have agreed, after considerable discussion, that the publication of such a journal is both eminently desirable and wholly possible. We therefore resolve to set up the machinery for such a publication."[68]

It was the aim of the journal to be a medium through which "island theologians could publish their ideas."[69] While it was not confined to local island writers, it was decided that articles be written in "simple English" to enable more local people to contribute, but without negating the need to "stretch the minds of the readers."[70] Importantly, the focus of the content of the journal was to be "the theological foundations of the life, witness and problems of the Church in the Pacific,"[71] and suggestion was made that contributors might address such things as "the biblical theology of land tenure, marriage customs, sacraments, church and colonial government, church architecture in the Pacific, liturgy, the place of the laity, sects in the Pacific, the understanding of 'the kingdom of God.'"[72]

The journal continued through the 1960s, but struggled to sustain both content and administrative support. This first attempt at a local journal of theology came to an end in 1970. Charles Forman reports that "there was not yet a sufficient number of Pacific theologians to support the venture," and that "most of the writing was done by a small group of European missionaries."[73] His comments are pertinent in that both the support required to sustain such a publishing project, and the writing task, are alien to the oral cultures of the South Pacific, and therefore not easily fulfilled by Pacific Islanders.

Some two decades later the journal was revived. It was re-launched in 1987, with a first volume in the second series coming out in 1989. By this time, there was a new generation of educated Islanders who were capable of articulating their ideas in literate form. Notably, the editorial of the first volume in the revived journal, written by the President of South Pacific Association of Theological Schools (SPATS), Larry Hannan, describes the journal's aim as "promoting Pacific Theology." He continues, "The Journal also provides an opportunity for closer contact between the sixteen member schools, scattered around the Pacific."[74] Hannan appeals for the journal "to be owned by its members, so that it can be authentic and truly reflect the

---

68. TEF, "Theological Education," 33.

69. Forman, "Finding," 115.

70. TEF, "Theological Education," 33.

71. TEF, "Theological Education," 33.

72. TEF, "Theological Education," 33.

73. Forman, "Finding," 32–33; Forman, *Voice,* 32–33

74. Hannan, "From the SPATS President," 2.

theological concerns and aspirations of SPATS." This would then mean "a regular flow of articles from Pacific writers."[75]

The journal has continued to the present day under the auspice of SPATS, with the majority of input now provided by Pacific Islanders themselves, still noting, however, that this mode of theology relies upon the capacities applicable in literate cultures.

The second major journal, contributing to the contextualizing of theology within the South Pacific, has been the Melanesian Journal of Theology. The loss of the Pacific Journal of Theology in 1970 had left the Pacific without a local theology journal through the formative period of the 1970s, and into the 1980s. It was during this era that the development of the contextualizing of theology was reaching its peak around the world. While there was some hope that the PJT might be revived, nothing eventuated through that time. At its meeting in March 1984, the all-Melanesian membership of the executive of the Melanesian Association of Theological Schools (MATS), based in Papua New Guinea, made a decision that they would await the revival of the earlier journal no longer, and would "go it alone and create something characteristically Melanesian."[76] The agreement was "to launch a journal for the specific purpose of developing indigenous theology in Melanesia."[77] Under the editorship of John D'Arcy May,[78] and with the administrative support of the Melanesian Institute in Goroka, the first edition of the Melanesian Journal of Theology appeared in 1985. Its first editorial explains the background of the journal, the theological and ecclesial context within which it was launched, and the urgency of "the need for a community of theological discourse, a forum for critical collaboration in Melanesia."[79] May concludes his opening editorial noting that "Time will tell" as to whether the journal will "bear the weight of responsibility thus foisted upon it."[80] The content of the whole of the first volume was given to papers from the March 1984 meeting of MATS on the theme, "Melanesian Theology: Melanesian Theologians at Work." It represented an impressive start to the newly launched journal.

Nearly thirty years later, the journal is still operating, with two volumes annually. Over that period, there has been a great wealth of contributions

75. Hannan, "From the SPATS President," 2.

76. May, "Editorial," 2.

77. May, "Editorial," 2.

78. May was a Roman Catholic Missionary of the Sacred Heart. He was later appointed to be Director of the Irish School of Ecumenics.

79. May, "Editorial," 2.

80. May, "Editorial," 3.

from a wide network of Pacific Islanders and expatriates. In that sense, the journal has substantially met its original purpose. The editor, Doug Hanson, in his survey in 2008 of the first twenty-four years of the MJT, itemizes the main themes that have appeared. These have included Melanesian culture (including tribal feasts, dancing, marriage, polygamy, music, wisdom, tribal fighting, and reconciliation) and Melanesian theology (including topics Christology, salvation and eschatology). In addition, there have been multiple articles on themes of leadership, mission, church history, education, politics, and the environment.[81]

However, the MJT shares with the PJT the same assumptions of literate capacities, perhaps even more so. There has been a conscious and notable change in the journal towards a more strictly formal and Western academic style. When the journal was first launched, the breadth of theological expression evident in the cultural context of the South Pacific was recognized as having a valid contribution to make:

> The MJT . . . is to concentrate on theology in all its manifold aspects, from exegesis to doctrine, including worship and evangelization, ethics and pastoral practice, with emphasis on the thoughts and feelings of Melanesians as they struggle to map out the intellectual structure of a theology for their unique situation. It is taken for granted that these efforts will draw on the already existing oral sources of indigenous theology in Melanesia, whether in Pidgin or in local languages: the stories and songs, the adaptations of myths, the solutions to practical problems found by prayer and consensus.[82]

While the journal still remains committed to the development of Melanesian theology, or more precisely, "the dialogue of Christian faith within Melanesian cultures,"[83] there has been a significant shift. The revised editorial policy of the journal is "to stimulate the writing of theology in Melanesia," with contributions to be "of scholarly standard."[84] This shift constitutes a significant obstacle to the contextualizing of theology. The journal, while promoting contextual content was now advocating a mode that was limited to literate cultures, or to those few who, coming from oral cultures, had learned how to succeed in using a literate mode. As such, the success of the journal as a medium for theological expression within the local cultural context has been compromised.

81. Hanson, "Twenty-Four Years."
82. May, "Editorial," 2.
83. Hanson, "Editorial Policy," 2.
84. Hanson, "Editorial Policy," 2.

In addition, it is observable that the success of the venture over the years has rested heavily on the involvement and resources of expatriates. It is they who have carried the editorial role, with the administrative support coming from one of the existing centers for theological education in Papua New Guinea, first the Melanesian Institute, and then the Christian Leaders Training College. It has to be concluded that overall, the MJT has made an ambiguous contribution to the process of contextualizing theology in the South Pacific.

In addition to the above two prominent journals, is the publication, "Point." Point is a series of books, produced by the Melanesian Institute, for the purpose of "researching, teaching and publishing on all aspects of Melanesian cultures."[85] Publications began in 1977. Each volume is of academic quality and devoted to a special theme relevant to Melanesia. Topics are approached from different points of view by specialists in the fields of theology, anthropology, sociology, economics, politics, and the arts. They have served a useful theological purpose by providing high quality and informed material on a range of Melanesian themes, and across a number of disciplines, even if the primary focus has not been strictly theological.

While it could not be argued that this journal has been one of the more important instruments for the development of contextual theology in the South Pacific, it has been an invaluable resource for providing insight into aspects of the Melanesian context. Some of the earlier volumes remain standard reference resources for such information.[86] However, the contributions have come from expatriate members of the Faculty of the Melanesian Institute rather than from Pacific Islanders, and in that sense, its contribution to the contextualizing of theology has been limited.

Not so much a journal as a magazine, "Catalyst" is published quarterly also by the Melanesian Institute. Publications began in 1971 with the express purpose of preparing people for mission work within Melanesian cultures, and for promoting a deeper understanding of Melanesian culture and religion, so as to resource effective mission practice. Each journal issue contains a variety of articles on a variety of themes concerned with culture, politics, economy, religion and social issues in Melanesia. When the more focused theological journal, MJT, was launched, Catalyst had already been in existence for well over a decade, and there was initially some anxiety expressed that the two would overlap in content and purpose, and so compete with each other. However, in his editorial of the first volume of MJT, May is concerned

---

85. See the website of the Melanesian Institute, "Melanesian Institute IPG."

86. One good example of such a reference is Whiteman, *Introduction*.

to dispel the impression, which is bound to arise, that MJT is an unnecessary duplication of Catalyst. . . . Implicit in the MATS decision, however, is that the time has come for differentiation of roles, and specialization of tasks: MJT is envisaged as complementary to Catalyst, because it is to concentrate on theology in all its manifold aspects.[87]

While most articles have been provided by expatriates, there have been a good number of Melanesian contributors over the years. Because of the broad range of topics covered, the journal is a valuable resource across various disciplines. However, the MJT, with its more exclusive attention to theology, is of greater significance in the emergence of theology in the South Pacific, despite the concerns about "compromise" expressed above.

TWO FURTHER STIMULI TO THE CONTEXTUALIZING OF THEOLOGY

1. *The Role of Chiefs in South Pacific Cultures*

Across the cultural groups in the South Pacific, there is a diversity of forms of leadership, and a diversity of powers, exercised by leaders.[88] In structural terms, broadly, the two common forms are "hereditary" leadership and "big-man" leadership. While the former is dominant in Polynesian communities, and the latter is recognized to be the norm in Melanesian communities, both forms are apparent in Vanuatu, and for both forms, the generic title "chief" is widely used. The chief of a tribal community in the Pacific not only speaks to his community, but his voice is the voice of his community. As such his voice carries the community along with him. In a context where church leaders are perceived in the same way as tribal chiefs, such leaders play a particularly influential role in molding the shape of their church institutions and communities.

Thus, it is fair to say that much of the development of a local theology within the South Pacific has come as a result of the particular contributions of such indigenous leaders. These earliest pioneers of contextualization were attributed with chiefly status and they provided inspiration for those who came afterwards. Had it not been for this early generation of indigenous chiefly leaders, who took upon themselves the agenda of contextualizing

---

87. May, "Editorial."

88. For more detailed insight into leadership, especially in Melanesian communities, see the insightful paper on this topic, Chao, "Leadership," 127–48. Chao, a Roman Catholic Sister of Mary, is an anthropologist who taught at the Melanesian Institute. See also Chowning, "Leadership in Melanesia," 66–84.

theology, there may have been no local ownership of the theological task, and nothing that could be described as an authentic contextualizing theology within the South Pacific.

Those who took up such a status in the earliest period of the emergence of Pacific Theology included Sione 'Amanaki Havea from the Methodist Church in Tonga, Ilaitia Sevati Tuwere from the Methodist Church in Fiji, Leslie Boseto from the United Church in the Solomon Islands, Patelesio Finau from the Roman Catholic Church in Tonga, and Jovili Iliesa Meo, a Fijian Methodist. Each of them has played a part in giving shape and momentum to the contextualizing of theology. Although the following chapter will explore in detail their particular contributions to the contextualizing of theology, recognition of their overall influence as chiefly figures is warranted at this point.

Sione 'Amanaki Havea was President of the Methodist Church of Tonga, the first chairperson of the Pacific Conference of Churches, and the first local Pacific Islander to serve as the Principal of the Pacific Theological College (1977–81). That makes him a very influential figure in the development of the contextualizing of theology. He was prominent in moving Pacific Island churches away from an uncritical acceptance of inherited Western theology, and of giving pioneering leadership to the unique content of Pacific theology. He led the way in the historic consultation on theological education in 1985 in Suva, and again at the consultation in Papua New Guinea in 1986.

Despite this significant place assigned to Havea in the development of theology within the South Pacific, Forman comments, "Havea was not so much a contributor to Pacific theology as he was an instigator, one who saw the need and got people interested in the subject."[89] Few would agree with this modest assessment. In a more recent tribute and critique, Ma'afu Palu speaks of Havea as "the architect" of Pacific Theology."[90] Referring to Havea's role in the Pacific Conference of Churches, and as the one who took up the battle against the planting of foreign Western theology, Palu credits Havea with "setting forth the foundational principles for Pacific Theology."[91]

Ilaitia Sevati Tuwere was also a leader of his own church, and of the regional Pacific church. Described by an Indian colleague at the PTC as an "outstanding Fijian theologian,"[92] he was the second indigenous Principal of the PTC (1982–88), and held the positions of General Secretary and

---

89. Forman, "Finding," 116.

90. Palu, "Dr. Sione 'Amanaki Havea," 68.

91. Palu, "Dr. Sione 'Amanaki Havea," 68.

92. Chandran, *Cross and the Tanoa*, v.

President of the Methodist Church of Fiji. Tuwere's doctoral dissertation focused on the topic of "land" and was published under the title "Vanua: Towards a Fijian Theology of Place."[93] Tuwere's engagement with these theological ideas overlapped with periods of major unrest within his own nation, and it fell to Tuwere to integrate his theological thought with testing conflicts between church and state. He was led to critique both. In this way, he "kept a precarious balance and has been a voice for moderation in strife-ridden Fiji."[94] His contribution to theology in the Pacific is comparable to that of Havea.

Leslie Boseto combined a strong commitment to the village communities of his own people while, at the same time, holding positions of leadership both within and beyond the national church. He served as Bishop of the United Church of Papua New Guinea and the Solomon Islands, and was the first Melanesian to serve as Moderator of his church. He was a cabinet minister in the national government and was a member of the Central Committee of the World Council of Churches.

It was Boseto who was "the authentic voice of the Pacific at international gatherings."[95] He was a champion of the indigenizing of theology; for him, while the gospel is universal, theology must be local, and the gospel must be interpreted in terms of the local culture. Particular theological themes taken up by Boseto included the centrality of the local community in the theological task in the Pacific (this connected with what he called "grass roots theology"), the importance of the environment and social ethics, and the unity of the church.[96]

The fourth of the leading Islander theologians is the Tongan Roman Catholic, Bishop Patelesio Finau. Along with the previous three, Finau held positions of significant leadership within and beyond his own church and nation. Tragically, he died suddenly while chairperson of the PCC in 1993.[97] He was seen as a prophetic figure and more: "He was a champion of action in society. His great effort was to get the churches out of their ecclesiastical closets and into the public life of the society. . . . Finau, however, was not just a social activist. He gave strong theological foundations to his ethical demands. The Hebrew prophets were his examples."[98] In summariz-

---

93. Tuwere, *Vanua*.

94. Forman, "Finding," 116.

95. May, *Living theology*, xii.

96. See for example, Boseto, "Challenges of the 1980s"; "God as Community."

97. A special volume of the *Pacific Journal of Theology* was produced to honor Finau. See the tribute in the opening editorial, Walker-Jones, "Tribute," 1–6.

98. Forman, "Finding," 117.

ing the contribution of Finau, Forman speaks of "his inspiring influence on young theological students and the younger priests and pastors," and acknowledges him to be "the only Roman Catholic man who has been a major figure in island theology."[99]

Jovili Iliesa Meo, like Tuwere, is also a Fijian of Methodist background. He was Principal of the Pacific Theological College (from 1996–2001) during a period of great upheaval caused by Fijian political interference.[100] While he has received less public recognition than others as a leading theologian in the Pacific, he has been a leading advocate for the contextualizing of theology, and a firm supporter of the emerging role of women in this task. His own theological contributions have embraced a range of local issues.[101]

There is a group of three other outstanding islanders who are worthy of mention at this point. The first is Lalomilo Kamu from Samoa, who did a doctoral dissertation at the University of Birmingham in the United Kingdom while working on the teaching Faculty at Selly Oak Colleges.[102] In his dissertation Kamu deals with themes of land, community, and God, exploring what it means to have an effective engagement between traditional cultural themes and the Christian gospel. There is a strong connection between the theological and cultural ideas of Kamu and those of Tuwere.

The significance for theology of the New Caledonian, Pothin Wete, is that he writes out of the context of the Kanak struggles for identity and liberation. Wete is "an ardent champion of the Kanaks,"[103] committed to their independence in a land colonized and controlled by the French. The thrust of his own book is on the themes of liberation, rooted in the Hebrew prophets and their call for freedom, and in the Christian hope for a new creation.[104] Wete, like other key islanders mentioned, also served on the teaching Faculty of the Pacific Theological College, and as such, exercised a significant influence on the younger generation of church leaders across the Pacific.

The last of the Islanders is Samoan, Ama'amalele Tofaeono, whose dissertation is a further illustration of a serious engagement with issues of the Christian faith and traditional culture. The focus of Tofaeno's earlier writing

99. Forman, "Finding," 117.

100. Nokise and Szesnat, *Oceanic Voyages*, 36–39. Nokise notes the significant cost on Meo's health as a result of the turmoil.

101. See for example Meo, *Developing*; "Smallness and Solidarity"; "How Do We?"

102. Forman, "Finding," 117. After Kamu's untimely death, his dissertation was revised and published posthumously by his wife under the title, "Samoan Culture and the Christian Gospel."

103. Forman, "Finding," 117.

104. Wete, *Le Developpement*.

is on the concept of "aiga," a fundamental and all-embracing traditional cultural term that refers to the whole family of God's creation.[105] Using this theme, and the insights that come from his own cultural heritage, Tofaeono addresses the urgent issues of eco-theology. He calls for a wider vision of the Christian faith that embraces, not only the human family, but also the family of the whole of God's creation—"aiga." In affirming Tofaeono's influence as "the most recent major theologian to emerge in the Pacific," Forman concludes, "Tofaeono's thoughts carry a challenge to Christianity far beyond the bounds of Samoa."[106]

2. Weaving the Voice of Women into a Man's World

Although not part of the early emergence of contextualizing theology in the South Pacific, the most significant stimulus in the last generation for the contextualizing of theology in the South Pacific has come through the introduction of Pacific women's theology.

Across the diverse and numerous cultures of the Pacific, the cultural context, almost without exception, is etched with the vivid distinction in roles between men and women.[107] "Women accepted their roles as mothers and housewives and men welcomed their roles as heads of families, defenders and decision-makers."[108] In such a prescribed cultural context, the fact that women began to step into the arena of public debate in the life of Pacific churches, is of historic moment.

The medium for this momentous step has been the organization, Weavers. Weavers was created in 1989 at the end of a regional consultation held in Tonga, on the topic, "Women and Ministry in the Pacific." The consultation was convened by the South Pacific Association of Theological Studies, with the specific objective of promoting the theological education of women in the Pacific. "It was recognized that the low participation of women in the official ministries of the churches could only be changed if more opportunities and encouragement were given to women for theological education, both formal and informal."[109] This recognition went hand-in-hand with the already recognized fact that "issues surrounding the role

---

105. Tofaeono, *Eco-Theology.*

106. Forman, "Finding," 118.

107. Chowning, *Introduction*, 41–62.

108. Tongamoa, *Pacific Women*, 88. The final chapter, titled "Overview," provides a more detailed summary.

109. Meo, "Weaving Women," 11.

of women in church and society have surfaced in recent years as a major concern in Pacific Island churches."[110]

The founding of Weavers set in train a Pacific-wide movement that has been a catalyst for establishing an influential role for women in the shaping of Pacific theology, and in locating Pacific women and their concerns within the wider global movement of women's theology. Following the 1991 consultation on "Women and Ministry" in Fiji, Lydia Johnson-Hill writes, with obvious enthusiasm about the response of women to the opportunity to contribute to the theological task: "We quickly discovered that there is no shortage of theologically sophisticated, articulate Pacific women who are eager to write, and who have significant things to say. The fact that we are able to present to the public so many of their statements, for the first time ever in print, makes this a truly historic document in South Pacific church history."[111]

The emerging role of Weavers in contributing to the shape of theology in the South Pacific was recognized by the President of SPATS, Jovili Meo. As sponsor of the 1995 Weavers' consultation on "Women's Theology—Pacific Perspectives," he welcomed the women by encouraging them to pursue a theology that takes their unique situation, lives and role seriously. He urged them to become the subjects of their own history, to re-read the Bible through their own reality, so that, "what the Dalits and Minjung theologians have experienced, that is, rediscovering the gospel, will also happen here in the Pacific. . . . Only in your struggle together as people of God will you be able to begin and reflect theologically and come up with a women's theology that is unique to the Pacific."[112] In his own reflection at the end of that second gathering, he comments on his excitement at the way the women "were to theologize about their life experiences, their knowledge and their beliefs."[113]

More will be said about the specific contribution by women to contextual theology in the South Pacific but it is sufficient at this stage to note that their inclusion into the movement from the late 1980s has been a most significant factor in the pursuit of the contextualizing of theology.

THE MOMENTUM IS SUSTAINED

The global pursuit of the contextualization of theology has continued, opportunities for trans-continental exposure have remained frequent,

---

110. Johnson-Hill, "Beyond the Story," 1

111. Johnson-Hill, "Beyond the Story," 1.

112. Meo, "Weaving Women," 14.

113. Meo, "Weaving Women," 12.

theological colleges have continued to grapple with the challenges of developing the next generation of theologians, Pacific Islanders have continued to engage together about local theological challenges, and consultations on theology have been regular. The list of such consultations from 1990–2005 clearly illustrates the point, as also does the list of particular topics and themes that have shaped the official gatherings of the PCC through its history from 1966 to the present.

By way of example, the PCC General Assembly, held in Honiara as recently as 2013, commissioned a group to do a feasibility study on the proposal to unite the three major Pacific Institutions—the PCC, the PTC and SPATS—into one Pacific Ecumenical Council. It was thought that, among other outcomes, this would stimulate further development of the theological agenda across the Pacific. Notably too, the final resolutions of this gathering focused heavily on contextual issues challenging the Pacific region, in particular political independence for Tahiti and West Papua, climate change, seabed mining, HIV-AIDS, the arms trade, and nuclear weapons.[114] These indicate an ongoing commitment to the contextualization of the theological agenda, at least on matters of content, if not on matters of methodology.

SUMMARY

It is clear that many factors have combined together to determine the birth and growth of the movement to contextualize theology within the region of the South Pacific. This movement flowed on from the parallel movements of contextualization that first erupted in Asia, Africa and Latin America through the 1950s and 1960s. At the same time, there were factors distinctive to the South Pacific that were important in establishing and sustaining the momentum for contextualizing theology. While the above section identifies these influences, it says little about the detail of the particular content and particular shape of this local theology. Neither does it offer any commentary on how effective it has been in contextualizing theology.

This brings me to the heart of this book, namely to a more specific exploration and critique of what South Pacific Islanders themselves have understood and articulated as a theology that is genuinely contextual. What have South Pacific Islanders been aiming to do in developing a theology that is contextually appropriate for their own peoples and cultures? As those who are the rightful subjects of such an undertaking, it is their voices that most deserve to be heard.

---

114. WCC, "Pacific Conference of Churches Resolutions."

3

The Voice of South Pacific Islanders

On the Definition, the Content, and the Methodology of Theology

THE NOTION OF ANY sort of theology seemed at first to be remote, even absent from the minds of Pacific Island Christians. Uriam reports that there was modest exploration of the indigenization of particular aspects of Christian life and practice, but there was no real interest in, nor attention given to, the indigenization or localization of theology. He comments, "In the Islands, before Pacific Theology came to the fore, attempts at the indigenization of aspects of Christian life were made. Structures, worship, and ministry were and could be indigenized; but theology somehow was left alone—it was as though it does not belong to the faith. It was seen more as a Western scholarly exercise to explain the Christian faith."[1]

Even the discussions around the establishment of the PTC in 1961 did not envisage a key role for the college in the emergence of a localized theology. While there was a commitment to develop the quality of theological education of the students, there was no indication of interest in the pursuit of a Pacific theology as such:

> The establishment of a central Theological College was supported as a way of bridging the isolation across the Pacific and providing opportunity for cooperative and communal approach to theological education, of pooling resources for theological education, of enabling people to train within their own cultural

1. Uriam, "Theology and Practice," 146.

70

environment, and of having a curriculum which was related to the special context of the Pacific.[2]

Perhaps the closest hint of the possibility of a local theology was in the preamble, which expressed hope that "the type of training will be such as to make these studies deeply relevant to the changing social conditions of the Pacific world."[3] But even that was some distance from any sort of contextualization of theology.

Given that the global movement towards the contextualization of theology was in its very early stages at this time, this lack of attention in the South Pacific is hardly surprising. What is surprising is that at the 1985 launching of the MJT, by which time the global movement of contextualization had gained great momentum, the strangeness of the contextualization of theology for the South Pacific was still apparent to some local theologians and church leaders, even if the ideas were becoming more familiar:

> The task of creating a Melanesian theology has been slow in coming. Perhaps our difficulty has been that we were not quite sure as to where we should start and how we should go about it. We should appreciate and praise our missionaries for the interest and encouragement they have shown in their attempt to guide us but we Melanesian theologians must be involved in the task. And the task is not simply "buying and selling" of modern theologies.[4]

This slowness in engaging with contextualization in the South Pacific may well be a reflection, as Uriam suggests, of the identification of theology as something that belonged only to the Western world. Equally, the heritage of theology may have been seen as part of the overall missionary package, and thus to be received without question. It may be expected then that any initial moves towards the contextualization of theology in the Pacific might be slow in coming, requiring recognition of the need to create critical distance from the inherited Western missionary theology. This recognition began to gain some momentum through the 1980s. Forman reports on this period:

> Along with Western culture, Western theology comes in for its share of criticism. It is common to argue that Western theology is relevant only to Western conditions. To try to apply it to the Pacific is to engage in theological imperialism. Theology must

2. TEF, "Theological Education," 13.
3. TEF, "Theological Education," 15.
4. Hagesi, "Towards a Melanesian Christian Theology," 17.

be reformulated for each time and place, and the would-be universal theologies from the West are ineffective for Oceanians.[5]

Dr. Sione 'A. Havea offers evidence in support of Forman's observation. "Pacific Theology should not be either a duplication of or transfer
from Western thinking, but should be home grown and nurtured in the
local soil . . . [it] should be an effort to acquaint the gospel and culture."[6]
The question arises: What then has come to emerge from this local "effort to acquaint the gospel and culture" so that Pacific theology might be
genuinely "home grown"?

What follows below is a documentation of the views and perspectives
of South Pacific Islanders under three headings: first the definition of theology, secondly the content of theology, and thirdly the methodology envisaged for theology. While these three themes are inevitably interconnected,
it is crucial for the purpose of this book to explore them separately. To do
so will enable clearer appreciation of both the strengths and the limitations,
in the pursuit of a contextually appropriate theology for the South Pacific.
This will then pave the way for identifying those particular issues that, I will
assert, need to be addressed in pursuing a theology for the South Pacific,
one which is more genuinely and thoroughly contextual.

For each of the three headings, I will trace their evolution over the
period from the 1960s into the early years of the twenty-first century, providing a brief summary at the end for each. While there will be some level of
duplication across the three sections, the focus on the distinction between
the three themes will be maintained. Each of the three themes will be explored in three periods, with 1985 identified as a central or climactic point
in the development; the periods before and after 1985 constitute the first
and third periods. The importance of this delineation, although somewhat
artificial, will become clear.

THE DEFINITION OF THEOLOGY

Before 1985

Despite the fact that some early hints towards a Pacific theology may be identified from the 1960s, there seems to be no accepted definition of what might
be meant by the term. More deliberate attempts to offer a definition start
to appear only in the 1980s. Through this decade, several significant events
took place, in part by way of special gatherings, and in part through written

---

5. Forman, "Finding," 120.
6. Havea, "Quest," 9.

publications that gave opportunity for Pacific Islanders to engage in serious conversation and reflection about a contextual theology for the Pacific.

The meeting of the Pacific Conference of Churches held in Tonga in 1981 was arguably the inaugural and most important of such gatherings. As such, it warrants some detailed consideration. The overall theme of the Fourth Assembly was "The Challenges of the '80s and the Mission of the Pacific Churches." There was a sense in which this Assembly more than others was a deliberate attempt to explore thoroughly the calling of the Churches for the future decade. This gave weight to all the topics on the agenda including theological education and potentially also theology. It had already been agreed at the previous PCC Assembly in 1976 that "theological education" would be a key agenda item for the 1981 conference. Minutes from that 1976 Assembly rather understate the sense of priority that was emerging for Pacific church leaders to look seriously at their own local approach to theological education. The minutes state, "This Assembly requests that more time be given when it next meets to the discussion of theological education."[7]

Follow-up of this 1976 decision was referred to the PCC Executive and members for consideration and action. Thus, in preparation for the 1981 Assembly in Tonga, a questionnaire on theological education was sent out by the PCC Executive to the churches in the region, with a view to gathering and collating the material in time for the Assembly. Five key areas were identified for response in the questionnaire: theological education in the Pacific context, theological education and the scientific approach, theological education and the church, ecumenical dimensions of theological education, and ministerial formation.[8]

Although the focus is clearly on theological education, the responses also included some particular deliberation about the definition of theology. The collated report of the pre-Assembly questionnaire remarks notably that

> There seemed to be several strands to the meaning of theology: i) Theology means the message of the gospel about God and man; ii) Theology is a process of making the message of the gospel relevant in the Pacific context by the use of cultural expression. Hence the suggestion of "Coconut Theology"; iii) Theology means the bringing of the Good News to the oppressed; iv) Theology is the life of the church as articulated and lived.[9]

7. Pacific Conference of Churches, "Third Assembly," 58.

8. A full report on the processes and the findings is written up in Pacific Conference of Churches, "Fourth Assembly," 215–21.

9. PCC, "Fourth Assembly," 216–17.

Later in the same summary report, it records that by the end of the gathering,

> There was no agreed understanding of the term theology. . . . Those who saw theology as being carried on by the church, understood theology as the church living its life and articulating that life through its self-reflection. Those who saw theology as independent of the church saw theology as an independent scientific investigation, which challenges the church.[10]

In addition to the questionnaire, a background collection of papers was prepared and distributed beforehand to Assembly delegates.[11] It included three articles that in one way or another addressed the definition of theology. The most pertinent was titled "Theological Education in the Pacific in the 1980s." It is something of an apologia written by Dr. Salesi Havea, a Tongan on the Faculty of the Pacific Theological College. The paper sets out to clarify the task of theology and theological education. In terms of a definition of theology, Havea asserts, "Theology is and can only be defined in terms of our attempts to study the revelation of God. Indeed it involves the scientific investigation of faith and personal commitment so that the believer can better understand the mechanisms of his belief in God."[12]

This definition establishes that the focus of theology is "the revelation of God," that the enterprise of theology involves serious study, that theology is carried out by a suitably educated person of faith, that it involves the use of the tools of scientific insight, and that the outcome of doing theology is to increase understanding of one's belief. Perhaps what is significant here is that the definition suggests nothing that is specific to the context of the South Pacific. In fact, the definition seems to sit rather awkwardly in the South Pacific context, and rather more comfortably in the context of the Western world, where critical scientific study had its origins, and where theology is commonly an intellectual exercise carried out by an individual.

As anticipated, the actual Assembly meeting that ensued gave significant attention in its agenda to what it called "Pacific theology." On the very first page of the Assembly minutes, it is noted, "A lively debate on the nature of theology engaged all members of the Assembly. Inevitably, the final statement adopted by the Assembly will not be able to reveal the richness and color of the debate."[13] In his own personal report of the gathering, Charles Forman records: "Probably the greatest enthusiasm of the Assembly cen-

10. PCC, "Fourth Assembly," 217–18.

11. PCC, "Background."

12. PCC, "Background," 62.

13. PCC, "Fourth Assembly," 1.

tered around the idea of a Pacific theology. One evening was devoted to discussion of this subject and that evening's session ran longer than any other because so many people were eager to speak."[14]

The report of the "lively debate" that took place includes attempts by the various delegates at a definition of Pacific theology.[15] Father John Foliaki, from the Church of Melanesia, spoke of Pacific theology as "looking at Pacific issues from the Pacific man's point of view"; Dr. Sione 'A. Havea of Tonga proposed that Pacific theology is "not an end in itself, but a vehicle . . . using Pacific images to help reveal the hiddenness of God"; Baiteke Nabetari from Kiribati spoke of Pacific theology as "the challenge to think of God in terms of Pacific culture."[16] A consistent and predictable focus, emerging in these spoken definitions, is the particularity of the Pacific as the context within which the theology is to find expression.

Prominent Roman Catholic ecumenist, Bishop Patelesio Finau from Tonga, apparently wary of the risks of over-emphasizing a focus on the Pacific, pointed out the need for a more generic systematic approach to theology. He indicated that his own understanding of theology was best represented in the pre-Assembly paper written by Father Etuale Lealofi. This paper sets out the Roman Catholic view of theology, and is recorded in its entirety within the Assembly report.[17] Calling upon his own church heritage, Lealofi writes,

> Theology is essentially "faith seeking understanding" as St Augustine [sic] puts it rather pithily . . . it seeks to explain the nature of the faith relationship between man and God . . . it is the expression of the verbalization of the community's faith . . . and an aid towards the deepening of this faith . . . as the scientific and systematic study of Revelation, it is necessary as a means of articulating the meaning of the experience of faith.[18]

This overlaps with the earlier definition offered by Dr. Salesi Havea in his paper. Commonly they have a focus on the pursuit of "understanding" God's self-revelation, using an approach which is both "scientific and

14. Forman, "Pacific Conference of Churches," 2.

15. In the evening session of May 7, a panel group of six, comprising four Pacific Islanders (Dr. S. A. Havea, the Rev. Baiteke Nabetari, the Rev. Albert Barua, and Fr. John Foliaki) and two overseas representatives (Dr. Charles Forman and the Rev. Ned Ripley) opened up the discussion on Pacific Theology. The minutes record some of the conversation which took place.

16. PCC, "Fourth Assembly," 26–30.

17. Lealofi, "Some Thoughts," 228–32.

18. Lealofi, "Some Thoughts," 230–31. Note that in fact it was St. Anselm—and not St. Augustine—who introduced the notion of "faith seeking understanding."

systematic," with a view to making pronouncements about the meaning of faith's experience. The difference between the two definitions lies in the focus given by Lealofi on the faith of the community.

Subsequent to this lively opening session, ongoing discussion took place in small groups that were required to report back in the second week of the Assembly. What emerged from the groups was that broadly speaking, there were two distinct voices in response to the question of a definition of Pacific theology. One voice wanted to speak of theology as the way in which "ordinary people speak of God and His ways" which can take place in formal and informal settings; the other spoke of theology as "a systematic study, like a science, which is best done by professionals who draw their measures from the scriptures, history and tradition, and from contact with the present Christian community, including its various cultures."[19]

Responding to the energy created during this Assembly, the final outcome included six resolutions that expressed the commitment to proceed further with the task of exploring a Pacific theology[20]. It was agreed to encourage lecturers in theological colleges around the Pacific region to convene a workshop on Pacific theology, to follow this up with regional seminars held on the main themes arising from the workshop, to urge theological colleges then to incorporate these within their curriculum for theological education, and to publish any papers which resourced the workshop and seminars. All of this was to be under the guidance and sponsorship of the PCC. In this way the momentum for exploring the nature of Pacific Theology was to be formally maintained.

In some respects, it may be said that little progress was made at this 1981 Assembly. No agreement was reached on a definition of Pacific theology. The diverse viewpoints and the areas of tension concerning the make-up of Pacific theology, which were apparent prior to the Assembly, were debated in the Assembly proceedings without resolution. The same divergent voices remained, and beyond the common commitment to give an important place to the actual context of the Pacific, it was left unclear as to what it might mean to speak of Pacific theology. However, Uriam's reflection on this assembly includes an optimistic, and perhaps overstated attempt to draw these diverse perspectives into something of a consensus. He comments that

> no particular theological position was adopted, though there was a general consensus that theology was an illustration or a statement of an analysis of human relationships and human

19. PCC, "Fourth Assembly," 233.

20. PCC, "Fourth Assembly," s.v. "Resolutions."

situations in which God or the truth could be revealed. In other words, a truly Christian theology for the Islanders was one that begins with the people and their context.[21]

Despite a lack of a concluding agreement in measurable ways, the opportunity for church leaders, across the diverse cultures around the Pacific, to gather in one place for such a discussion, would have provided a great stimulus for the leaders themselves, and their churches, to think more seriously about the nature of a Pacific theology. The passion for the pursuit was evident in the nature and length of the discussion on theology. In that important sense, the 1981 Assembly in Tonga served an invaluable purpose. Further developments that took place through the 1980s and beyond may well owe their stimulus, if not their origins, to this Assembly.

The Year 1985

It is a good illustration of the practical challenges faced by Pacific Islanders in convening regional meetings across the vastness of their many thousands of dispersed and tiny islands, that the 1981 commitment to hold further consultations on Pacific theology did not eventuate until four years later. In fact, through the year 1985, there were three independent and coincidental events of particular relevance to the development of Pacific theology, in retrospect, making 1985 a watershed year for the evolution of Pacific theology. Two of the three events were to do with publications, brought to fruition by the Melanesian Institute in Papua New Guinea, and dedicated to the promotion of Melanesian Theology. The third was the convening of a special consultation in Suva, Fiji on the topic of Pacific theology, as had been proposed by the 1981 Assembly. All three events deserve attention because of their focus on the meaning and the task of a Pacific theology, not least in relation to its definition.

In the editorial to the very first volume of the Melanesian Journal of Theology (MJT), John D'Arcy May describes the journal as "a new venture by the Melanesian Association of Theological Schools (MATS): to launch a journal for the specific purpose of developing indigenous theology in Melanesia . . . to create something characteristically Melanesian, while participating in the Pacific theology which is slowly but surely emerging."[22]

This very first volume in April 1985, appropriately, is dedicated entirely to an exploration of Melanesian theology, and it contains some careful and deliberate attempts to offer a definition of the term. The two most

21. Uriam, "Theology and Practice," 72.
22. May, "Editorial," 1.

helpful and focused definitions appear in the early part of the journal. Peter Miria[23] writes,

> Theology is faith which seeks to understand itself. Since faith in Melanesia is grounded in the concrete flesh and blood of the Melanesians, Melanesian theology is Melanesian believers seeking to understand the meaning of their faith. Thus doing theology in the Melanesian context is the reflection and the articulation of the faith experience of the Melanesian community of believers. Theology thus arises out of the community of faith which is the local church and so is at the service of the church.[24]

This definition overlaps with other contributions from Roman Catholics reported above. In common with those, it has a focus on theology as an enterprise in understanding the experience of faith. However, it notably omits any reference to "systematic" and to "scientific" and puts a clear focus on the community of believers. It suggests that theology arises from and addresses the local church community, in this way being a servant of it. With these distinct points, Miria is alert to the accusation that theology is a remote academic exercise, carried out by individual professionals, who have little connection with the issues facing local village communities. His own personal commitment to local parish ministry doubtless informs his views.

Equally thoughtful in this publication is the definition offered by Robert Hagesi.[25] In order to ensure a Christian focus to theology in Melanesia, his paper begins by arguing for the use of the term Melanesian Christian Theology over against three other possibilities—Betel Nut Theology, Melanesian Theology and Coconut Theology.[26] He then deals with three themes: terminology, the meaning of Melanesian theology, and methodology in theology. He then offers this definition:

> By Melanesian Christian Theology I mean the reflective expression and understanding of the Christian faith in the cultural, social and religious experience of the Melanesian Christian people within the Melanesian context, as decisive for the existence of

---

23. Miria, "Christian Faith," 14–17. Miria, a Roman Catholic Priest, was from Bereina Diocese in Papua New Guinea. He did post-graduate studies in Belgium, was a lecturer in theology, and Vice-President of MATS. Shortly before writing this article, he returned to parish ministry "to renew his contact with the people and their problems." May adds, "A sign of a true Third-World theologian."

24. Miria, "Christian Faith," 14.

25. Hagesi, "Towards a Melanesian Christian Theology," 17–24. Hagesi, an Anglican priest, was Warden at the Bishop Patteson Theological Centre in the Solomon Islands.

26. Hagesi, "Towards a Melanesian Christian Theology," 20.

the Melanesian Christian communities. . . . It is equally true and important to say that theologizing should be a Christian community involvement.[27]

There are similarities here with Miria's definition, both of them requiring a reflective approach that seeks to understand the experience of faith, and both of them giving a focal role to the community of believers. However, Hagesi's definition goes further than Miria's in emphasizing the role of the local Christian community. For Hagesi, the community setting is the "locus" for theology; the community actually engages in the theological task, and the outcome is "decisive" for the ongoing existence of the community, although in what way is not made clear.

While each of the two articles, especially that by Hagesi, goes on to say more about the nature of Melanesian theology, further input is best left to the sections below where I give more detailed and specific attention to the separate elements of content and methodology in Pacific theology.

The second of the two publications from 1985 is an anthology, *Living Theology in Melanesia: A Reader*.[28] As editor of this volume as well, May introduces the book with what may seem an ambitious declaration:

> The publication of this Reader by the Melanesian Association of Theological Schools and The Melanesian Institute marks a turning point in the development of indigenous theology in Melanesia. I do not think it is too much to say that with this anthology, the first to contain expressions of faith and theology entirely by Melanesians, theology in Melanesia comes of age, if by "theology" we mean the communication of experiences and insights regarding faith, scripture and the church to the wider Christian community.[29]

Although definitions of theology are implicit in the content of many of the contributions, the book is oddly non-specific in offering particular statements of definition, as were recognizable in the inaugural edition of the MJT. However, the book does contain a range of valuable contributions that speak of each of the content and the methodology envisaged in Melanesian theology. For this reason, the insights into theology from this second publication are preferably left to the two major sections that follow this section on the definition of theology.

27. Hagesi, "Towards a Melanesian Christian Theology," 20.

28. May, *Living Theology*.

29. May, *Living Theology*, ix.

The third of the major events from 1985 was the convening of a consultation of church leaders and teachers in Suva, Fiji from July 8–12. The report of the consultation is written up under the title, "Towards a Relevant Pacific Theology: The Role of the Churches and Theological Education."[30] The actual title of the report is instructive. It did not attempt to set out a definitive statement on Pacific theology, nor to create such a theology. Rather "it was designed to allow both the churches and theological schools in the Pacific, through discussion as well as through writing, to move towards a theology."[31]

The report is written up under six headings. The first, and most important for our purposes, is "Pacific Identity and Pacific Theology." The remainder are: Pacific Women and Theological Education; Peace and Justice; Christian Spirituality; Communication; Theological Education. Under the first heading, there is again considerable attention given to the nature and form of Pacific theology.

The most specific attempt at an actual definition comes in a paper from Dr. Sione 'A. Havea.[32] He begins with a very general definition: "The study of Pacific theology is an effort to understand theology in the context of the Pacific."[33] Without any reference to the language and ideas of the TEF, but in a way very similar to the TEF explanation, it is notable that Havea introduces the terminology of "contextualization." He distinguishes it from "indigenization" in that the former term includes the latter while adding to it also "current sociological, political, and environmental events of the past, present and even the future."[34] It is within the same paper that he suggests that all theology is contextual, noting in particular that, "most of the recognised European theologians such as Bonhoeffer, Tillich, Barth and Brunner were victims of war, and their theological perspectives were based on crisis backgrounds."[35] For Havea, endorsing the ideas of respected Solomon Island theologian Leslie Boseto, Pacific Theology cannot and must not simply be a "transplanted" Western theology, but rather one that grows from within

30. Lang et al., *Towards.*

31. Lang et al., *Towards,* v.

32. Havea, "Pacific Theology," 21. It is important to note that this paper is, with very minor modification, identical to the article that appears in the book "South Pacific Theology" under the title "Christianity in the Pacific Today." This latter publication is a collection of papers presented to a consultation held in Papua New Guinea in January 1986, just six months after the consultation in Fiji. See Havea, "Christianity in the Pacific."

33. Havea, "Pacific Theology," 21.

34. Havea, "Pacific Theology," 21.

35. Havea, "Pacific Theology," 21.

the local soil.[36] At the same time, Havea wants to avoid any suggestion that Pacific Theology is disconnected from the theologies which emerge in other contexts. "The term Pacific is limited to its region, but the term theology in general refers to a wider range which must be viewed in its global and universal context."[37] Accordingly, he adds, "Theology, therefore, must not be compartmentalized exclusively to one region but be seen as a vehicle to convey to the believer the quality and richness in our quest to know God in His hiddenness."[38] Suggested by the uniqueness of the Pacific cultural context, Havea then proposes "Theology of Celebration" and "Coconut Theology," as illustrations of what he means by an authentic Pacific theology.[39]

While again it is notable that Havea's definition focuses on the importance of understanding, his clear concern is to hold in balance both the particularity of the Pacific context and the universality of the Christian faith. He is clearly wary of a theology that is so localized that it becomes sectarian, by isolating itself from the unity of the catholic faith, shared by the Christian church, in all its local diversity, across the world. His two examples, and the way in which he explains them, illustrate the definition he offers. Both "celebration" and "coconut" are very familiar deeply rooted Pacific cultural realities, and so a theology that centers on these themes localizes the theology and authenticates it as "Pacific." In his explanation of these theologies, Havea's focus is on the way in which these themes represent or embody theological and Scriptural themes that are part of the global territory of theology, those of the welcoming grace of God and the saving act of God, expressed and accomplished in the incarnation, death, and resurrection of Jesus Christ.

Thus Havea makes a substantial contribution to the redefining of theology for Pacific Islanders, emphasizing the requirement for it to be recognizable as contextually Pacific, and thereby picking up the language and ideas of contextualization already emerging in other parts of the world. The implications of this for both content and method will be explored further in those sections below.

Keen attention during the 1985 consultation was also given to a presentation by Russell Chandran, an Indian theologian, who was at the time a member of the Faculty of the Pacific Theological College in Suva. He brought into the meeting the experience and insights of Asian churches in giving shape to their own theologies. The value of this was that it represented

36. Havea, "Pacific Theology," 21.
37. Havea, "Pacific Theology," 21.
38. Havea, "Pacific Theology," 21.
39. Havea, "Pacific Theology," 21.

another voice from the Third World, and in this way it was illuminating and pertinent for the Pacific audience.[40] Chandran writes,

> By theology we mean the human activity giving expression to the systematic articulation or reflection of the faith-response to the once-for-all saving event in Christ. . . . The verbalizing of this faith response is contextual. . . . Theology is a human response, but a necessary response for understanding, interpreting and communicating the gospel in order that we may grow from faith to faith.[41]

Interestingly, this definition of theology has much in common with other definitions already documented, although Chandran perhaps gives more overt attention than others to a Christological focus. What is common with others is the view that theology is the response of the experience of faith, which seeks to understand that experience, and to give systematic explanation of it. The purpose of theology is that the believers might grow in faith. The contextual aspect of theology for Chandran is the fact that the experience itself, and the articulating of it, are contextual. It is notable that, unlike Miria and Hagesi, Chandran makes little direct mention of the role of the local Christian community in the theological task. The Christian community is the beneficiary by virtue of theology's purpose, as a growing "from faith to faith." It is also notable that Chandran, as an Asian theologian, has not taken up the views expressed by some of his Asian colleagues who were at the forefront of the movement of the contextualization of theology, and for whom theology necessarily addressed socio-political realities, responding to them with action.

From 1985 Onwards

Just six months after the consultation in Suva, World Vision International convened a consultation in Papua New Guinea on a comparable theme. The papers from this 1986 Papua New Guinea consultation were published under the title *South Pacific Theology*. The title is notable for two reasons: first, it includes the word "South" in an attempt to limit the focus more to Melanesian and Polynesian peoples, and secondly, it omits any idea of "towards," assuming that it is possible to speak confidently about the existence of such a theology.

A representative of the host organization records in the introduction to the publication, "The purpose of the consultation was to provide an

---

40. Chandran, "Asian Perspectives," 32–38.
41. Chandran, "Asian Perspectives," 33.

opportunity for Pacific Christians to discuss what God's message means for Pacific peoples, and how this message can be more effectively communicated."[42] While this does not claim to be a definition of South Pacific Theology, the fact that it introduces the publication suggests that intent. As such, it offers a very open statement that includes communal discussion by Pacific Island Christians, and discernment of the contextual message of God to Pacific Islanders, with the task of relating this, presumably, to the wider church and beyond. The local identity of the participants, and the local focus of the message, seem to provide the criteria for a South Pacific theology.

While there is little to be added from the articles in this publication by way of a definition of theology, they do reinforce definitions that have emerged through the previous years, particularly in wanting to step away from Western approaches to theology and to ground theology within the life of the local Pacific Island communities. As was the case in the previous consultation in Fiji in 1985, Sione 'A. Havea was again prominent in this consultation and he reiterated his pioneering views. In fact, his prominence as the leading Pacific theologian is recognized by the fact that he was invited to write the foreword for the publication, and his own input constitutes the first chapter of the book.

Twelve months after the gathering in Papua New Guinea, in July 1987, the Programme on Theological Education (PTE) of the World Council of Churches (WCC), and the South Pacific Association of Theological Schools (SPATS), jointly sponsored a consultation for the South Pacific on "Gospel and Culture in the Pacific." It was timely and generated widespread interest. Sixty-five members, representing all main churches across the South Pacific, except for the French-speaking island nations, participated in what was part of a global initiative of the WCC to promote such consultations.[43] This resolution was made at the Sixth Assembly of the WCC held in Vancouver in 1983. It was in recognition of the importance of grounding the Christian gospel within the cultural contexts of Christian churches across the world, and encouraging churches in non-Western contexts to move beyond the Western missionary era which had been marked by a denigration of local cultures and an uncritical imposition of Western culture. On behalf of the WCC, Dr. Samuel Amirtham spoke of the important task of theological education to equip local churches "to express the Christian faith and to communicate it authentically through the local culture." It was recognized that "the Gospel-Culture relationship is integrally related to

---

42. Johnson, "Introduction," 9.

43. Chandran, *Cross and the Tanoa*, 1.

this quest for Pacific identity and Pacific theology."[44] As such, the consultation encouraged the view that any definition of Pacific theology required the grounding of the Christian gospel within the cultures of the local people. Much attention was given to what this means and how in fact it might happen. Across the range of presentations, the general approach assumed the universality of the Christian gospel, its expression in local cultural images, and a gospel critique of varying elements of local cultures as life-affirming or life-denying.[45]

Notably, the consultation also recommended the "revival of the Pacific Journal of Theology," and that the topic of "Gospel-Culture" should be included in the syllabus of all theological colleges.[46] This consultation reflected a growing movement towards a definition of theology that assumed the centrality of local cultures and local Christian communities in any theological enterprise within the South Pacific. As such, it constituted a significant step in defining the contextualization of theology.

In the late 1980s, the language of "contextualization" in theology in Melanesia, with some particular attention to the definition of that term, came from Dick Avi from Papua New Guinea.[47] Although, as noted, Havea had already picked up the language of the TEF in his paper of 1985, Avi is the first to do so in a more thorough way. Alert to the wider global trends in theology, Avi, quoting Shoki Coe, notes that the term "indigenization" is commonly used to describe the way in which the Gospel is articulated within the framework of traditional cultures, and therefore "the term is inclined to be past-oriented."[48] In his own critique of the term "indigenization," Avi notes further that it is used "only in relation to Third-World theologies." Because of this, "Third-World theologies become unduly preoccupied with the pattern of reaction against the theology of the West." He concludes, "The concept of indigenisation portrays the spirit of cultural self-containment, prejudice and to some extent opposition against the theologies of other peoples."[49]

He expresses a firm preference for the notion of "contextualization" because, reflecting "the contextuality of the gospel," it is a term that

44. Chandran, *Cross and the Tanoa*, 5.

45. See, for example, Rakau, "Wholeness of Life," 80–98. See also the summary of findings from the consultation in Chandran, *Cross and the Tanoa*, 14–17.

46. Chandran, *Cross and the Tanoa*, 16–17.

47. Avi was a prominent Pacific theologian. He was a lecturer at the Rarongo Theological College and President of The Melanesian Association of Theological Schools (MATS). See Avi, "Contextualization in Melanesia."

48. Avi, "Contextualization in Melanesia," 7.

49. Avi, "Contextualization in Melanesia," 9.

automatically applies to all theology, including in the West. "Theology cannot be done in a vacuum"[50]; it is about "responding to the immanent revelation of God and his concern with the realities of a particular context . . . the incarnation demonstrates this quite clearly."[51] Avi shares the view that every theology has grown out of contextual encounters with this God; this is evident in the theologies of the early church, as well as Liberation Theology, Black Theology, Water Buffalo Theology, Death of God Theology, Secular Theology, Ecological Theology, Mystical Theology. In fact, "all theologies are contextually conditioned. If theology is not contextual, it would fail to communicate . . . it would not be historical."[52] Avi then offers a summary definition of what it means to speak of the contextualization of theology. Not simply referring to a particular method, nor to particular content,

> "Contextualization" should be felt as a process in which the decision and actions are directed at local situations seriously. Thus theology rises from being the word of God to responsible and active involvement in the work of God as proclaimed in Jesus Christ, the incarnated Word of God, to bring about His purpose in a particular local situation. Theology, in other words, comes alive in a particular context.[53]

The overall thrust of Avi's paper is to adopt the definition of theology as embraced by the TEF in its use of the language of contextualization. It is a definition that suggests that theology is an enterprise that belongs at the heart of the church's vocation as it seeks to respond, in words and in actions, to the ongoing revelation of God. This is the God who, incarnate in Jesus Christ, has responded, and continues to respond, to human struggles in particular context. In doing so, this God invites a participation in specific acts of renewal and liberation, as an expression of the ultimate renewal of the whole of creation. In this articulation, Avi integrates both words and actions; he also integrates both the contextual particularity and the universality of theology. Thus he adds a Pacific voice to the chorus of other voices expressing, with increasing volume and harmony, such views about the nature of theology. Notably, however, outside its contextual location, there is nothing in Avi's approach that suggests any uniquely Pacific character to the practice of theology. This emerges later.

Further developments in defining the contextualization of theology find expression in two major consultations in the 1990s, sponsored by the

50. Avi, "Contextualization in Melanesia," 9.

51. Avi, "Contextualization in Melanesia," 10.

52. Avi, "Contextualization in Melanesia," 11.

53. Avi, "Contextualization in Melanesia," 12–13.

Pacific Chapter of EATWOT. The Pacific Chapter was established in September 1994, marked by an inaugural meeting in Fiji with the theme, "A Preferred Future for Pacific Theology." At that meeting, Sevati Tuwere offered the first paper. It begins with a definition of theology as "essentially a reflection on history in the light of the Word of God . . . our consciousness in history is brought to meet with the awareness of God."[54] The task of theology, he continues, alluding to Romans 8, is "to translate and transform into articulated speech the 'groanings' of the spirit of God in the struggle of the community in which the theologian lives. Theology is an expression of the human being and language or speech is a mark of this."[55] Tuwere then presents a new proposal, that, for the sake of "meeting the need for a common framework" for a local theology, there be "a shift (in language) from 'Pacific' to 'Oceania.'"[56] For Tuwere, this is not an incidental shift of terminology, but one that is symbolically important for the nature of theology. The word "Pacific" is of colonial origins and carries with it the heritage of colonial history and all that is implied. In contrast, the term "Oceania" means, "We are the sea. We are the ocean."[57] The significance of the shift for Tuwere is two-fold. First, the word "Oceania" more properly represents the true home of island peoples, and secondly, it recognizes that in theology in the South Pacific, the fullness of Oceanic life and history meets with the wholeness of Christology. What Tuwere has in mind is that with the use of the word "Oceania," there is nothing of local life and cultures excluded from theology, and no longer can there be a dual approach that divides salvation history, on the one hand, from the "dark" history of culture, on the other.[58]

The definition of theology offered by Tuwere intends to expand previous definitions in two important ways. First it embraces the whole of creation as understood and experienced in Pacific life, and secondly, it embraces Pacific cultural histories into the saving work of God. Notably, the discussion following Tuwere's paper and the subsequent conference deliberations did not come to any agreement on the use of the term "Oceania" to replace the word "Pacific." However, his lasting contribution to the content of theology will become apparent in the next section.

The subsequent meeting of EATWOT—Pacific Chapter, two years later, on "The Quest for a Pacific Theology," added little to definitions of

54. Tuwere, "Agenda," 6.

55. Tuwere, "Agenda," 6.

56. Tuwere, "Agenda," 8–9. Tuwere's first call for an "Oceanic Theology" may have been as early as 1990. See Tuwere, "He Began in Galilee," 4–9.

57. Tuwere, "Agenda," 9.

58. Tuwere, "Agenda," 11.

theology. It was more a matter of particular points of emphasis rather than any point of innovation, and it gave primary attention to the content of theology. Jovili Meo, editor of the PJT volume that records the papers and the report from the gathering, indicates that "the need was evident in our last EATWOT meeting three years ago (in September 1994) that the question of gospel and culture needed to be addressed again."[59] In doing so, this second conference gave particular attention to the changing cultural context of the Pacific, and the impact of globalization.[60]

The next major stage in the defining of Pacific theology came with a comprehensive four-year programmatic commitment to consultations on "Contextual Theology," sponsored by SPATS and to be held around regions of the Pacific. The very commitment to such a series of consultations is significant, indicating a growing acknowledgement that the agenda for theology is now directed to the task of the contextualization of theology within Pacific cultures. The language of "contextualization," which by now had become normative across many parts of the world, was becoming the accepted language in the Pacific.

The first of the consultations was held in Fiji in October 2001. The record of the consultation contains papers which were presented on three basic questions: "What is contextual theology?, Why do we do contextual theology?, and How do we do contextual theology?"[61] It was Tuwere who again provided the key input, and added further to earlier Pacific voices on the defining of theology. He chose, as the title of his paper, "What is Contextual Theology? A View from Oceania." He begins with a definition that states quite simply that theology "is essentially a human construction or reflection . . . an engagement where one is invited to faithfully speak about God on the one hand and really speak about Him on the other. And the God about whom we speak in theological discourse is none other than Him who in freedom manifested Himself in Jesus Christ as attested to us through the Holy Scriptures."[62]

His dual reference to the expression, "speak about God," suggests both a need to be consistent with traditional speech about God ("faithfully speak"), and the need to speak afresh out of a living engagement with God ("really speak"). This definition also reinforces the tradition that, at the heart of theology, is the God who was incarnate in Jesus Christ, and that the Scriptures constitute the authoritative witness to Jesus Christ. In "contextualizing" his

59. Meo, "Introduction," 2–3.
60. Gaudi, "One Gospel."
61. Tofaeono, "Editorial."
62. Tuwere, "What is Contextual Theology?," 8.

definition, Tuwere then reaffirms his view that human speech about God is not a matter of metaphysical speculation and philosophical reflection, but takes place "at concrete and particular moments in concrete and particular contexts . . . each is characterised by specific social relations, hopes, dreams or fears of people."[63]

Tuwere, like Havea and Avi before him, and consistent with the TEF statement, rejects other familiar terms (for example, indigenization) in favor of the term "contextualization."[64] He adds, "By contextualization we mean the wrestling with God's word in such a way that the power of the incarnation, which is the divine form of contextualization, can enable us to follow his steps to contextualize."[65] In something of a summary definition of contextual theology, he writes, "Authentic contextual theology is carried out with a deep sense of commitment of faith to God and for his cause, which finds explicit expression in Jesus Christ. This commitment is developed and nurtured in the community of faith that is the church. It accepts the primacy of the gospel story and seeks actively to live in the world in accordance with this story."[66]

Such a series of definitive statements offers a succinct summary of what is important in Tuwere's view of theology. Theology as "contextual" belongs to the life of the worshipping community of faith; it is grounded in the depths of human experience and need; it is an act of faithful response to God, and exists for the sake of nurturing and activating the community of faith; it gives commitment to the priority of what God has accomplished in Jesus Christ, in such a way that this story illuminates all other contextual stories. Therefore, while theology is contextual, it cannot be captive to, nor domesticated by, the context. It plays a prophetic role in critiquing and re-forming the context in the light of the overarching contextual story of God's act in Jesus Christ. This is where contextual theology ends, as it begins, from what God has already done in Jesus Christ, remembered and celebrated in the church, which is the community of faith.[67]

As he had done in the 1994 consultation, Tuwere reiterates his call for the term "Oceania" theology, and proposes "four principles of theological discourse" which he adopts from Asian contextual theology: Situation (the particular reality), Hermeneutics (the interaction between Oceanic situation and Christian gospel), Missiology (equipping the community of faith

63. Tuwere, "What is Contextual Theology?," 8.

64. Tuwere, "What is Contextual Theology?," 8.

65. Tuwere, "What is Contextual Theology?," 9.

66. Tuwere, "What is Contextual Theology?," 11.

67. Tuwere, "What is Contextual Theology?," 11–12.

for mission), and Education (informing the educational task for the church and for theological education). In this way, he sets up a clear framework for the future theological task in "Oceania."[68]

WOMEN DEFINING THEOLOGY

It was the second consultation, held in Suva in July 1991, on "Women and Ministry in the Pacific in the 1990s," that saw the first real contribution coming from Pacific women about a definition of theology. In an editorial summary of the conference, Lydia Johnson-Hill writes, "The underlying orientation that seemed to inform almost every contribution was a narrative approach to the doing of theology in the Pacific context."[69] This approach to theology prompted the use of "new theological symbols" and "a refreshing honesty about where we have been and where we may be going as Pacific Christians."[70] The outcome was a theology that was marked by a unique focus on the context and struggles of women in the Pacific, with a call for the liberation of women from cultural forms of oppression and dehumanization. The highlight of the consultation was a groundbreaking paper from Keiti Ann Kanongata'a on liberation. Such liberation, she claimed, means "not that we women need to become like men—oh no!—but to participate in the life and the work of the community."[71]

In her own paper, Johnson-Hill actually claims a "refreshing newness" in the contribution by women to Pacific theology. She challenges the predominance in Pacific theology and in Pacific seminaries of "symbols within the conceptual framework of Western theology," which requires "the mastering of concept/doctrine/principle first, then see if they can retranslate it somehow and apply it to their own contexts."[72] In contrast, the women's narrative approach to theology represents "a truly indigenous theology," it "tends more towards orthopraxy than orthodoxy," it "grapples with real life" and enables "a direct link with the Christian story."[73]

The structural three-fold partition that I have made in this chapter of the book between definition, content, and method becomes problematic at this point. The proposal of theology as narrative, not only carries with it a distinctive definition of theology, but it implies also its particular content and particular methodology. "Pacific women doing theology can restore to

68. Tuwere, "What is Contextual Theology?," 14.

69. Lydia Johnson-Hill, "Editorial," 1.

70. Johnson-Hill, "Editorial," 1.

71. Kanongata'a, "Pacific Woman's Theology," 11.

72. Johnson-Hill, "Beyond the Story," 46.

73. Johnson-Hill, "Beyond the Story," 46–47.

their male counterparts the art of storytelling as a theological act."[74] Clearly this affirmation by Johnson-Hill suggests substantial elements of content and of methodology as well as definition. Through their attention to honest personal narrative, it is the overall character of theology that is here redefined by the women.

This contribution to the definition of theology is given strong public reiteration just three years later. With the emerging voice of articulate women theologians impacting increasingly on the theological scene around the Pacific, women were welcomed into the inaugural meeting of the EATWOT—Pacific Chapter in 1994. It was the very first occasion when women were in a mixed-gender public arena, formally addressing the topic of "A Preferred Future for Pacific Theology." It is significant that the second of three key papers presented to this meeting, was offered by a woman, Keiti Ann Kanongata'a, who had delivered "a ground-breaking paper" at the 1991 Weavers conference. Kanongata'a was, at the time, Superior General of the Sisters of Our Lady of Nazareth congregation (an indigenous order in the Pacific islands), a teacher at the Pacific Regional Seminary, and was involved in establishing the PCC's Women's Desk and the SPATS women's advocacy group Weavers. She gained a doctorate in missiology at Pontifical Urban University, Rome. In defining theology, Kanongata'a calls for an "authentic and inculturated theology," which she describes as, "Theology that springs from the grass-root level, theology that is first lived before it is explained, theology that expresses women's true experiences, theology that is life-giving . . . in other words, theology that makes sense and is meaningful to Pacific women."[75]

Kanongata'a, emerging as the spokesperson of Pacific women's theology,[76] also offered one of the key presentations at the first major consultation on "Contextual Theology" in 2001. In that presentation, consistent with a narrative approach, she recounted five personal stories, extracting from each certain conclusions about contextual theology, and setting that in contrast to what she calls "traditional theology." Doing "traditional theology" means "engaging in philosophical thinking, translation, adaptation, application from European traditions to our Pacific situation. . . . We need a theology which begins with the people for the people."[77]

---

74. Johnson-Hill, "Beyond the Story," 48.

75. Kanongata'a, "Pacific Woman's Theology," 21.

76. The term which recurs in the literature is "women theology" rather than "women's theology."

77. Kanongata'a, "Why Contextual?," 28.

For this articulate Roman Catholic Sister from Tonga, "Women theology is giving a lead in Contextual Theology." She explains, "We began our women theology by telling and coming into touch with our own women stories. Today, we do not just tell our stories, we have launched into actually making things happen."[78] She summarizes, "Contextual theology is people's theology lived in human society."[79] In this way, Kanongata'a, on behalf of the women of the South Pacific, points her male colleagues to an understanding of theology that offers for the South Pacific a particular and innovative approach to contextualization.

SUMMARY COMMENTS ON THE DEFINITION OF THEOLOGY

Across the myriad of local voices, articulated primarily at regional gatherings and through the major theological journals, there is a clear line of development in the defining of theology in and for the South Pacific. This development moves from a sense that theology is an alien notion belonging to Western missionaries and irrelevant to Pacific Island churches, through a period of application of Pacific symbols to an inherited missionary theology, towards a recognition of the importance of pursuing a distinctive theology that belongs to the South Pacific, and then to an articulation of theology represented by the internationally emerging normative parameters of contextualization.

When compared with other Third World peoples, Pacific Islanders may have been tardy in taking initiatives in the contextualization of theology. However, the decade of the 1980s constituted an era of significant momentum for, and commitment to, such a theology for the South Pacific. This was further consolidated in the 1990s, giving rise, in the early years after the turn of the century, to a programmatic series of workshops specifically directed to the contextualization of theology for the South Pacific. Over this period of two decades or more, there has developed an increasing awareness of the cultural and social realities of the local people, and a growing trend towards the importance of theology as communal rather than individual, as local rather than institutional. In particular the voice of women has highlighted the centrality of human experience and personal story as a core ingredient in the definition of theology.

As indicated earlier and as is already clear, any discussion on a definition of theology cannot be separated from consideration of both the content

78. Kanongata'a, "Why Contextual?," 35. Note the author's expression "women theology" rather than "women's theology"

79. Kanongata'a, "Why Contextual?," 37.

and the methodology of theology. In order to gain an adequate picture of how South Pacific Islanders wish to give their own shape to the contextualization of theology, and the key issues and challenges to achieving this, it is now crucial to explore each of these in turn.

THE CONTENT OF THEOLOGY

In terms of the content of theology, the process of contextualization has involved a coinciding two-fold movement. On the one hand, there has been a conscious effort to move away from the heritage of Western theology, and on the other hand, various initiatives have been taken towards a deliberate engagement with the cultures and contexts of South Pacific peoples.

Before 1985

At the official opening of the Third Assembly of the Pacific Conference of Churches in 1976, Sir John Guise, Governor-General of Papua New Guinea, challenged the Assembly delegates in a speech that was to be long remembered as an historic moment in the struggle for a uniquely Pacific content to theology:

> There is one thing you must do even if you do nothing else; this Pacific Assembly must reveal to us and to the world the Melanesian Christ, the Polynesian Christ, the Micronesian Christ. If you like, we can call him the Pacific Christ. Many thousands of Christians in the Pacific believe in the Christian faith, but they believe in Christ in an abstract form because Christ was not born in any of the Pacific countries; he may still be someone who does not belong to the soil of the Pacific. But the Christian faith, and Christ himself, must become a living reality in our villages, in our culture as well as in our lives. The Christian Church must be involved in all these village festivities instead of turning their backs and preaching damnation and hell to the people from church pulpits or at their village church meetings, telling the people that their traditional festivities are sinful. The traditional festivities will become part of the Christian church only if the church and Christ become part of them.[80]

In some ways, the significance of this speech was circumstantial. Papua New Guinea had become independent just one year earlier, and there was a strong sense of pride and self-determination around this newly independent nation. Guise himself was the first indigenous Governor-General, and was

80. PCC, "Third Assembly," 10.

knighted on the occasion of his appointment. His call to the churches in the Pacific mirrored the mood of post-colonial autonomy among his own people. It was a call that recognized the alien nature of Christ and the Christian faith, as it had been received from the Western missionary tradition. It was a call that reclaims the heritage and cultures of the Pacific as the defining ingredients and context for a post-colonial Christian faith. As such, it forecasts this changed content for a localized theology. The 1976 Assembly that followed on from its opening, did not fulfill the hopes of Guise, but it did make a clear commitment to pursue the topics of Pacific theology and Pacific theological education so as to ground these within Pacific soil.

The dual move—on the one hand, away from the heritage of the Western missionary tradition, and on the other hand, towards the Pacific—is evident also in the Melanesian Institute Point Series of publications in this same period. In 1977, it published a paper by Joe Gaqurae, a vocal Solomon Island student at Rarongo Theological College in Papua New Guinea. The paper had been delivered to a workshop sponsored by the Melanesian Institute and held in Goroka on November 28—December 3, 1976. In it, Gaqurae speaks out boldly against the heritage of Western theology.[81] He asserts, "The Church at present needs to empty itself of all the unnecessary elements of Western heritage and pitch her tent in Melanesia."[82] Quoting Allan Tippett, he claims that a church is indigenous "when the indigenous people of a community think of the Lord as their own, not a foreign Christ."[83] Gaqurae advocates for the idea of using Melanesian cultural terms to speak about the significance of Jesus Christ. He grounds this in the theological significance of the incarnation of God in Jesus of Nazareth, that in being incarnate, albeit as a Jew, Jesus identifies with each and every cultural context. On these grounds, he says, it is important to speak of a "Melanesian Christ," to counter the problem that people think of Christ as a white foreigner.[84]

This approach has become a regular theme of Pacific Theology as a way of addressing a deep sense of the foreign-ness of the Christian faith among Pacific Islanders, and of encouraging a contextual Pacific response to the question asked of Jesus to his disciples, "Who do you say that I am?" (Mark 8:29) The same themes are picked up again in the 1981 PCC Assembly. In his important paper written, "to clarify the task of theology and theological education," Tongan lecturer, the Rev. Dr. Salesi Havea, accepts the criticism that "theological education has been too theoretical, academic and a carbon

---

81. It was first published in 1977 and republished in 1985.
82. Gaqurae, "Indigenization," 148.
83. Gaqurae, "Indigenization," 148.
84. Gaqurae, "Indigenization," 207–17

copy of Western culture." He goes on to say that while theological education needs to be "grounded within biblical knowledge, exegesis, historical and systematic theology and praxis," it must also "seek to dialogue with social sciences, relate to the contemporary realities of church, society and world, and be carried out in the context of Christian spiritual life."[85] In another of the background papers, Dr. Sione 'A. Havea, noting that "the days of mission-control are moving behind us," writes,

> In the past the missionary churches had to accept and believe what the missionaries believed, and use their forms of liturgies and worship. We had to speak their languages in order to be efficient in our ministry; even dress like them and adopt their customs. We had to read Brunner and Barth and Bonhoeffer (the three B's) to be a theologian. But I think we have as much or more to contribute from the Pacific to theology as we have to learn from the West.[86]

In further evidence of a commitment to a uniquely Pacific content for theology, the report from the pre-Assembly questionnaire documents the voice of "theological educationalists." These voices suggested that "there should be a marriage of theology and culture in an 'indigenous' theology," noting "a great sense of need for a pastoral theology which springs from the grass-root level of values found in the gospel and the cultures."[87] In listing something of what might actually make up "grass roots values of the cultures," various issues gain attention. "There were strong suggestions that the theological programs should look into contemporary issues facing the Pacific . . . human development, the abandonment of traditional customs in favor of western influences, growing materialism, alcoholism, break-up of family life and the suppression of women."[88]

In the conclusions of the Assembly, the core contents of a home-grown Pacific theology were identified. They include five ingredients: (1) upholding the central elements of Christian theology (e.g., Christology, Scriptures), (2) using Pacific language and symbols to describe core elements of the Christian faith, (3) giving focused attention to addressing issues affecting the lives of Pacific peoples, socially and culturally, (4) embracing personal and communal stories of suffering and struggle into a theological act for personal, cultural and social renewal, and (5) embracing the unity of human life with

---

85. PCC, "Background," 62–63.
86. PCC, "Background," 70.
87. PCC, "Fourth Assembly," 217.
88. PCC, "Fourth Assembly," 217.

all creation in an Oceania theology of re-creation.[89] In the proposed follow-up, it is notable that the commitment was to be content-based, "especially in the areas of Christian faith, issues of the '80s, and culture."[90]

Looking back over the generation that followed this gathering in 1981, the agreement to prioritize consideration of theological education and theology was decisive in shaping the content of such a theology. At the same time, the struggle to break away from a Western heritage continued.

The Year 1985

In the very first volume of the *Melanesian Journal of Theology*, Esau Tuza, lecturer in Church History at Rarongo Theological College, expresses the power of the heritage of Western theology, and the corresponding difficulty of forging any real local content of a Pacific theology:

> So much has been imparted in Melanesian minds that names such as Luther for the Lutherans, Thomas Aquinas for the Catholics, John Wesley for the Methodists, and John Calvin for Presbyterians, etc., have become almost as traditional as the names of our ancestors. We inherit, as Melanesians, the "end-product" of western theological thinking, so that it is at times difficult to venture into new areas ourselves to speak about new truths in theological matters.[91]

In the same volume, Robert Hagesi asserts that "the theologies which the missionaries imported from the Western World or First World are not relevant and intelligible to, or not even functional in the various situations, cultures and issues in the Third World."[92]

There is little further progress in this volume towards the content of a South Pacific theology. However, in the publication of the anthology *Living Theology in Melanesia: A Reader*, the actual content of a Melanesian theology forms the focus of the section titled, "Theology in Melanesia." It contains three papers all of which are relevant to the development of the content of theology.

The first reproduces the landmark paper, referred to above, by Joe Gaqurae. Tragically, Gaqurae died an untimely death in March 1985, "a great loss to theology in Melanesia."[93] His paper of almost a decade earlier

89. PCC, "Fourth Assembly," 233–34.
90. PCC, "Fourth Assembly," s.v. "Final Resolutions."
91. Tuza, "Instances," 48.
92. Hagesi, "Towards a Melanesian Christian Theology," 17.
93. May, *Living Theology*, 306.

was considered worthy of inclusion in this publication as "a prophetic statement" which "brings our Reader to the threshold of theology unmistakably Melanesian."[94]

The other two papers are illustrations of Gaqurae's advocacy for taking particular cultural themes or practices, and using them to localize the Christian gospel. Simon Apea's "Footprints of God in Ialibu"[95] speaks of the presence of God in terms of the tribal god Yakili, of ancestral spirits, and of power. Penuel Ben Idusulia's "Biblical Sacrifice through Melanesian Eyes,"[96] does what the title suggests, namely connects traditional cultural practices of sacrifice with themes of sacrifice in Scripture, referring in particular to the death of Jesus. The greater significance of these two papers is two-fold. First, they begin to give quite specific cultural content to the "incarnation" of the Christian faith in Pacific cultures, and secondly, they counter the view that traditional Pacific cultures, per se, are at odds with the Christian gospel.

At the 1985 consultation on theological education in Suva, Sione 'A. Havea, in calling for a theology which is grounded in the soil of the Pacific, writes, "In contextualizing theology we look to our history, culture and customs to illustrate in the light of the Good News, what God is like and is doing to us in his saving acts of revelation and salvation."[97]

It is in this light that Havea then introduces a "theology of celebration" and "coconut theology,"[98] in which he applies two familiar cultural images to illustrate the central features of the Christian faith. In this way he connects the content of theological expression with the common experience of Pacific Island people. At the time, the significance of Havea's proposals for a theology grounded in local soil could not have been anticipated. The notion of "coconut theology" captured people's imagination such that in subsequent years, this came to be adopted within and beyond the Pacific as the hallmark of Pacific Theology. Palu speaks of "coconut theology" as "the most distinctive formulation of Pacific Theology"[99] and of Havea as "the most influential theologian of the twentieth century in the Pacific region . . . the father of contextualization."[100] He restated his views even more strongly ten years later.[101] The place of "coconut theology" on the international stage

94. May, Living Theology, xii–xiii.

95. Apea, "Footprints of God," 218–55.

96. Idusulia, "Biblical Sacrifice," 256–303.

97. Lang et al., Towards, 22.

98. Lang et al., Towards, 22–24.

99. Palu, "On Pacific Theology," 35.

100. Palu, "On Pacific Theology," 33.

101. Palu, "Dr. Sione 'Amanaki Havea."

is noted further in 2007, at the ninth PCC Assembly, when the WCC President for the Pacific region, John Taroanui Doom, called on Pacific islanders to be more assertive in bringing their voice into international forums. He cited "coconut theology" as the example of a "Pacific theological insight," worthy of international consideration alongside those that emanate from Europe.[102] Clearly it deserves close attention in exploring the content of the contextualization of theology.

First Emerging Topic in Contextualization:
Coconut Theology

Uriam devotes nine pages of his thesis to the development of, and debates around, Coconut Theology, which took place during the formative period of the 1980s.[103] Apart from Coconut Theology, he considers that all other localized Pacific theologies to have been no more than "outlines," and "although they developed in response to finding a better way of communicating the Christian message to the changing conditions in the Islands . . . they were really applications of other influential theologies from outside the Pacific."[104]

The coconut as an image lends itself to an insightful and profound statement of Christian theology in the Pacific Islands. There are good reasons why such a theology might speak powerfully to Pacific peoples.[105]

First, the coconut pre-existed the arrival of inhabitants in the Pacific Islands.[106] This "pre-existent" aspect of the coconut parallels the confession that the presence of God in the South Pacific precedes, not only the coming of the missionaries, but also any known human occupation. In this sense, the coconut is genuinely resident, and rooted in Pacific soil, and reflects the residence of God in the soil of the Pacific Islands.

Secondly, the coconut tree is found everywhere throughout the islands; there is almost no island of the South Pacific where the coconut tree is not found. This aspect of the coconut mirrors the universal character of the Christian faith.

---

102. Gold, "Pacific Churches."

103. Uriam, "Theology and Practice," 145–54.

104. Uriam, "Theology and Practice," 149.

105. Prior, "I am the Coconut."

106. Archaeologist Matthew Spriggs has identified remains of a coconut on the island of Aneityum in Vanuatu dating back 6,000 years, leading to the conclusion that the coconut was native to the islands of the Pacific. See Spriggs, "Early Coconut Remains," 71–76.

The third point relates to the actual use of the coconut plant. Apart from the obvious value of the fruit of the coconut as a source of food, the coconut tree, as a whole, has the most broad and varied of uses and purposes for local island people. Its trunk is used for the pillars of homes; its crown of leaves is used for thatching of roofs, for walls of dwellings, and for weaving both mats and fishing nets, and its bark contains an oil which is used for medicinal purposes. The outer husk and the inner shell are used as a source of firewood; the outer husk is also used for weaving a twine or rope while the inner shell is also used as a drinking vessel. In more recent times, the coconut has also been a significant contributor to the economy of South Pacific countries, being smoked and exported as copra, for the purposes of perfume production. The fruit of the tree is a ready source of both food and drink. When the fruit is young and green, it offers good quantities of the most refreshing cool drink; when older, while the juice is less desirable for drinking, the inner flesh of the coconut is a basic ingredient for cooking (normally grated and "milked" and then mixed with root vegetable to be cooked in a ground oven). That the coconut is put to such a broad range of basic uses in sustaining the daily life of the people, is understood to mirror the diverse ways in which the gospel serves and sustains human life. In that sense the coconut represents the gospel of Jesus Christ and "the one thing needful" for living (Luke 10:42).

Apart from what might be true about these diverse uses to which the coconut tree is put, it is the life cycle of the coconut that is perhaps the most expressive of the significance of the Christian gospel. This is the fourth point of reference between the gospel and the coconut plant. The fruit of the coconut grows at the very top of the coconut tree and is inaccessible to human reach, thus representing the transcendence of God, unreachable to humankind. In its own time, the coconut ripens, then falls to the ground, rolling to the lowest point, at which it then comes to rest. This is understood to represent the descent of God to the world in the person of Jesus Christ, a descent that was to the lowest and most humble points of human life. If the coconut is left at that point, the interior of the coconut undergoes a transformation whereby the juice dries out, the flesh expands, roots are sent out into the ground, and a shoot forms the beginning of a new coconut tree—what in Vanuatu is known as a "navara." The connection between the life-cycle of the coconut fruit, and the incarnation, death and resurrection of Jesus, is, to the Pacific Islander at least, an obvious one. The connection is completed by two further elements: first, the fact that, at the end from which the juice of the coconut is drunk, a de-husked coconut has a "human face" in the form of three points, which are referred to as two eyes and a mouth; secondly, the fact that the coconut tree has a life-span comparable to the life-span of a human, living for up to seventy-five years of age, and bearing its best crops between twenty-five and fifty years.

It is hardly surprising then, that in the South Pacific, the coconut has also been used for the elements of the sacrament of the Lord's Supper. In fact, its liturgical significance in the sacrament has been much greater than simply making use of the flesh and the juice as a form of bread and wine. At the 1979 workshop on "Culture and Faith" in the New Hebrides, an indigenous liturgy for the Lord's Supper was developed, using the coconut.[107] It included using a local bush-knife to de-husk the outer shell of the coconut, during prayers of confession, to represent confession of the sinful acts of humanity in rejecting, stripping and killing Jesus Christ. Later in the liturgy, the same knife is used to break open the husked coconut to expose both the flesh and the juice, the latter spilling out expressively into a bowl—the broken body and poured-out blood of Jesus.

Such an approach to localizing theology, where local theologians identified specific cultural features and used them as a means of expressing an aspect of the Christian faith, was set to become a pattern from this period onwards. While the coconut remained the most prominent and evocative theological image, Uriam reports that

> Throughout the 1980s all sorts of theological reflections or interpretations about the Island way of life and Pacific realities emerged, and all sorts of symbols were used to illustrate these human relationships and experiences in the new Pacific: there was the canoe, the outrigger, the pandanus, the tavaala, the kava, the sea, the land, the gap, the grassroots, migration, celebration, and a lot more others.[108]

This constituted one notable step towards the contextualization of the specific content of theology in the South Pacific. But other equally significant moves were also now occurring.

From 1985 Onwards

At the 1986 "Consultation on Pacific Theology" held in Papua New Guinea, the papers presented reinforced the main themes from the preceding occasion in Fiji. However, there is one matter worthy of mention for its innovative and controversial theological content.

---

107. The liturgy has been developed further in Vanuatu and is recorded in detail in Prior, *Contemporary Local Perspectives*, 147–49. See also Uriam, "Theology and Practice," 146.

108. Uriam, "Theology and Practice," 73.

As part of his pioneering theology, Havea, recognizing that "Pacific theology is relatively new,"[109] makes the bold claim that "the Good News" of the Christian faith was already within Pacific cultures long before the arrival of the missionaries; the missionaries simply identified what was already present.[110] Havea grounds this claim in the story of the first Pentecost (Acts 2:1–11) when, through the visitation by the Holy Spirit, the gathered apostles proclaimed the good news in such a way that Jews from every nation under heaven heard it, each in their own native language. On this basis, Havea asserts that while the content of the "Good News" is the particular historical and contextual story of Jesus Christ—his birth, his life, and Calvary—it was through the Holy Spirit at the first Pentecost that "the effectiveness of these events was immediate and simultaneous to every part and every people of the world."[111] In making this claim, Havea not only contradicts the missionary heritage, that cultures of the Pacific were void of any "Good News" until their arrival, but he locates the "enlightenment" of Pacific cultures in the event of the first Pentecost. The missionaries brought nothing new into the Pacific context; they merely illuminated what was already present.

This is not a theological approach that was quickly endorsed in subsequent Pacific consultations; in fact, it has come under strident criticism by some as being "far removed from the historically accepted accounts of the work of the nineteenth century missionaries to Tonga."[112] However what did gain greater traction was the claim of God's self-revelation in Pacific cultures prior to the arrival of missionaries, a claim grounded in God's act of the creation of all things. While some would stand with Havea in asserting the pre-missionary presence of the gospel within the traditional cultures of the people, the notion of the pre-missionary presence of God has been less controversial, and has become increasingly supported by Pacific voices over the years, providing a key addition to the content of a Pacific theology.

These matters were addressed further in the 1987 Consultation on Gospel and Culture.[113] While this 1987 consultation did not add much to the actual definition of theology in the South Pacific, it did make measurable headway in attending to the content of such a theology.[114] Several years later,

109. Havea, "Christianity in the Pacific," 11.
110. Havea, "Christianity in the Pacific," 12.
111. Havea, "Christianity in the Pacific," 12.
112. Palu, "On Pacific Theology," 39.
113. Chandran, *Cross and the Tanoa.*
114. See Rzepkowski, "Stepping Stones."

at the EATWOT conference in 1994, prominent Pacific theologian, Tuwere, highlights this 1987 consultation as one that had significant influence on the agenda of theology in the South Pacific.[115] It was the first occasion on which a conference on this topic had been held involving a wide cross-section of Pacific Island representatives, along with international visitors. The background to the conference was the growing global recognition that the Western missionary era had led to the denigration of the "receptor cultures," and it was now important to engage, in a new way, with the global missiological question of the interaction between the gospel and cultures.

It was Tuwere who chaired the event. In his opening welcome, he explained the purpose of the gathering: "We have been called together to wrestle with this great and important theme and we hope that it will be an occasion when we understand one another properly and deeply. We are invited to get into the deeper meaning of what the gospel is all about, what culture is and how gospel and culture interact with each other."[116]

Five background papers and three key addresses, representing a range of voices across the Pacific, and a diversity of themes, resourced the conference. At the end of the three-day gathering, a consensus was reached among the participants with a range of significant affirmations and implications. It was acknowledged that the relationship between the gospel and cultures is "dialectical," involving a fluid interaction between the gospel and the cultural context that "demands constant reference to God's action in Jesus Christ and the discernment of his presence and action in the enhancement of the quality of life of humanity and the enrichment of human life in its totality."[117] Consistent with this affirmation, the consensus then endorsed "the possibility of discerning the presence of Christ even before the Missionaries had brought the gospel." This is not the same point as the one made by Havea in the 1986 consultation. In this case, the consensus statement goes on to say, "The missionaries did not bring Christ to the Pacific. They came to bear witness to Christ and brought the knowledge of Christ as revealed in Jesus of Nazareth."[118] This "possibility" was provided by the "positive elements in the different island cultures" that included "the practice of hospitality, and corporate responsibility for one another, the principle of sharing and caring, the tradition of resolving conflict situations through processes of reconciliation."[119]

---

115. Tuwere, "Agenda."

116. Chandran, *Cross and the Tanoa*, 1.

117. Chandran, *Cross and the Tanoa*, 15.

118. Chandran, *Cross and the Tanoa*, 14.

119. Chandran, *Cross and the Tanoa*, 14.

At the same time, it was recognized that the gospel brings judgment on other elements of local cultures, without any of these being identified. Some traditional cultural elements were left for further exploration. These included practices of the drinking of kava or yaqona, betel nut chewing, chiefly systems, the role of women.[120] In a statement that is odd for its assumption, it was proposed that practices that "appear to be incompatible with social economic progress" also required further exploration. These included bride-price payment, funeral and wedding feasts, gift giving and the extended family system.[121] The "oddity" is the inference that "social economic progress" is consistent with the gospel; in fact it may rather be an aping of Western cultural commitments to the importance of economic progress.

Nevertheless, the recognition that the topic of "Gospel and Culture" was now to become an agreed priority for the theological agenda for the Pacific, is found in the wide-ranging recommendations that were referred for action to be taken by SPATS. This would commit the churches to raising the profile of this topic in all theological colleges and in church programs, both locally and regionally. It would also lead to the production of written educational resources for local congregations, and the promotion of the use of cultural symbols in worship.[122] It is notable that the "culture" to be embraced included, not only the traditional practices of Pacific Island communities, but also the emerging changes impacting on Pacific cultures by virtue of colonialism and globalization. "SPATS should initiate a program of political education, providing adequate tools for social analysis for enabling the people in their reflection, meaningfully relating the socio-political situations to the gospel faith."[123]

In terms of the contextualization of the content of theology, the overall benefit of the consultation was three-fold. First, it provided theological authenticity for the view that the cultures of the Pacific testified to the presence of God, prior to the arrival of the missionaries. Secondly, it endorsed the view that the gospel and cultures are in ongoing dynamic relationship, in such a way that the gospel takes root within the cultural context of Pacific peoples, and the culture provides both the ingredients for the expression of the gospel, and the context for the experience of the gospel. Thirdly, it set the theological task primarily within the life of the local village communities and their cultural identities. With each of these three insights, significant aspects of the

120. Chandran, *Cross and the Tanoa*, 15. Kava is a root crop which, when squeezed for its liquid content, produces a drink which is used in custom rituals. Yaqona is the Fijian alternative name for Kava.

121. Chandran, *Cross and the Tanoa*, 15.

122. Chandran, *Cross and the Tanoa*, 16–17.

123. Chandran, *Cross and the Tanoa*, 17.

heritage of Western missiological presuppositions were identified and countered. In that sense, the conference was indeed significant for its contribution to the contextualization of the content of theology.

It is clear that the outcomes of the consultation on Gospel and Culture stimulated the further contextualization of theology across the Pacific in particular ways. Culturally contextual ways of expressing the content for a theology among Pacific Island theologians, and students of theology, expanded rapidly through the following decade, leading into and beyond the turn of the century. A perusal of articles published in each of the PJT and MJT reflects this normalizing trend.[124] In the 2008 publication of the MJT, editor Doug Hanson commemorates the first twenty-four years of the journal by helpfully making a summary list of the contents of the journal from its beginnings in 1985. He notes in his introductory comments that a prominent trend through this period has been a growing focus on particular cultural themes. He cites by way of example, "tribal feasts, dancing, marriage, polygamy, music, wisdom, tribal fighting, and reconciliation." He may also have added pig-killing, spirits, chiefly system, and traditional healing. A reading of the articles indicates that these cultural themes and practices have provided specific contextual content to theology in the Pacific.[125] In a similar way, a perusal of the topics for research theses among the students of the Pacific Theological College, leads to the same conclusion about the normalizing of contextual content.[126]

Through this same period, one of the more notable contributions to the further contextualization of the content of theology came in a 1988 article by Dick Avi, "Contextualization in Melanesia." Addressing the growing awareness, in the Third World, of theology as contextual, Avi identifies three factors "which inspired theology in the Third World to take particular contexts seriously."[127] He then applies them to the Pacific. First, says Avi, theology is not abstract, but responds to the liberating presence of the God who, in Jesus Christ, continues to engage with human realities—the problems of poverty, hunger, disease, ignorance, war, exploitation, and crime. Quoting from Romans 8:22–23, he sees the revolutionary struggles of the Third World as

124. See, for example, Tuwere, "Theological Reflection"; "Emerging Themes"; Havea, "Reconsideration"; Boseto, "God as Community"; "Towards"; Meo, "Advocacy"; Sala, "Attempt"; Halapua, "Fakakakato."

125. Hanson, "Twenty-Four Years," 4.

126. See, for example, Siolo, "Quest"; Kuru, "God's word"; Tufarina, "Contextual Study"; Zecharie, "Exploration"; Toap, "Melanesian Theology"; Qionivoka, "Fijian Traditional Healing."

127. Avi, "Contextualization in Melanesia," 10.

signs of the painful groaning of humanity toward an ultimate redemption.[128] Secondly, he affirms that theology has always grown out of contextual encounters, "whether that be theologies of the early church or more recently the theologies around the world—the theologies of the West and of the Third World."[129] Thirdly, he affirms that "contextualization involves a critical awareness which, in the language of Liberation Theology, is conscientisation."[130] In expanding this third point, and picking up the language of Liberation Theology from Latin America, Avi claims that genuine theology necessarily involves "an awakening to context so that people ask questions about poverty, unemployment, crime, separation, sickness . . . in such contexts, where problems, questions, and struggles happen, theology emerges as a way of seeking and building human life on earth."[131] Avi thus makes a direct connection between the content of theology and the struggles of people for fulfilment; in fact, it is the struggles of the people that provide the starting point for the content of theology. All contexts, he says, are marked by "conditions of captivity" and anticipate "an ultimate future."[132]

Avi then grounds these declarations in the particularity of the local context of Papua New Guinea. As current issues of human struggle, and therefore of theological engagement, he names the ongoing colonial oppression, a growing emphasis on material wealth and individual freedom,[133] the religious background of animism with its belief in spirits,[134] the fragmentation of church denominations, the missionary heritage which proposed that traditional cultures be eradicated, the imposition by the missionaries of the separation of the physical and spiritual over against a Melanesian view of life as a whole.[135] In the face of these struggles, he affirms the Christian hope for "a concrete fulfilment of the Kingdom," and sets this over against the false hopes articulated in the popular cargo cults.[136]

He then addresses an important theological issue of contextuality represented in the use of language. He calls for the term, "a Christian Melanesian" to be used, over against the familiar term, "a Melanesian Christian." The former is one whose life as a Melanesian is renewed by faith in Christ,

---

128. Avi, "Contextualization in Melanesia," 10.
129. Avi, "Contextualization in Melanesia," 11.
130. Avi, "Contextualization in Melanesia," 11.
131. Avi, "Contextualization in Melanesia," 11.
132. Avi, "Contextualization in Melanesia," 11.
133. Avi, "Contextualization in Melanesia," 14–15.
134. Avi, "Contextualization in Melanesia," 16.
135. Avi, "Contextualization in Melanesia," 19.
136. Avi, "Contextualization in Melanesia," 21.

and who lives out the truth of the incarnation in the particularity of the Melanesian context. The latter speaks of one who has migrated into a space called "Christianity," uprooted from cultural context, one for whom the gospel is distant from, and irrelevant to context. Avi concludes his paper with the affirmation that "those who call themselves Christians cannot be worthy of the name unless their lives bear that Cross in the struggles for freedom and unity of human society. This is true contextualization—theology contextualized in the world."[137]

Avi's contribution in the pursuit of contextualizing theology is to direct attention to "the challenges to the freedom and unity of human society" that arise from two discrete sources: first, traditional Pacific cultures, and secondly, contemporary socio-political forces. Both intra-cultural and external forces, for Avi, create their own forms of "captivity" among Pacific peoples. It is these that then become the ingredients for theological engagement, in such a way that the theological task involves an awakening to these realities, and a struggle for appropriate expressions of freedom and reconciliation. Any sense of separation between theology and such struggles of the people, has no place in Avi's view of the content of a theology for the Pacific. It is the very struggles themselves that determine the agenda for contextualization, and the orientation of this contextualization is the "freedom and unity of human society."[138]

What is notable in Avi's approach is his strong connection with the theological agenda that had shaped contextual theology in Latin America under the influence of Liberation Theology. This influence was subsequently to find expression in a range of ways across the Pacific, most particularly in the face of the broader contemporary socio-political issues impacting on the life-style and identity of Pacific peoples. The 1992 publication of the PJT illustrates this well. The editorial introducing the volume, reports that "the Pacific Journal of Theology has until now never attempted in a single issue to identify and reflect systematically upon conflict situations in the Pacific. In this issue, we make a first effort."[139] While acknowledging that only a selection of "the regional social ills" can be addressed in one issue of the journal, and noting the omission of relevant issues such as "the tragedy of the high incidence of suicide in Samoa and parts of Micronesia, or the ongoing struggle for independence in Kanaky," it does include "the upsurge in violence, growing gap between rich and poor/powerful and powerless, racial tensions, dependency on foreign entities, threats to the environment, French nuclear testing

137. Avi, "Contextualization in Melanesia," 22.

138. Avi, "Contextualization in Melanesia," 22.

139. Johnson-Hill, "Editorial," 1.

in French Polynesia, the Earth Summit, the shift to a money economy, the rise of AIDS, Fiji's military coup, justice and peace, the gospel of economy, reconciliation and violence in Bouganville."[140]

The breadth and diversity of these issues displays the extent to which the categories of Liberation Theology had come to impact upon the South Pacific. Although the beginnings of such influence was already recognizable from the 1970s—in the struggles for decolonization and political independence across the Pacific Island nations—it has come to influence the content of theology in the Pacific across a much wider array of socio-political and cultural issues in the later post-colonial era. As such, it stands alongside Coconut Theology in its influence, and is worthy of further examination as an expression of contextualization.

SECOND EMERGING TOPIC IN CONTEXTUALIZATION: LIBERATION THEOLOGY

Uriam identifies Liberation Theology as "the most popular form of a theology which originated from outside the Pacific and which has found effective application within the Pacific."[141] This feature of local theology emerged initially through the period when island nations took up their fight for political independence. No doubt influenced by a cultural heritage which saw matters of religion and social ordering as part of an integrated whole, indigenous church leaders were seen as leaders of their people in all aspects of their life. It was only natural that these church leaders would then be the ones to embody and represent the aspirations of their people to gain independence from colonial powers. Liberation theology provided the framework for movements of independence within their own countries and in the countries of their neighbors.

This engagement in social and political action extended beyond the pioneering role in the achievement of national independence. In his survey of the emergence of theology within the South Pacific, Forman gives attention to particular indigenous leaders whose theological commitment called them "to address the major social and economic problems of the Pacific and the world."[142] Such theologians include Tongan Bishop Finau[143] and indigenous New Caledonians,[144] most prominently Pothin Wete.[145] They all had in com-

---

140. Johnson-Hill, "Editorial," 1.

141. Uriam, "Theology and Practice," 152.

142. Forman, "Finding," 118.

143. Forman, "Finding," 117.

144. Forman, "Finding," 117.

145. Forman, "Finding," 117.

mon that their actions were integrated with a Christian faith built upon the cry for justice and freedom in the face of oppression, and upon the hope for a new creation. By way of illustration, Forman describes the turmoil in New Caledonia in the late eighties leading Wete to become an important figure across the Pacific as an activist, theological leader and teacher—he was on the Faculty of the PTC and so exercised a significant influence in theological formation of that generation. Forman describes Wete as "an ardent champion of the Kanaks" and "a theological thinker rather than an activist but whose thinking points clearly to vigorous action."[146]

The dynamics of Liberation Theology have continued to be applied in the South Pacific in three distinct areas: (1) the ongoing struggles for particular nations to achieve independence; (2) the struggles of the whole region to avoid exploitation and manipulation by global powers; (3) the struggles against the impact of traditional cultural attitudes and practices.

In relation to the first, the ongoing struggles on behalf of the peoples of New Caledonia, Tahiti and West Papua routinely appear on the agenda of local and regional church gatherings. On the second of these, the Pacific Conference of Churches has maintained its commitment to protect the South Pacific from various forms of exploitation at the hands of foreign powers; this continues to be the theme of regional conferences. The 2013 PCC Assembly held in the Solomon Islands provides a perfect illustration. Its final resolutions are directed almost exclusively to such issues. Apart from the call for zero-tolerance to nuclear testing, the resolutions call for a stop to all seabed mining, an end to the stigmatisation of those suffering from AIDS, further research into climate change and its impact, and a commitment to monitor the arms trade following reports that gun ownership in the Pacific was escalating.[147]

On the third of the above, Liberation Theology has found a home also among those who struggle against gender captivity promulgated from within their own traditional cultures. "Women in the Islands tend to see Liberation Theology as the most appropriate way of thinking about their Christian faith in the Islands today. . . . Island women tend to see themselves also as oppressed people and that is why Liberation Theology is very suitable for them."[148] In pursuing the agenda for liberation in the context of such cultural oppression, Uriam identifies the right of women to be ordained as leaders of the church, equality in family life and in decision-making, the end of abuse both at home and in the work place, and exclusivist male-oriented language,

---

146. Forman, "Finding," 118.

147. WCC, "Pacific Conference of Churches Resolutions."

148. Uriam, "Theology and Practice," 149.

as some of the main issues to be addressed. The oppressors of the women are variously identified as men, traditional culture, and the church.[149] In 2003, the women's group, Weavers, produced its own publication giving expression to the liberation theology of women in the South Pacific. It is a collection of twenty-three essays, from women across the region, and represents a forthright articulation of their struggles and hopes.[150]

A further key contribution to the contextualization of the content of theology through this period came from Sevati Tuwere, and involved the unique Pacific understanding of land as represented in the word "vanua." While this was not entirely absent from earlier contributions to contextualization,[151] it formed the focus of Tuwere's doctoral thesis,[152] as a result of which he found himself being identified as the leading proponent of this theme. For Tuwere, the Pacific notion of "land" was not simply one of many relevant features of Pacific cultures, but it lay at the very heart of the Pacific Islander's worldview. In this sense, the process of contextualization for the Pacific took a particularly important further step, represented for Tuwere in the call for an "Oceania theology." He articulated his views first at the Weavers" conference in 1991, then at EATWOT in 1994, and later at the programmatic four-year Pacific-wide forums on "Contextual Theology."[153]

THIRD EMERGING TOPIC IN CONTEXTUALIZATION: OCEANIA THEOLOGY

For those of Western cultural origin, the significance of land for Pacific Islanders is difficult to comprehend. Tuwere speaks on behalf of cultures across the Pacific in his assertion that for Fijians, the importance of land "cannot be overemphasised."[154] It has both literal and symbolic meanings, which are "inextricably tied together."[155] The literal meaning refers to specific location or place, including everything in it—house, garden, and people in community—while the symbolic meaning refers to livelihood, identity, time, event, history, ancestors, and creation.[156] There is a profound sense in which the people and the land are soul-less without each other.

---

149. Uriam, "Theology and Practice," 149–50.

150. Johnson-Hill and Filemoni-Tofaeono, *Weavings*.

151. Kamu, *Samoan Culture*; Boseto, "Do Not Separate Us."

152. Tuwere, *Vanua*.

153. Tuwere, "Emerging Themes"; "Agenda"; "What is Contextual Theology?"

154. Tuwere, *Vanua*, 11.

155. Tuwere, *Vanua*, 33.

156. In chapter 2 of his book, Tuwere offers a rich and detailed description of the centrality of the land in both its literal and symbolic senses for the people of Fiji. See Tuwere, *Vanua*, 33–51.

Thus, connection with the land is fundamental to the identity of Pacific Islanders. Land is not simply a location on which to live and to plant food. To be without land is to be uprooted as a human being, in other words, to be dehumanized. In Vanuatu, it is commonly said, "Land, hem i mama blong mi" (that is, "the land is my mother"). What is contained in this declaration is the affirmation that human life is lived and nurtured within the "womb" of the land, and that to be dislocated from one's land is to be deprived of life. Over the years, changes and challenges to the cultures of Pacific peoples have in no way diminished this understanding. "The land we live on is like a mother with children. The children live out of the hand of the mother, day and night."[157]

Notably, a Pacific-wide workshop, on "Pacific Indigenous Peoples' Struggle for Land and Identity," was held in Fiji to mark the beginning of the new millennium. The statement from participants at the end of the workshop declared, "To us as Pacific Indigenous Peoples, we say that the land as our mother, known as vanua, fenua, enua, hanua, fonua, whenna, te aba, etc., is life, our soul and identity: land is people, resources, cultures, beliefs, spirituality, languages, chiefly system and sea."[158] Recognizing that "land" includes also the surrounding seas and the land beneath it, the statement continues, "Our theological understanding of the land in the water is one of 'God's garden.' . . . There is a place for everyone in the garden and for every tool to be used. The purpose of the garden is to grow, to bloom, flower and to give fruit.[159] It then concludes, "The issue of land, history and identity is the main burning issue of the region. . . . The theology of the land needs to be articulated as soon as possible."[160]

In accord with this concept of land as mother, it is pertinent that the primary catalyst for independence in Vanuatu was a growing awareness that the traditional lands of the local people were being taken away from local people and acquired by expatriates. In his autobiography, Peter Taurakoto, one of two people instrumental in founding the New Hebrides Cultural Association, identifies the issue of land takeover by foreign interests as the single most important catalyst for the birth of the independence movement. He writes: "We decided on the establishment of the New Hebrides Cultural Association and we organized a peaceful demonstration on Thursday

---

157. From the 2002 workshop group who took "Land" as the priority issue of "Gospel and Culture" facing their local communities. Prior, *Voice of the Local Church*, 97.

158. Workshop Participants, "Pacific Indigenous," 96.

159. Workshop Participants, "Pacific Indigenous," 96–97.

160. Workshop Participants, "Pacific Indigenous," 97.

19 August 1971 to stop the sale of the islands and subdivisions."[161] The return of those lands back into the hands of indigenous people was one of the primary aims of, and one of the most significant aspects of, political independence in Vanuatu. It was not arbitrary that the name selected for the newly independent nation was then "Vanua-tu."[162]

Given this intricate connection of land with the very identity of Pacific Islanders, it is hardly surprising that the topic of land, and, with it, the accompanying themes of creation, environment, ecology, and climate change, have now come to feature prominently in theological discussion and writings within the South Pacific. This found its earliest and clearest articulation in Tuwere who has set the agenda for others to pursue.[163] At the inaugural meeting of EATWOT in September 1994, he explained how, as Principal of PTC, he had re-shaped the curriculum of theology to be consistent with this Pacific world-view. He outlined a theology that uses the notion of "vanua" (land and sea) as indicating four things: "means of livelihood, making sense of time and event, place of traditions and ancestors, a reassuring of identity."[164] He then goes on to claim, "What is expected of us as theologians of the churches is to seek for the restoration of the presence of God within the created order. . . . This view has always been an integral part of our belief and value system in Oceania and is essentially a Christian idea."[165]

For Tuwere, this invites theologians from Oceania to "claim back parts of their cosmos that were rejected during the missionary and colonial period. This lost cosmos is experienced through our people who now find it difficult in many cases to remember their myths and legends, their dances and idioms, their thought categories and symbols."[166] This has powerful connections with the heart and hope of the Christian gospel. In "An Unfinished Agenda," Tuwere asks,

> Is there a vision of the future that we can all claim to feed our imagination and empower our zeal? Is there a dream that we can all dream together as we each seek to proclaim Christ and let his way be followed? . . . I believe there is. It is the eschatological vision of the reuniting of all things in Christ as found in Ephesians

---

161. Taurakoto, *Fighting for a Proper Passport*, 91, 113.

162. From the word "vanua," meaning "land."

163. See also Boseto, "Do Not Separate Us"; Tofaeono, *Eco-Theology*; Everi, "Eco-Theology"; Halapua, "HIV/AIDS."

164. Tuwere, "Agenda," 10.

165. Tuwere, "Agenda," 11.

166. Tuwere, "Agenda," 10.

1:10: as a plan for the fullness of time, to gather up all things in
Him, in heaven and things on earth.[167]

For Pacific Islanders, this expands the heritage of Western missionary
theology and its culturally limiting focus on the action of God in human
history, and the conversion of individuals to the Christian faith. For the
Pacific world-view, the saving work of God in history embraces the whole
of creation, and the theological task is oriented to the renewal of creation.
Over the last generation, this has become a normative feature of theology in
the Pacific. Its significance is more than the fact that it identifies "land" as
a central feature of the context of Pacific peoples; it establishes an Oceanic
world-view as the essential frame of reference for the contextualization of
the content of theology within the Pacific. In that sense, it constitutes an
important leap in the contextualization process.

WOMEN ON THE CONTENT OF THEOLOGY

Pacific women's contribution to theology emerged from the beginning of
the 1990s, following the formation of Weavers. Their unique contribution to
the content of theology presented a challenge to the common assumptions
about the core content of a Pacific theology. Johnson-Hill remarks, "The
two regional consultations on Women and Ministry (1989 and 1991) have
generated intense debate and soul-searching, especially in the seminary
community."[168]

In relation to the content, women advocated strongly for a theology
that, at its heart, took up the situations and struggles of women and their
rapidly changing roles in Pacific cultures. "Issues surrounding the role of
women in church and society have surfaced in recent years as a major concern in Pacific Island churches."[169] The contextualization of theology was
to involve, not only these more general issues of cultural change and challenge, but also the particular personal stories of women in the midst of this
cultural turmoil. Theology is not about general issues, ideas or concepts, but
it is "the life and experience of simple and poor women"; it is this concrete
reality that is "the basic content of theological thinking and doing."[170]

In her 1991 paper, Kanongata'a takes up the issue of the oppression
of women. With reference to the engagement between Jesus and Mary
in Luke 10:41–42, she calls upon the church to embody a community of

167. Tuwere, "Agenda," 12.
168. Johnson-Hill, "Editorial," 1.
169. Johnson-Hill, "Editorial," 1.
170. Kanongata'a, "Pacific Women," 31.

reconciliation in which women are no longer subservient to men. "Jesus allows Mary to break the shackles of subservience. He breaks the barrier of gender. His coming is a call to women to enter into communion with him, to be his disciples and to be fully liberated. . . . Jesus and Mary had the courage to break the shackles which bound women to an inferior position in society."[171] Kanongata'a extends this agenda by asserting that women in the Pacific are becoming more aware, not only of concerns specific to themselves, "but also with problems of wider significance such as inadequate education, poverty, exploitation of the poorer classes in society, nuclear proliferation, militarism and ecological concerns."[172] She identifies "two prominent religious issues which women of the Pacific must address urgently—equality and the ordination of women."[173] Observing the increasing problems and materialism of the world, she says that "to theologize our life in the Pacific, in a visionary way, means a call to fashion an alternative way of living in the world. This is a way of covenantal responsibility. . . . It calls for a total metanoia."[174]

Drawing attention to the central place of Scripture in Women's Theology in her later paper, Kanongata'a focuses on Jesus' personal relationships with women. "Women were among his disciples and his closest friends. Women were lifted up, affirmed, accepted, healed and encouraged."[175] Mirroring the framework of a theology of liberation, she continues, "Jesus was not on the side of women because of their gender—but rather because women were among the "little people" of the time. Jesus was always on the side of the people who were treated unfairly or oppressed by others . . . these people were the true inheritors of the kingdom."[176]

There is a further aspect of women's experience which informs Kanongata'a's advocacy for the unique experience of women to be formative in the contextualizing of the content of theology. In her 1991 presentation to the Weavers consultation, she uses the image of a woman's womb to represent the birthing of women's theology. "The Pacific woman is emerging from a life of confinement in a womb to a new world of complex realities."[177] Noting the inter-relationship in Hebrew between "womb" (*rehem*) and "bowels," the seat of God's mercy (*rahmim*), she comments:

171. Kanongata'a, "Pacific Woman's Theology," 8.
172. Kanongata'a, "Pacific Woman's Theology," 9.
173. Kanongata'a, "Pacific Woman's Theology," 10.
174. Kanongata'a, "Pacific Woman's Theology," 11.
175. Kanongata'a, "Pacific Women," 27.
176. Kanongata'a, "Pacific Women," 28.
177. Kanongata'a, "Pacific Woman's Theology," 4.

"Women theologians are seeking to recover the word 'Rehem' (womb) to express the relationship between the womb and God's mercy. God's female maternal womb enables our birthing to come about with force and firmness but also with creativity and gentleness, without violence."[178] In her later paper in 1994, she asserts that if God meets people in their humanity, "then the women's femineity [sic] is part of and parcel of her total world and situation where God finds a home."[179]

Kanongata'a then locates her approach within the wider Pacific worldview identified in Tuwere's notion of the land, but without naming this. She reminds her audience that "The center of our focus, though, must be the 'image of God' . . . the God-given plan for all of creation. . . . This is the eschatological image of the peaceable kingdom when wild animals and little children can play together in harmony. Perhaps lions and babies are easier to imagine at peace than human males and females."[180] In the section, "Where do we go from here? Towards a Contextual church," Kanongata'a describes the rapidly changing and challenging situation of the world and the Pacific. She calls for the reclaiming of traditional cultural values of Pacific peoples:

> As Pacific people . . . our values frequently are contrary to the anti-values of the "first world." In other words, we have the potential to humanise because at least, in principle, and often in practice, we offer community instead of individualism, simplicity instead of opulence, helpfulness instead of selfishness, creativity and spontaneity instead of enforced slavery, celebration instead of mere enjoyment, and openness to transcendency instead of dull pragmatism.[181]

In the subsequent EATWOT meeting in 1996, women were again active contributors to the topic, "The Quest for a Pacific Theology." The affirmations that had been offered previously by Kanongata'a were reiterated in the major paper presented by Samoan minister, Marie Ropeti, who was then working for the PCC in Resources Development.[182] Ropeti surveys the situation of women around the Pacific and highlights the oppression they feel, and the struggles they have. She challenges the male domination of theology and of biblical interpretation. She criticizes the colonial impact on culture, including the separating of religion and politics. She concludes with a call for women to be recognized as equal contributors with men,

178. Kanongata'a, "Pacific Woman's Theology," 7.

179. Kanongata'a, "Pacific Women," 21.

180. Kanongata'a, "Pacific Women," 32.

181. Kanongata'a, "Pacific Women," 29.

182. Ropeti, "Women's Theology."

for the promotion of women's participation in church leadership, and for women to be given equal opportunity in theological education. Her paper was met with some discontent from the men in the consultation, but her input made it clear that the issues impacting specifically on Pacific women were becoming normative for the agenda for contextualizing theology in the South Pacific.

By the turn of the millennium, women were being recognized as key contributors to the theological task in the Pacific. Kanongata'a was again invited to present a paper on the occasion of the first major workshop on Contextual Theology, held in Fiji, as part of the four year plan sponsored by SPATS across the Pacific. Not wanting to "reproduce what Contextual Theologians from Africa, Asia and Latin America have written on the subject,"[183] Kanongata'a, with customary forthrightness, offers her own overview of the key elements of the content of a theology for the Pacific. The impact of colonization has been to "rape us of our cultural honor," and to put the colonized into "subordinate positions in society and the church." This has been perpetuated in worship with English tune music, Sunday black coats, white hats, Roman vestments, and rituals."[184] It is this legacy that "demands contextual theology." What is needed is "a theology that allows us to tell our own stories . . . we need a theology that will uplift us from our powerlessness to our God-given dignity . . . and never be ashamed of our 'nakedness' and 'nativeness.'"[185]

While the focus is clearly on the stories and struggles of women, the suggestion is that anything of Pacific culture and human experience may potentially form the ingredients of contextualization. "The traditional question of 'How can we adapt theology to our needs?' will have to be changed to, 'How can our needs be theologized?' Our needs become the raw material for doing theology. We are our needs and thus we are the 'clay' for moulding theology."[186] With a sense of being authorized by the nature of the Christian gospel as "incarnational," Kanongata'a quotes Latin American Rene Padilla, "Because of the very nature of the gospel, we know this gospel only as a message contextualized in culture."[187]

While giving central place to the cultural realities of Pacific Islanders in any contextual theology, for Kanongata'a, there is no risk of idolizing the culture. Arising from the experience of women, she asserts that "every

183. Kanongata'a, "Why Contextual?," 24.
184. Kanongata'a, "Why Contextual?," 24–25.
185. Kanongata'a, "Why Contextual?," 25.
186. Kanongata'a, "Why Contextual?," 27.
187. Kanongata'a, "Why Contextual?," 30.

culture needs purification and that is why there is a need for faith to encounter culture. . . . Although we need a strong cultural identity, we need to be on guard against doing a theology that places too much emphasis on cultural identity."[188] After again affirming Tuwere's Pacific world-view that recognizes the importance of cultural history and of creation as truly "sacramental," and "revelatory,"[189] she concludes with the declaration, "It will demand that we have confidence to do this in 'the Pacific Way.'"[190]

In terms of the contextualization of the content of theology, the contribution of women is to draw attention to the particular situation in which women find themselves. It is both the unique experience of women as child-bearers, and the oppressive cultural roles expected of women, which dominate these discussions. In this distinctive way, they add their own voice to the number of male voices, which have called for a substantial shift in the nature, and content of theology in the Pacific. It is a call for a clear detachment from the heritage of Western theology, and a firm embracing of Pacific cultures and context as the authentic and core ingredients in such a theology.

SUMMARY COMMENTS ON THE CONTENT OF THEOLOGY

Over the decades from the 1960s, there has been significant development in the way in which the content of a theology in the South Pacific has been contextualized. While assuming the central place of the Scriptures and the life of Jesus Christ, this contextualization of the content of theology has moved in a series of discernable steps, even if that movement has not been deliberate or smooth. It can be summarized in the following way:

1. The adoption of Western theological content as imparted by the missionaries

2. The adaptation, at first tentative, and then more confidently, of Western theological content into the language and symbols of Pacific cultures

3. Giving focused attention to addressing issues affecting the lives of Pacific peoples—socially and culturally

4. Engaging with socio-political struggles inherent in colonization, in search for liberation and political independence

---

188. Kanongata'a, "Why Contextual?," 37.
189. Kanongata'a, "Why Contextual?," 30.
190. Kanongata'a, "Why Contextual?," 38.

5. A growing readiness to take up the task of shaping a theology which is embedded in Pacific cultures and experience

6. Embracing personal and communal stories of suffering and oppression, particularly as represented by Pacific women

7. Reclaiming a Pacific world-view, of the unity of human life with all creation, into an "Oceania" theology

Set out in this way, the advancement over the years since the 1960s has been decisive, and has come to match the advancement in other parts of the Third World. However, this advancement continues to be accompanied by the tensions created by the persistence of the Western heritage of the content of theology, as introduced in the missionary history of the South Pacific. In addition, the development over these decades has not been without its critics. The most outspoken in recent times has been Tongan Ma'afu 'o Tu'itonga Palu.[191] Palu's primary assertion is that the steps towards the contextualization of the content of theology have meant that the unique authority of the content of the Scriptures has been supplanted by the authority of the Pacific context. Such a theology, he says, cannot claim to be Christian. This criticism goes hand in hand with Palu's claim that the Western missionary tradition has been falsely represented. For Palu, the Western missionaries were exemplary in upholding the centrality of the Scriptures, and what they have stood for is now seriously jeopardized.

What may be at issue here is not so much the centrality of the Scriptures, but what it means for the Scriptures to have a central role. Palu reflects an approach to Scripture that borders on textual literalism, in comparison with an approach that regards Scripture as unique witness to the primary Text, who is the living Word of the Gospel. In that sense, there is no serious threat to "the centrality of the Scriptures" in the voices of those leading the movement towards a contextual theology in the Pacific. Such voices consistently assume the centrality of the Scriptures. Tuwere himself exemplifies this. "Contextual theology ends as it begins from what God has already done in Jesus Christ, remembered and celebrated in the church which is the community of faith."[192] The Scriptures, not as a collection of texts, but as the normative testimony to the Good news of Jesus Christ, remain utterly central here.

Palu's criticisms will be voiced again, and more strongly so, in relation to the third of the categories under consideration, namely on the methodology of theology. To that category, we now turn.

191. See Palu, "On Pacific Theology," esp. 35–38.
192. Tuwere, "What is Contextual Theology?," 11.

THE METHODOLOGY OF THEOLOGY

In coming to this final of the three areas of exploration of the contextualization of theology in the South Pacific, we approach what is the most problematic and challenging element in the contextualization agenda. In the period being surveyed, there has been much discussion among Pacific Islanders about theology and its contextual character. However, there has been little focused attention given to the matter of contextualizing the methodology of theology. Even when attention is given to this, it is often in a more general way, rather than to any specific workings of a methodology.[193] For some, it seems sufficient to use the term "contextual" with the word "theology," assuming that this then indicates adequately a theological methodology. It is uncommon to find a paper by anyone from the South Pacific that offers any detail about a methodology that is culturally accessible and appropriate. Mostly, the methodology proposed seems implicit rather than explicit.

Defining Methodology

In his classic publication, "Models of Contextual Theology," Stephen Bevans identifies three primary questions that need to be brought to the matter of theological methodology: (i) What form does theology take? (ii) Who does theology? (iii) Can a non-participant in a context do contextual theology?[194] Given that the focus in this book is on the voice of indigenous peoples, the last of these is not relevant here. However the first two questions are important. Alongside these, I want to add two further questions of equal importance, namely, "What is the primary location for the theological task?" and "What is the primary purpose of theology?" Each of these four questions is critical to the contextualization of the methodology of theology within the South Pacific. Thus it is these four questions that will be included in what is understood as theological methodology.

Before 1985

From the 1970s, there was a frequently articulated assertion that any theology that could claim to be contextual to the South Pacific must be integrated with the life of local village people. While this is asserted and endorsed by many, there is no real follow up as to how this might be implemented. By way of illustration of this point, Theodore Ahrens declares that the task of doing theology involves the minister in learning the theology of the people, engaging

193. In his 1992 article examining the progress towards a Pacific Theology, Rzepkowski states, "But what is still lacking is a suitable theological methodology," 44.

194. Bevans, *Models*, 17–21.

in dialogue with the people, helping the people to come to new awareness, and himself being open to learn. The process involves the whole community in doing theology.[195] Ahrens offers significant pointers here about what the calling to do theology involves, but he does not go on to give any specific indication as to how this might work within the community; it seems sufficient simply to set out certain broad markers, albeit important ones.

In the evolution and consolidation of a home-grown or contextual Pacific theology, one of the major challenges is precisely the question of methodology. Having identified what is important in the nature and content of a contextual theology, how then is this to be worked through fruitfully within a given local context? The article by Ahrens, which speaks at the same time of "doing theology" and "the minister as a change-agent," might be expected to say more than it does on the concrete detail of a methodology.

The same lack of detail about methodology is apparent in most of the primary material about theology in the South Pacific. In the concluding section of the report of discussions at the 1981 PCC Assembly, in dealing with the question, "What is Theology?," two distinct and different voices from the Assembly members are noted. One voice is from those who want to emphasize that theology belongs with "ordinary people" who "know God and speak of Him and His ways." The other is the voice of those for whom theology is "a systematic study, like a science, which is best done by professionals."[196] What follows is a series of seven statements under the heading "Is there a Pacific theology?" While the statements suggest that certain specific things need to be done to achieve the stated purposes (e.g., "All aspects of life including custom and culture should be brought to the center . . . to understand Christ," Bible translation which "is clear and in the language of the people . . . relevant to the culture and situation of the people," and "we must teach using stories, parables, meaningful human encounters"), that is as far as the text goes in terms of a methodology of theology.[197]

A more specific suggestion of a methodology for theology appears in an earlier 1976 article by James Bergquist, a visitor to Papua New Guinea who, as a member of the Theological Education Fund of the World Council of Churches, had surveyed theological education in the emerging Third World. He brings the findings of his global survey into a poignantly titled article addressing theological education in Melanesia.[198] He claims that theological

---

195. See Ahrens, "Doing Theology," esp. 71–73. Although not a Pacific Islander, he speaks out of a deep immersion in the Pacific context.

196. PCC, "Fourth Assembly," 233.

197. PCC, "Fourth Assembly," 233.

198. Bergquist, "Theological Education in Ferment," 5–15.

education in the Third World faces a crisis as a result of a "post-colonial revolution" that marks the beginning of the end of Western world dominance.[199] With this "revolutionary" change, Bergquist is confident that the structures of theological education, put in place during the missionary era, cannot be sustained by local churches. He calls for a form of theological education that follows the model of Latin American educationalist Paulo Freire. With specific reference to pedagogy, he then writes, "At every school I have visited recently, one is immediately struck by the growing dissatisfaction with their pedagogical procedures: over-dependence on the lecture method, the isolation of the student from 'life issues,' attempts to cover too much in too little time, the inability of the schools to develop satisfactory methods of promoting critical and independent study."[200]

Then, citing Paulo Freire, he calls for a dramatic change in the methodology of theological education (and by implication, also of theology) across the Third World, including Melanesia: "Freire insists that the student is a subject—not an object—and that learning takes place in the dialogical inter-change between teacher and student. . . . Education will either confirm him as an object or it will become the practice of freedom where men learn to participate in the transformation of the world."[201] Without giving details as to how this model might be worked out in local Pacific communities, he sees this approach to be "a truly living theology authentic to the local culture."[202]

Also wanting to stimulate ways of doing theology that make it a task undertaken by local Melanesian communities, is Albert Burua, Principal of Rarongo Theological College in Papua New Guinea. In 1980, having returned from a three-month European trip including six "eye-opening" weeks in Switzerland where he was exposed to the wider ecumenical church,[203] Burua sets out five guidelines for the development of a more indigenous theological education. Two of these are relevant for our consideration of a methodology of theology:

1. Theological reflection in a Melanesian context. Melanesian students have a lot in themselves that can be used as the basis for theological reflection. Students have written articles, theses and essays. It is possible to collect some of these materials and use them as a basis for theological discussion?

199. Bergquist, "Theological Education in Ferment," 7.
200. Bergquist, "Theological Education in Ferment," 12.
201. Bergquist, "Theological Education in Ferment," 13.
202. Bergquist, "Theological Education in Ferment," 15.
203. Burua, "Theology and Melanesia," 9.

2. Group work by scholars in theology. Within seminaries we have people who are theologians. Is it possible for these people to work together
as a team, collecting and discussing issues that are being raised by our
churches?[204]

Because of Burua's leadership role in theological education, the recommendations refer more directly to life in the community of the theological
college rather than to the wider life of the church, or to village church communities. His primary concern is to promote ways in which the theological
task might be taken up more effectively, within and by the college community. His proposals imply quite specific and achievable means of developing
a more contextualized theology. However, it is notable that, while his second
point refers to communal and oral activity by scholars, with a focus on current issues in the community of faith, his first point refers to their written
articulations as a basis for discussion. In other words, although it hints at
some ideas that might be embraced in the college community, it assumes a
competency in literacy. As such it does not engage seriously with the pedagogical challenges posed earlier by Bergquist.

The Year 1985

The deliberate purpose of the Melanesian Journal of Theology was to foster
the development of theology for and by Melanesians. In honoring the ordinary activities of a local Christian community as a focus for theology, the
purpose of the journal is,

> to concentrate on theology in all its manifold aspects, from ex-
> egesis to doctrine, including worship and evangelization, ethics
> and pastoral practice, with emphasis on the thoughts and feel-
> ings of Melanesians as they struggle to map out the intellectual
> structure of a theology for their unique situation. . . . [These ef-
> forts] will draw on the already existing oral sources of indigenous
> theology in Melanesia, whether in Pidgin or in local languages:
> the stories and songs, the adaptation of myths, the solutions to
> practical problems found by prayer and consensus.[205]

The most specific and impressive setting out of a methodology for theology appears in the first volume of the journal. It merits close scrutiny. It
comes from Robert Hagesi in his paper, "Towards a Melanesian Christian
Theology."[206] In the final of three sections of his paper, headed "Methodol-

---

204. Burua, "Theology and Melanesia," 9–12.
205. May, "Editorial," 2.
206. Hagesi, "Towards a Melanesian Christian Theology," 17–24.

ogy," he is one of few people who tackles, in any deliberate way, the particular challenge of how Christian theology might become culturally Melanesian in its methodology. Taking his lead from Bernard Lonergan, and the latter's insights about cross-cultural communication,[207] Hagesi sets out what he calls "propositions for a methodology" for Melanesian theology, namely that it

> be formulated in the language of our people, not merely in terms
> of the words used but in the people's terms of reference in their
> culture; use a set of procedures which make sense in that cultural
> context, and be inclusive; address itself to issues and questions
> that are real to the people (and ignore those that are not relevant);
> use appropriate literary forms and genres . . . such as poetry, wise
> words, or religious terms of Melanesia; evolve from the Christian
> community, and all the members of the community be involved
> in the task; be open and free to invite the Christian community
> to suggest and to make constructive verbal expressions; avoid
> syncretism and the tendency to confuse or make the gospel be-
> come culture-bound. It must allow the gospel to transcend and
> transform our Melanesian cultures; be Christocentric, biblical,
> prophetic and use hermeneutical methods, and should avoid
> simple buying and selling of existing theologies; be open-ended
> and subject to the guidance of the Holy Spirit.[208]

Hagesi displays a consistency between his understanding of the meaning of Melanesian Christian Theology, its content and its methodology: "The term Melanesian Christian Theology would suggest a Christian theology or knowledge of God as experienced, expressed and understood in a Melanesian context."[209] He emphasizes the importance of the local Christian community as the context for participation and reflection in theology. Then, quoting John Macquarrie's Principles of Christian Theology,[210] he also emphasizes the need "to express its reflection in the clearest language and thought forms of the community involved. . . . Language is the most important medium of communication without which theologizing can never be done."[211]

---

207. Hagesi, "Towards a Melanesian Christian Theology," 22.

208. Hagesi, "Towards a Melanesian Christian Theology," 22–23.

209. Hagesi, "Towards a Melanesian Christian Theology," 18.

210. "Theology may be defined as a study which, through participation in and reflection upon a religious faith, seeks to express the content of this faith in the clearest and most coherent language available" (Hagesi, "Towards a Melanesian Christian Theology," 18).

211. Hagesi, "Towards a Melanesian Christian Theology," 20.

Acknowledging the oral character of Melanesian communities, Hagesi continues, "But at the same time there is no harm in having oral theology which can be communicated in the form of story-telling. Melanesian custom stories, myths and legends have been preserved and passed on from one generation to another in this way. Why not Melanesian Christian Theology?"[212] Hagesi then asks, "What is now the criterion for developing such a theology?" In making reference to Paul Tillich's language of "ultimate concern," he then posits his own response, "If it is to be Christian in meaning and Melanesian in form then the criterion by which we articulate it is that it should be based on the biblical faith and what really concerns us in our Christian communities."[213]

Putting these several statements together, with the series of particular proposals for a methodology, Hagesi provides a number of helpful guidelines in terms of the methodological development of a "Melanesian Christian Theology." The value of his insights is that he offers concrete steps in the approach to theology that are culturally contextual within a village community. While he does not give any particular illustrations of the practice of this theology, his proposals for how it might work are some of the most clear and helpful offered by a Melanesian.

Following Hagesi's contribution to the contextualization of the methodology of theology within a local community of faith, it is somewhat surprising that there is little indication of any follow-up to his input, despite the growing emphasis in subsequent years on the importance of the contextualization of a theology for the South Pacific.

In explaining the ordering of the four parts to the book, "Living Theology in Melanesia" the editor John D'Arcy May writes,

> The structure of this anthology is a statement of its priorities. Part I devotes considerable space to what my colleague Esau Tuza suggested we call "village theology," on the analogy of what has been called "peasant theology" in the Philippines, and Minjung or "people's theology" in Korea. . . . The real life setting (sitz im leben) of Melanesian theology is the prolonged discussion on the beach, under a tree or round the fire, the singing (festival) or lotu (worship). The community does theology by reaching a consensus in reflecting on its practice.[214]

The particular section on "village theology" then includes certain village-based practices of Christian life and Christian communities: traditional

212. Hagesi, "Towards a Melanesian Christian Theology," 20.

213. Hagesi, "Towards a Melanesian Christian Theology," 21.

214. May, *Living Theology*, ix–x.

Melanesian prayers, hymns, sermons, a drama of the conversion of a sor-
cerer, a creed set in the context of traditional culture, and a moving story by
Bernard Narakobi recounting the death of his mother, titled "A Truly Noble
Death."[215] Although this is only one of four parts to the anthology, and there
are other views about theology in the remaining three parts, priority is given
to the recognition of these normal involvements and experiences of a local
Christian community as an important manifestation of both the content
and mode for theology in Melanesia.

Again, it is notable that there is no concrete detail as to how these
modes may be pursued or developed in village communities, but it is clear
that the term "theology" includes local village articulations of the Christian
faith, for example through prayer, hymn, sermon, and narrative accounts
of Christian living and dying. These suggest something of a concrete methodology for theology as it may be practiced within such village settings. It
relocates the theological enterprise, from its confinement within the walls of
theological institutions, into the life of the wider church. It also redefines the
nature of theology, away from its missionary heritage into something that is
more culturally contextual.

The 1985 consultation in Fiji is illustrative of the general fact that,
when it comes to consultations on Pacific theology, it is the definition and
content of theology, rather than the methodology of theology, that receive
greater attention. There was no specific paper, nor portion of a paper, that
engaged directly with issues of methodology. Any reference was indirect or
by way of implication.

Prominent Fijian Government Minister and Christian layman, Mahe
U Tupouniua was invited to open the consultation. He did so by speaking to
the conference topic, "Towards a Relevant Pacific Theology." His presentation highlighted the challenge facing the participants. Acknowledging himself to be a layman, Tupouniua reinforces the view that theology is a body
of knowledge that belongs solely to a professional group of people. As such,
it is "something a layman would rather leave to students and teachers of
theology."[216] Its relevance is only of marginal interest to the church; indeed,
"the church can still get by reasonably well without it."[217] Nevertheless, "The
layman would like ministers, pastors and members of the clergy to know
something about theology."[218] There is little here to encourage any sense of

215. May, *Living Theology*, xi.
216. Lang et al., "Towards," 9.
217. Lang et al., "Towards," 10.
218. Lang et al., "Towards," 9.

the vitality of theology in the life of the church, let alone any suggestion of a contextual methodology.

Subsequently, however, there was a good deal of emphasis at the consultation on the importance of theology being integrated with "Pacific identity,"[219] and grounded "in the local soil and in the local context."[220] Considerable discussion took place on the way in which the gospel and the cultural context might interact,[221] and how elements of Pacific life—coconut, celebration, and kava—can be used to localize theology.[222]

Within the summary reports offered by the working groups, there are some hints as to what is important in methodology. Included in these are a call for theology to be "of the people"[223] and that "laity be equipped with the confidence and ability to think theologically about their life experience."[224] While there is much energy given to other important questions related to the quest for a Pacific theology, further issues of methodology receive little attention.

From 1985 Onwards

The papers presented at the gathering in Papua New Guinea in 1986 add little to the issue of a contextual methodology. However, there is one paper worthy of particular mention. Mohenoa Puloka, exploring Pacific theology in the context of rural Tongan communities, begins his paper as follows: "The basic assumption of this paper is that since the Tongan context is predominantly rural, the Tongan Church must acknowledge that its ministry must always consist in the continuous interaction between the gospel and the struggles and aspirations of the rural community. . . . The Tongan Church must as a top priority develop and implement an applicable theological methodology."[225] Puloka notes, with further reference to the cultures of Tonga, "The relatively late emergence of written language in Tonga (begun in 1826) . . . and mostly the lack of a taste for writing in general, has made theology in Tonga exist largely in verbal form as oral tradition. The absence of any great theological work in this case is not surprising."[226]

---

219. See the paper specifically on Pacific Identity in Lang et al., "Towards," 14–19.

220. From the paper on "Pacific Theology" by Havea. See Lang et al., "Towards," 21.

221. Lang et al., "Towards," 25–7.

222. Lang et al., "Towards," 27.

223. Lang et al., "Towards," 29.

224. Lang et al., "Towards," 31.

225. Puloka, "Attempt at Contexualizing," 82.

226. Puloka, "Attempt at Contextualizing," 84–85.

The thrust of the remainder of his paper is on the methodology of theology. He declares that he is "particularly concerned with the methodology by which theology, in general, can respond most meaningfully and effectively to every aspect of human existence."[227] He then makes the point emphatically that the only appropriate methodology is represented by the notion of contextualization. "Contextualization is a theological methodology. It encourages the development of an authentic understanding of the Christian faith in particular cultures. . . . In applying this methodology to the Tongan context, the Tongan Church must understand contextualization as the inevitable inter-action between the text and the Tongan context."[228]

Puloka sees this approach to be "the most important mandate which has emerged out of the experiences of the younger churches of the Third World." The author sees the methodology of contextualization being grounded in the incarnation of Jesus, as the event in which God and human context intersect. He quotes Philippians 2:5–8 as an affirmation of this Christological grounding, and sees contextualization "as a theological methodology in which the Tongan church can participate meaningfully in the interaction between the gospel and the Tongan context."[229]

What is of interest here is Puloka's commitment to a particular methodology appropriate to the Tongan rural situation, and by implication to local village communities across the Pacific. It represents a methodology, namely "contextualization," which has been prominent in other parts of the Third World, and so connects the Pacific with this global theological movement. However, while the general principles of this methodology are firmly set forth, the concrete steps involved in its implementation are not clarified, nor does he indicate what might give this methodology its unique Tongan character. In his paper, Puloka seems then to shift his focus, away from rural Tongan communities, to developments of liberation movements in the Third World, and so the latter part of his paper takes up issues of social change, justice and liberation. In his conclusion, Puloka asserts that "The theology of the Church must be liberated from the shadow of the so-called "missionary theology" and Western theology in order that it emerges freely out of its own roots. . . . Contextualization is the serious scrutiny of the immediate local context for the purpose of determining the extent to which it fosters the full actualization of justice, liberation, and the development of the wholeness of life for the whole person."[230]

227. Puloka, "Attempt at Contextualizing," 87.
228. Puloka, "Attempt at Contextualizing," 83.
229. Puloka, "Attempt at Contextualizing," 88.
230. Puloka, "Attempt at Contextualizing," 99.

While rapid social changes have impacted powerfully across Tonga, including its village communities, we are left wondering how Puloka's approach might be implemented in the Tongan rural context, the very context that he sought to address.

Over the following generation of consultations on theology and theological education, and in published articles, there is growing support for the notion of "contextualization" of theology in the Pacific. However, with few exceptions, any discussions on methodology are focused on the broad principles of such contextual approaches to theology. There is little attention given to the particular features of a theological methodology that would be culturally distinctive and effective in achieving this contextualization for Pacific peoples, especially for local village contexts.

At the same time there remains continuing concern, even anguish, about the gap between formal theological education and the life and struggles of local church communities, and about the alienating influence of the heritage of the methodology of Western theology. These concerns appear at the 1994 inaugural meeting of EATWOT's Pacific Chapter. In the opening keynote paper,[231] Tuwere starts with the acknowledgement, "There is no doubt that a very real gap exists between theology and theological education on the one hand, and the churches on the other. And this gap can widen further if theology does not do anything to address the church's and society's real needs."[232] While the content of theology takes the form of "articulated speech," such theological speech ought to be the articulation of the work of the Spirit as it comes to expression "in the struggle of the community in which the theologian lives."[233] Given his own role in theological leadership, it is with brave honesty that he then confesses, "But, it has not really been translated into the language of the ordinary people; it remains the speech of the educated elites."[234] Tuwere concludes his paper by looking ahead to the future. Under "An Unfinished Agenda," he identifies three "areas of concern for future discussions." Among these is what he calls "People's theology," adding the important note, "A theology of the laity (church and secular laity) which I do not hear very much in the Pacific today, needs to be revisited."[235]

In the discussion that followed his paper, Tuwere's concern was widely and firmly endorsed. In the report on the "discussion highlights," there is agreement among the meeting participants of "the need to identify

231. Tuwere, "Agenda," 5–12.
232. Tuwere, "Agenda," 5.
233. Tuwere, "Agenda," 7.
234. Tuwere, "Agenda," 7.
235. Tuwere, "Agenda," 12.

whose task doing theology really is and for whose benefit it is done; concern about those Pacific theologians who are trained overseas who then need to reclaim their Pacific tradition, and the need to make theological education, ministry and theological reflection more relevant to the lives and needs of the people."[236]

To address effectively the "very real gap" to which Tuwere refers at the opening of his paper, and the endorsed need for a theology that belongs within the life of the church ("the laity"), the confession by Tuwere of the confinement of theology to "educated elites" will need to be addressed as a priority. It is not so much an issue of the content of theology, as Tuwere seems to suggest, it is more an issue of the nature of theology and its methodology. By restricting the expression of theology to "speech"—spoken or written—and the sort of "speech" that requires formal articulation by individuals within an academic environment, the task of theology will remain biased towards, if not captive to, "educated elites" (noting here that the term "education" is used in a Western cultural sense). Unless the issues of the nature and methodology of theology are addressed, the gap between theology and local church communities, and with it the sense of the irrelevance of theology to the church, most especially in rural locations, will remain unchanged.

As suggested already, the methodology represented in Latin American Liberation Theology appeals to some as a genuine option for the Pacific, particularly in the light of the impact of globalization. At the second meeting of the Pacific Chapter of EATWOT, Haraki Gaudi offers a paper on the impact of globalization and the consequences of this for Pacific theology.[237] In it, he responds to some of the concerns raised by Tuwere at the first meeting, engaging with the question of a methodology that involves local Christian communities in the theological task. He does so by advocating in the Pacific for the particular form of Liberation Theology which, grounded in the conscientisation ideas of Paulo Freire, emerged in Latin America. Having noted the growing impact of globalization on the Pacific, and supporting "a programme of conscientisation as advocated by Freire," the task of theologians is to "make the poor number one on the agenda of theological enterprise. . . . We need a type of theology that is read and interpreted at the grassroot level in a language they can understand."[238]

236. Tuwere, "Agenda," 12.

237. Gaudi, "One Gospel." Gaudi was Head of the Department of Anthropology in the University of Papua New Guinea and a consultant for the PCC.

238. Gaudi, "One Gospel," 73.

For Gaudi, this has implications for what happens in theological colleges and its theological curriculum. "This must be a serious agenda of theological colleges for Oceanic reflection. Theologize the situation of the people, then they come to the personal praxis. We cannot propose praxis unless people are educated first to know who they are and what they can do."[239]

While Gaudi's proposals suggest a way of bringing together the formal theological task and the church community as "subjects" in the theological process, they risk importing a foreign theological framework that may, or may not, be effective in local South Pacific communities. Uncritical attempts to import Latin American forms of Liberation Theology into other cultural contexts have met with strong opposition on the grounds of a lack of contextual integrity and contextual appropriateness.[240] In that sense, this approach to theology cannot be described as a genuine contextualization of theology even if, as we have already seen, elements of its methodology may be well suited to some aspects of the South Pacific situation. What it does not offer, as will become clear, is a methodology, which can address fundamental issues of the cultural world-view of local village communities. Nor does it offer a means by which theology can be owned by such local communities.

One of the more creative and illuminating consultations in contextual methodology was a lower-profile event, convened by the Aotearoa New Zealand Presbyterian Church, on the topic, "Doing Theology in Oceania; Partners in Conversation."[241] It came just one month after the second EATWOT-Pacific conference. Expatriate, Philip Gibbs, wrote the conference report.[242] Making clear that the consultation deliberately focused on a theological methodology that was not aping Western theology, but directed to the cultures of the Pacific, Gibbs, perhaps reflecting his own preferences, states that "it was not a conference dominated by tedious academic papers, but rather an interweaving of creative presentations from participants grouped according to culture."[243] He raises a series of methodological questions, "What is special and unique about the way we do theology

---

239. Gaudi, "One Gospel," 74.

240. See Pears, *Doing Contextual Theology*, 170–73. Pears documents reactions around the world to the uncritical importation of Liberation Theology in various contexts, as well as noting the limitations of this theology within Latin America.

241. It was held at Otago University on November 17–21, 1996, and attended by over 150 participants from around the South Pacific, including Australia.

242. Gibbs, "Conference Report," 62–66. Gibbs was a Roman Catholic priest and lecturer in Theology and Anthropology in Papua New Guinea.

243. Gibbs, "Conference Report," 62.

in Oceania? Who does theology? Where, When, Why, How?"[244] He then outlines examples "from the more formal theology done in the seminary setting, to the theology found in prayer, dance and song coming from rural communities."[245] In addition, there are "oral reflections and discussions on marriage, death, hospitality, land, birth, struggle."[246]

On the pursuit of a contextual methodology for the South Pacific, this 1996 gathering offers a significant contribution. Steering away from the more formal approaches that have dominated other gatherings, it takes account of particular elements of Pacific cultures. Among these is the preference for orality over literacy, a communal rather than individual approach, and ritual modes of drama, dance, song and ceremony. In this way, the event suggests some particular ways ahead for the contextualization of the methodology of theology for the South Pacific. Apparently aware of this, Gibbs offers the following pertinent comments in conclusion, "It was obvious at this conference that theology can be done differently. . . . The questions were many, often leading to further questions about the nature of the theological enterprise. Often it seemed as though we were only beginning. . . . Traditional sources of theology have their place. But those attending this conference couldn't help but be impressed by the rich diversity of theological resources in Oceania."[247]

Just short of one year after this gathering, in October 1997, South Pacific Islanders gathered for a workshop on "Evangelization and Communication: Voicing the Gospel in the Pacific Islands." Most notable was a paper by the Tongan pastor and theologian, Tevita Mohenoa Puloka,[248] whose insightful attention to the question of a contextual methodology, given at the 1986 consultation in Papua New Guinea, has already been noted. On this subsequent occasion he expands his views further.[249] Observing the need to move from a "pot-plant gospel" to a localized gospel, it is "incumbent" upon the Pacific churches, he says, "to formulate a specific theological methodology" which serves this process. "Contextualization, as a theological methodology is our response to the demand of the gospel to be understood and made meaningful in the light of our Pacific cultural milieu."[250]

244. Gibbs, "Conference Report," 62.

245. Gibbs, "Conference Report," 63.

246. Gibbs, "Conference Report," 65.

247. Gibbs, "Conference Report," 66.

248. Puloka, "Evangelization."

249. Puloka, "Evangelization," 46.

250. Puloka, "Evangelization," 47.

Criticizing an approach that separates the text from the context, Puloka claims that the seminary, separated as it is from the life of the local people, cannot be the primary place for contextualization. Rather, "the work of contextualization is better served at the local church. It is where the pastor and the laity come face to face with the force and the peculiar demands of the Gospel of Jesus Christ."[251] He then deals with "three factors in contextualization of the gospel." The first is "rootedness" (a personal encounter between God and the "believer"); the second is "particularity" (the gospel addresses specific situations); the third is universality (particularity must go with "global vision and a solidarity with the whole human family").[252] He concludes by concurring with what has been learned in Latin America, namely that theology is "praxis" and involves "doing the truth."[253]

As was Puloka's input in 1986, so this paper is challenging in addressing issues of a methodology for the South Pacific. Perhaps because he defines himself as a pastor rather than as a theologian, he promotes a view that the primary location for a contextual theology in the South Pacific cannot be within theological colleges. It can only be within the community of faith, since the purpose of theology is the transformation of life, and such transformation takes place within the life of the local community of faith as gospel and people interact. Theology is not an intellectual exercise of educated ("elite") individuals but a pursuit of the local community; it is not a matter of reflection and speech, but it involves the "doing of truth." More than Gaudi, Puloka is reflective about what can be learned from Latin America, and selectively adopts the notion of praxis as methodologically suitable for Pacific theology. In his statement of the three factors involved in local theology, his advocacy for contextualization holds together both the particularity of the local situation and the universality of the theological task. His firm advocacy for such a contextual methodology brings serious challenges to the role to be played by theological colleges and the "elite" theologian in the shaping of contextual theology. What is not addressed in Puloka's paper is any detail as to how his theological methodology might find concrete expression within a particular community, or might have a uniquely Pacific character; in that sense, his proposals are not sufficiently followed through.

In a 1999 paper, pertinently titled, "Moving toward a Pacific Theology," and puzzlingly subtitled, "Theologizing with Concepts,"[254] Paulo Koria senses

251. Puloka, "Evangelization," 48.

252. Puloka, "Evangelization," 49–53.

253. Puloka, "Evangelization," 54.

254. See Koria, "Moving Towards a Pacific Theology."

a particular urgency about the need for an appropriate methodology. "It seems to me that the question of methodology is of fundamental importance to our theological endeavor, one that needs immediate and serious attention."[255] Affirming that "contextual or indigenous theology is by definition oriented to the cultural context and existential circumstances of people living in a particular historical locality,"[256] his paper then draws attention to a vast range of cultural media that might be called upon in the theological task.

> A Pacific theology therefore is at liberty to utilize and appropriate all available cultural resources for expressing the message of the gospel. What might these be? Pacific languages immediately come to mind. Linguistic idioms, proverbial sayings, imagery, symbolism, metaphors and the like, are all viable means for communicating the substance of the gospel message. Secondly, there are local stories, parables, island folk tales, legends, myths, narratives both oral and literary which our Pacific people have accumulated and treasured as a communal source of knowledge.[257]

To these, Koria adds "customs, social etiquette, traditions, philosophies, religious beliefs," which provide "a system of meaning by which life in the Pacific is lived," asserting that "because theology has to do with the totality of human life, all these resources are important for the expression and articulation of the Christian faith."[258]

This is doubtlessly an important contribution to the issues of theological methodology in the Pacific. It comes from a theological college lecturer who teaches in a field of theology (systematic) that is known for its conceptual and academic approach to the theological task. Koria advocates a wide range of traditional cultural resources, familiar to local communities, as the means of theological expression. He thus challenges the view of theology as articulated speech by educated individuals, a view that would inform the shape of his own theological college as well as his own field of teaching. The actual implications for theological education, and for his teaching practice, are not followed through in detail. Neither are the implications for the important questions of the nature, location and purpose of the theological task. As for others who explore the issues of theological methodology, so also for Koria, his engagement with the theme needs to go further into the practical applications of his ideas.

255. Koria, "Moving Towards a Pacific Theology," 4.
256. Koria, "Moving Towards a Pacific Theology," 4.
257. Koria, "Moving Towards a Pacific Theology," 4.
258. Koria, "Moving Towards a Pacific Theology," 4.

As an indication of the topicality of the concern for a contextual methodology, a helpful paper appears just one year later in the Melanesian Journal of Theology, written by Philip Manuao.[259] While Manuao is preoccupied with the effective communication of the gospel in local communities rather than with a contextual methodology for theology, nevertheless, what he says overlaps with Koria's input, and is relevant to this question. Manuao also identifies the importance of applying traditional cultural resources for the expression of the Christian gospel. He has in mind the concrete situation of a local community, where the people have few, if any, benefits of formal (Western) education. By exploring what processes might be implemented in local communities, his ideas go beyond the contribution of Koria. Manuao sets out to do four things, namely,

> to elucidate meaningful cultural forms as vehicles for getting God's message across to the illiterate and the semi-illiterate people in the church; to provide guidance for indigenous ministers of God to make good use of their meaningful cultural forms as they proclaim the word of God; to make the gospel message simple and relevant to the people so that this may lead them to Christ; to educate the indigenous church about applying the gospel to their context, and not to look outside for foreign methods which are irrelevant to the Melanesian context.[260]

Manuao then addresses two particular forms of communication, both of which are non-literate: the audible and the visual. Under "audible," he includes praying, sacrifice (leading into an approach to the sacraments of baptism and holy communion), worship, story-telling, music and songs, use of names, blowing conch shells, hitting wooden gongs and beating paddles. Under "visual," he includes fire, small sticks and decoration.[261] Influenced by the cross-cultural work of Kevin Hovey,[262] Manuao proposes drama-based storytelling, in particular, as a key method of communicating the gospel among his people. Noting the revival of this approach as a form of gospel communication, he asserts, "We need to apply the principles of storytelling in our preaching and teaching of God's word."[263]

More than most other local writers, Manuao understands the importance of orality in Melanesian communities, and the implications of this for communicating the gospel. Aware of the work of Herbert Klem among

259. Manuao, "Communicating the Gospel," 57–91.

260. Manuao, "Communicating the Gospel," 57–58.

261. Manuao, "Communicating the Gospel," 61–69.

262. Hovey, *Before All Else Fails*.

263. Manuao, "Communicating the Gospel," 71.

oral communities in Nigeria and Kenya,[264] and its relevance to his own local context, Manuao recommends the use of "indigenous oral media" in the teaching of the gospel. "If a denomination, which has a predominantly oral society, depends primarily upon written material for most of its Bible study and teaching, then, at the heart of its ministry, such a denomination is not indigenous."[265]

Again, more detail is needed for the actual working out of this approach in local village communities, but Manuao's work highlights a fundamental but much overlooked feature of Melanesian cultures, namely their oral nature. It has an importance not named so clearly by others, and has wide-ranging implications for an appropriate methodology for theology in the South Pacific. This character of South Pacific communities will be a key focus in the later examination of "The Gospel and Culture in Vanuatu" project.

After the turn of the century, during the four-year PCC program of workshops on Contextual Theology, the methodology for theology was given some further attention. In his paper presented at the first of these, held in Suva in 2001, Tuwere takes up matters that are critical to the topic.[266] The relevance of his input on this occasion is connected with the dynamic engagement between culture and gospel. He adopts his working definition of "culture" from the report of the WCC Assembly in Vancouver in 1983. "Culture is what holds a community together, giving a common framework of meaning. It is preserved in language, thought patterns, ways of life, attitudes, symbols and presuppositions and is celebrated in art, music and drama, literature and the like. It constitutes the collective memory of the people and the collective heritage that will be handed down to generations to come."[267] Then, quoting Lesslie Newbigin's seminal work, he asserts that "there is no such thing as gospel which is not embodied in a culture."[268] By necessity therefore, "every interpretation of the gospel is embodied in some cultural form. Culture shapes the voice that answers the voice of Christ. For this reason every theological reflection is contextual. It is shaped by the social milieu of a given culture and period of time."[269]

He then makes key affirmations that are important in theological methodology. After upholding the primacy of the story of the Judeo-Christian God as the story that embraces and illuminates all other contextual stories,

---

264. Klem, *Oral Communication*.

265. Manuao, "Communicating the Gospel," 86.

266. Tuwere, "What is Contextual Theology?," 7–20.

267. Tuwere, "What is Contextual Theology?," 9.

268. Newbigin, *Foolishness*, 3, quoted in Tuwere, "What is Contextual Theology?," 9.

269. Tuwere, "What is Contextual Theology?," 10.

he argues that the theological task is one that properly belongs within the community of faith, as the community which remembers and celebrates this one overarching story. It is grounded in the real needs of the people, always takes cultural expression, and leads to responsive faithful action.[270] As he has done before, Tuwere refers to theology in terms of reflection on discourse. However, on this occasion, he sets the methodology of this discourse, more clearly than he has done previously, within the context of the local Christian community and a calling to be faithful. The implications of this for the role of theological colleges, and whether such a methodology can be learned or practiced within theological colleges, is not addressed. Like others, Tuwere does not offer any particular detail as to how the local community of faith might pursue the theological task. These remain key questions.

Any survey of what Pacific Islanders say about the methodology of theology cannot be complete without noting the input of Maʻafu ʻo Tuʻitonga Palu.[271] Palu is one of the key protagonists of the emerging and dominant forms of contextualization in the South Pacific, and he is so for reasons of its methodology. In two substantial articles which appear in the PJT, in 2002[272] and 2003, he sets out his argument against what he sees are serious methodological flaws. The title of the 2003 paper indicates the thrust of the whole article, namely an alternative approach to the popularly accepted methodology of theology in the South Pacific.[273]

Drawing on the work of George Lindbeck,[274] Palu is critical of what he describes as a "context-dominating-text" methodology, and advocates for an approach that he calls "intra-textualization," or a "text-controlled approach to contextualization." Although it is not within the scope of this book to explore the details of Lindbeck's work, Palu's criticisms are so strident and relevant to the debates about the methodology of contextualization that a brief explanation of his accusations and some response are needed.

The first of his criticisms relates to the biblical text itself. For Palu, there has been a failure among Pacific Islanders to recognize that any biblical text is not culture-free but belongs to an historical and cultural context, which is "somewhat removed from our own."[275] Thus the text may not be immedi-

---

270. Tuwere, "What is Contextual Theology?," 11–12.

271. Palu, a Tongan, was lecturer in Biblical Studies at Saiʻatoutai Theological College in Tonga.

272. Palu, "On Pacific Theology," 21–53.

273. Palu, "On Pacific Theology—A Reconsideration," 30–58.

274. Lindbeck, Professor of Theology at Yale University, was a key figure in debates about the nature of (Western) theology through the last half of the twentieth century. See Lindbeck, *Nature of Doctrine*.

275. Palu, "On Pacific Theology," 26.

ately relevant or accessible to the contemporary context. He claims that to be faithful to the text requires an exploration of this original context in such a way that one enters into the world of the text and into its truths. The text is understood to open up an horizon of experience, a world in which one may live.[276] For Palu, this engagement with text is the one determining point in theological methodology.

The second of his criticisms relates to the local context. For Palu, there is a failure to recognize the innate limitations of any particular culture, "the sinfulness, finiteness and cultural spectacles"[277] that hinder the proper contextualizing of the biblical text; context has assumed a priority over text.

The combination of these two flaws leads, on the one hand, to the danger of the "fundamentalism of culture," whereby the culture actually defines the form and content of the gospel, and on the other hand, to the danger of a "cultureless Christianity," which overlooks the cultural context of the gospel and falls into the trap of proclaiming "biblical truths which are irrelevant to cultures."[278] The result is a de-historicizing of Jesus of Nazareth, a de-contextualizing of the gospel message, and a preoccupation with the immediate experience of the Christ of faith. In turn, theology is robbed of the possibility of self-criticism, as is the case "in most recent publications of Pacific theologians."[279] The end result is that rather than making such a theology contextually responsive and relevant to the Pacific church, the very opposite occurs. It "undermines the message of the Scriptures and has the effect of widening the gap between local church people and professional theologians as the latter are the only group who can apply the culturally oriented method to reading Scripture."[280] More fundamentally, as Palu asserts in his 2003 paper, such a contextual theology "ceases any longer to be a truly Christian theology."[281]

Palu argues instead for a methodology that begins with Scripture, not as timeless supra-cultural truth, but as text within its own context. The primary theological task then is to enter into the world of the text. Only then, as a second step, can the worldview of traditional Tongan culture— "my pre-understanding baggage"—be brought into question and changed by the worldview of the text. This is the kind of contextualization that will

276. Palu, "On Pacific Theology," 41.
277. Palu, "On Pacific Theology," 26.
278. Palu, "On Pacific Theology," 27.
279. Palu, "On Pacific Theology," 38.
280. Palu, "On Pacific Theology," 41.
281. Palu, "Reconsideration," 35.

finally be faithful to the text on the one hand, and insightful to the cultural context on the other.[282]

In order to ensure that his own methodology is relevant and accessible for his target audience—to local Christian communities—Palu sets out a concrete process by which local church readers of a text might enter the world of that text. What he proposes is that in any given Scriptural passage, the reader identify the main characters, understand their roles, establish who typifies Christ in the passage, and then take upon the character of the one who is addressed by Christ. "In assuming the role of a character in the biblical text I therefore 'enter the world' of the text and thus interact with God . . . and in so doing I interpret the world in terms of the literary framework of the Word."[283]

The voice of Palu in the debate about the methodology of Pacific theology needs to be heard. He is one of few people who give such deliberate attention to this aspect of the theological task. His paper is informed by serious scholarship and by a genuine commitment to a Christian contextual theology for the South Pacific. There are important elements to his rather strident and sweeping critique that should be noted. Timely are his warnings about the prioritizing and idolizing of culture, the loss of any external point of reference (and with it, the loss of cultural self-criticism), the failure to recognize that the text has its own cultural context, and a methodology that "gags" the text and therefore silences the message of the gospel. These are all genuine risks for those who engage in the task of contextualizing theology, whatever the context.

However, there are limitations to Palu's critique. The separation of biblical text and local context is somewhat contrived, as it does not adequately explain the dynamic by which the God, to whom the biblical text witnesses, is the one who continues to speak in, and to, any and every local context. This limitation is evident when Palu attempts to set out a concrete process by which a local Christian community might enact his proposed approach to text and to context. There is no guarantee that what he seeks to achieve in this process can be accomplished. There is also a tendency in Palu's approach to take a literalist approach to the text, that is, to confuse the priority of texts and the priority of the gospel to which the texts testify.

Palu's concerns are not entirely without precedent in the South Pacific debate on the contextualization of theology. Tuwere has spoken up strongly for the primacy of the gospel and the overarching story of God, as that which critiques all local contexts. In a statement that sounds much like the

---

282. Palu, "On Pacific Theology," 44.
283. Palu, "On Pacific Theology," 45.

voice of Palu, Tuwere writes, "True and authentic contextualization happens when the gospel is given its rightful primacy, its authority and power to penetrate every culture and to speak within each culture the Word which is both NO and YES *(his emphasis)*, hate and love, judgement and grace."[284] He then goes on, again in Palu-like affirmation:

> Where do we begin to theologize in contextual theology? Some would say "Begin with the aspirations of people." Authentic contextualization begins with what God has already done in the story of Israel and supremely in the story of Jesus Christ. This is the overarching story that must illumine all other stories within a context or culture. . . . Contextual theology is also critical theology. . . . In its critical role, contextual theology assumes a "hermeneutic of suspicion."[285]

As if responding to Palu's strident accusation about the irrelevance of the developments in contextualizing theology to local church communities, and about the failure of local theologians to recognize the sins of human cultures, Tuwere goes on to acknowledge that "the community of faith is nurtured in the gospel story through word, sacrament and fellowship, by which it inhabits the story of Jesus." He further acknowledges that, in our selfishness, we need constant correction. "This correction comes from those who share the life in Christ but inhabit different cultural situations. Contextual theology must accept corrections from others who share the same faith with us but who belong to another culture."[286]

While Tuwere's input is only one voice, it is a voice that within the South Pacific, has an authoritative and chiefly character within the circle of those who pursue the task of the contextualization of theology for the South Pacific. That is to say, Tuwere's voice carries the weight of one who speaks for and to the people, and establishes the framework by which the theological task is to be pursued. In that sense, it is a prominent local theological response that addresses and embraces the key elements of Palu's concerns.

WOMEN ON THE METHODOLOGY OF THEOLOGY

Focus on the methodology of theology has been given particular attention by Pacific Island women from the time of the founding of Weavers. In part, this is because of their impassioned concern to propose a form of theology that speaks out of, and into, the uniqueness of their own experience

---

284. Tuwere, "What is Contextual Theology?," 11.

285. Tuwere, "What is Contextual Theology?," 11–12.

286. Tuwere, "What is Contextual Theology?," 12.

as Pacific Island women. At the seminal 1991 Weavers consultation, Lydia Johnson-Hill claims that the dominant approach to Pacific theology has been essentially one which simply uses Pacific symbols within the alien conceptual framework of Western theology. Pacific theology coming through the local seminaries has taught "methodologies of conventional theologizing," by which she means "the mastering of concept/doctrine/principle first, then see if they can re-translate it somehow and apply it to their own contexts."[287] In contrast, the most appropriate methodology, at least for women, if not for all Pacific Islanders, is a narrative approach to theology. "Women in the Pacific simply tell their stories. . . . This implies a way of doing theology which is more honest than the 'graft-Pacific-themes-onto-western-models' approach."[288]

What makes this narrative approach more culturally contextual for Johnson-Hill is that narrative stories "tend more towards orthopraxis than orthodoxy." It is an approach that is "grappling with real life," and one that is "critically needed" in the Pacific. These life stories "create a more direct link with the Christian story."[289] There is an agenda and purpose beyond its personal significance, namely, it offers a critical approach to the society as a whole, one "that allows us to step aside and see ourselves, our cultures, our societies as they really are." Such an approach "welcomes insights also from the sciences and humanities alongside the Christian story."[290]

Kanongata'a, like Johnson-Hill, also advocates a narrative approach, and then draws the implications of this into a summary of the ingredients for a contextualized methodology for the South Pacific. It is an approach that "springs from the grass-root level," it is "first lived before it is explained," it gives expression to "women's true experiences," it is "life-giving," it is "for the service of the church" and "supports the mission of the church." As such, it is a theology "that makes sense and is meaningful to Pacific women." In summary, she concludes, "Theological method needs to always start and finish with people's experiences."[291]

What is offered here by Johnson-Hill, and more particularly by Kanongata'a, are indicators, rather than details, as to what this might mean in methodological terms, and how it might be enacted within a local community. Even without the details, however, it is clear that this approach offers a direct challenge to the dominant theology that is confined to theological

287. Johnson-Hill, "Beyond the Story," 46.
288. Johnson-Hill, "Beyond the Story," 46.
289. Johnson-Hill, "Beyond the Story," 46–47.
290. Johnson-Hill, "Beyond the Story," 48.
291. Kanongata'a, "Pacific Women," 21.

colleges, perceived to be distant from village life, alien to people's experience, and which finds expression only in literate academic ways.

Kanongata'a expands these affirmations about methodology in the first of the Pacific-wide consultations on contextual theology. Presenting one of the key papers at the 2001 consultation, she first recounts a story about a sermon preached by a new graduate of a Pacific Theological College that seemed utterly irrelevant to his congregation. She uses this anecdotal narrative to repeat her views about the methodology with which theology is commonly done in the Pacific. "Doing traditional theology means engaging in philosophical thinking, translation, adaptation, application from European traditions to our Pacific situation."[292]

She calls for a theology that is grounded within the daily life of the community of faith. "The depth of human experience is the data of practical theology."[293] In particular, Kanongata'a has in mind the experience of women. "We must begin by addressing the issues of village and town women's experiences."[294] Calling for women's theology to model the sense of community represented in Pacific cultures, she comments, "The strength of women's theology will be found in their solidarity with each other. When theology is done in communion and not in individual isolation it produces life."[295] She urges what might be referred to as a "praxis" approach to the theological task, that is, a methodology that requires commitment to change, "We began our women theology by telling and coming into touch with our own women stories. Today, we do not just tell our stories, we have launched into actually making things happen. The women are so much involved in the struggle against violence especially domestic violence against themselves and our children, in the struggle for justice and in the struggle for liberation from cultural and social enslavement."[296] The element of serious theological discourse is not overlooked in this methodology. Women theologians must "try to understand, to receive and to accept their stories, to hear their songs and lamentations and to translate these subsequently into articulate, rigorous, theological discourse."[297] Kanongata'a wants to uphold a particular part to be played by those who are formally educated. "It

292. Kanongata'a, "Why Contextual?," 27.

293. Kanongata'a, "Why Contextual?," 28.

294. Kanongata'a, "Pacific Women," 31.

295. Kanongata'a, "Pacific Women," 31.

296. Kanongata'a, "Why Contextual?," 35.

297. Kanongata'a, "Pacific Women," 31.

is the work of professional theologians to lead the way of theologizing and to develop this theology."[298]

In addressing more directly how institutions of theological education might embrace her proposed methodology, Kanongata'a recounts a story about a classroom experience.

> The whole class wanted to theologize on the burning issue of the day . . . a law to allow a casino in Tonga . . . and so, over a couple of weeks, the whole class workshopped through a series of stages . . . the final stage being the question: "Where is God in all this?" for which they used the process learned in the course—they searched the Bible, the traditions and practices of the Church for theological responses to the question—resulting in a letter of petition going to the Parliament.[299]

Kanongata'a suggests that, with this methodology, "women theology is giving a lead in Contextual Theology."[300] In her conclusion, Kanongata'a offers a summary of the key insights and issues that have come from the emergence of "women theology": People's experience must be the "locus theologicus"; while culture is the context for theology, there is a need for faith to encounter culture; we need to rediscover the power of ritual in expressing theology; because Pacific people are people in community, theology must rediscover "family" and the "unity in diversity" of our Pacific Island nations; we need also to be on guard against doing a theology that places too exclusive an emphasis on cultural identity; the contextualization of theology is an imperative for all contexts—it is part of the nature of theology itself.[301]

The primary contribution of women, in the discussion about theology, lies in their passionate call for a methodology that accords with the cultural context of the South Pacific. Such a methodology, whether it be expressed in narrative form as articulated by Johnson-Hill, or more expansively in the ways developed by Kanongata'a, will ensure that theology in the South Pacific is grounded in the personal, communal, social and cultural experiences of the people, and it will respond to these with action. In advocating such a methodology, Katongata'a is wary of the risks of cultural fundamentalism. She avoids this accusation by warning against a theology that over-emphasizes the importance of cultural identity. For this reason, the "professional theologian" has an important role. As one who needs to be within the community of faith, sharing their agonies and hopes, the theologically educated leader reminds

298. Kanongata'a, "Why Contextual?," 27.
299. Kanongata'a, "Why Contextual?," 34.
300. Kanongata'a, "Why Contextual?," 35.
301. Kanongata'a, "Why Contextual?," 37–38.

the community of the content of the faith, and so resources and facilitates the processes of contextualization.[302] This process, for Kanongata'a, is not a duplication of any foreign feminist liberation, but a form of contextual theology, to be done "in the Pacific Way." Therefore, the methodology will involve a communal process that upholds the unity of men and women, one where the struggles and hopes of the community are the "locus" of theology.[303]

The "women theology" that has emerged through the 1990s, and has been articulated primarily through Weavers, has led the way by embracing the unique struggles and experiences of women as the starting point for theology. In this sense, "women theology" does offer a methodology that, while not unique to women in the South Pacific, challenges the inherited Western-influenced methodology of theology that across the South Pacific still remains the dominant agenda. What Katongata'a also offers is a pedagogical approach that potentially could be adopted within the classrooms of theological colleges. It also contains some initial indication as to what might work within a local community of faith as the community begins to own and to engage in the theological task. How this might be so is not described in any concrete way, and so the risk is that this experiential approach to theology is not integrated with the life of the local church communities.

SUMMARY COMMENTS ON THE METHODOLOGY OF THEOLOGY

In some respects, the development of a suitable methodology for contextual theology has run parallel to the development of a contextual definition and of contextual content, as described in the previous sections. Some specific and notable attempts have been made to propose a methodology that is genuinely contextual within the South Pacific. These attempts have engaged with the four key questions of methodology, "What form does theology take?" "Who does theology?" "What is the primary location for the theological task?" and "What is the primary purpose of theology?" However, in comparison with matters of definition and content, the matter of methodology has been addressed far more spasmodically, by fewer contributors, and with little attention given to implementation. This lack of attention to implementation, both in institutions of theological education, and more particularly in local Christian communities, is apparent in each of the leading indigenous contributions.

Most importantly, the tensions involved in moving from the heritage of Western missionary theology, with all its presuppositions, into a culturally

302. Kanongata'a, "Why Contextual?," 37.
303. Kanongata'a, "Why Contextual?," 38.

contextualized theology in the South Pacific, come to much greater focus and to much greater challenge around this question of methodology. To attend to the key issues of methodology requires a clear understanding of the cultural influences that have dominated the methodology implanted through the missionary era, and an equally clear understanding of the cultural categories that constitute the identity of South Pacific Islanders. It is the clash of cultural presuppositions between the Western world, on the one hand, and the world of the South Pacific, on the other hand, that lies at the foundation of these ongoing tensions, giving rise to the following methodological issues that remain unresolved:

1. Whether theology belongs essentially as an activity of seminaries and colleges, or whether it belongs essentially as an activity of the local church community

2. Whether theology is an academic pursuit of knowledge and ideas, accessed through written texts and classroom lectures, and requiring critical thought, or whether theology is embodied, learned in context, grounded in experience and involving a praxis methodology

3. Whether the articulation of theology assumes a literate form, or may take a range of other forms

4. Whether theology is to be done only, or primarily, by those who are sufficiently educated—the "elite" or "professional"—or whether it is primarily the task of the whole community of faith

5. Whether theology is an individual or a communal enterprise

6. Whether the primary purpose of theology is to articulate the views of a "professional" within an academic world, or whether the primary purpose is to serve the local Christian community in its calling to be faithful to the gospel.

Each of the above questions is deliberately set out in dual form in order to highlight the contrasting cultural preferences which may be said to arise from Western and South Pacific cultures respectively. Their resolution is fundamental in establishing a methodology of theology, which is contextually grounded within the cultures of the South Pacific. It is towards such resolution that this book now turns.

4

Methodology: The Key to Contextualization

Three Fundamental Issues

WHILE IT IS CLEAR from the preceding survey that significant attention has been given to the task of the contextualization of theology in the South Pacific, the tensions around this pursuit, and the challenges that inhibit ongoing progress, remain substantial. This is particularly so in the matter of the methodology of theology. In making any further headway, there are three key issues, arising from the overall survey, that require deliberate engagement. Each of the three is grounded in the particularity of the cultures of the South Pacific, and their impact can only be properly appreciated from that perspective. While all three are interconnected, nevertheless each constitutes a fundamental issue to be addressed in its own right. Essentially it is one or more of these three issues that have undergirded the tensions and obstacles in the pursuit of the contextualization of theology, and continue to do so.

The first is the oral nature of South Pacific cultures. The second is the fact that South Pacific cultures have no direct heritage of the Enlightenment paradigm. The third is the separation of theological colleges from the life of the local church communities. While these issues have implications for the contextualization of the definition, and of the content, of theology in the South Pacific, their primary impact is upon the contextualization of the methodology of theology—they determine the responses to the four questions I have posed, namely who does theology, what form does theology take, what is the essential location for the theological task, and what is the primary purpose of theology.

My fundamental assertion is that unless these three issues are better understood and deliberately tackled, then the overall task of the contextualization of theology in the South Pacific will remain seriously flawed. To put the corollary, it is only an understanding of the impact of these three issues, especially on the matters of methodology, that a more grounded contextualization of theology in the South Pacific will be possible.

PRIMARY ORALITY

The most foundational issue for the contextual methodology of theology is the fact that the cultures across the South Pacific are essentially primary oral cultures. In contrast, Western cultures are primary literate cultures. There is a fundamental clash between the cultural world view determined by primary orality, and the world view existent in cultures of primary literacy. It is the latter, inherited from the Western missionary movement of the nineteenth century, that has come to dominate the methodology of theology in the South Pacific.

The dilemmas created by this clash have surfaced throughout the period of the struggle for a localized theology in the South Pacific, and they continue to the present day. The pivotal consultation in 1985, "Towards a Relevant Theology," recommended that "tapes be used in addition to books and articles as a vehicle for the expression of Pacific Theology; that the PCC provide writing workshops for theological teachers who want to publish their ideas but need help in the methods of writing; and that the churches initiate action by which the local congregations will be helped to reflect theologically through various art forms such as song, dance, drawing and decorating."[1] It concluded with the affirmation, "We believe that the Pacific churches have a contribution to make to the entire world in the use of these modes of theological expression."[2]

In the same vein, the comments by Mohenoa Puloka on the contextualization of theology in Tonga have already been noted, "The relatively late emergence of written language in Tonga . . . and mostly the lack of a taste for writing in general, has made theology in Tonga exist largely in verbal form as oral tradition. The absence of any great theological work in this case is not surprising."[3] Perhaps the word "literary," following the word "great," is meant. By way of further illustration, Anglican Franciscan Friar, Brother Silas, makes a pertinent general comment about theology in Melanesia,

1. Lang et al., "Towards," 146–47.
2. Lang et al., "Towards," 147.
3. Puloka, "Attempt at Contextualizing," 84–85.

> Melanesia is a region where one would expect to see intense
> theological activity. It has a high concentration of Christians in
> tight-knit communities, who talk about their faith. . . . I believe
> such activity is indeed taking place, but is often overlooked by
> church leaders and theologians because it is informal and pre-
> sented in an unconventional way. The people's theological in-
> sights should be welcomed and encouraged by the churches, but
> because they are not readily reduced to the language of formal
> theology they are often suppressed as wrong or relegated to the
> fringes of church life.[4]

In 1998, in a special publication of the PJT that was allocated to members of the Sia'atoutai Theological College in Tonga, on the topic of "Local
Theology," the guest editor, College Principal Adrian Burdon, acknowledges,

> In common with all of the islands of the Pacific, the traditional
> means of communication in the Kingdom of Tonga is oral. It is
> only relatively recently that the demands of western academia
> have required assessable pieces of written prose. . . . As theologi-
> cal educators in the Pacific we should be encouraging our stu-
> dents and scholars to explore the creativity of expression which
> arises out of the traditional ways of communicating.[5]

The struggle to make oral preference learners become more literate
is an agenda that is familiar to the teachers of theology across the South
Pacific, both indigenous and expatriate. For some, it generates constant
frustration with the students. Fa'atulituli Setu, lecturer in Church History
at Malua, declares, "I often seek out ministers for the use of their libraries. However, to my frustration, most of them do not have libraries. Most
ministers think that reading stops when one graduates with a Diploma of
Theology or a Bachelor of Divinity. Some think that reading is characteristically for the academics and lecturers."[6]

The clashes created by the contrast between the cultures of primary
orality and the cultures of primary literacy, and the superior place given to
the latter, is not exclusive to the South Pacific. It finds common expression
in other parts of the primary oral world, in particular, in the African experience, where primary orality is the cultural norm.[7] Aware of the tensions
in his own situation, and anticipating a change of approach in the mode of

4. Silas, "Solving the Problem of the Pigs," 63.

5. Burdon, "Editorial," 2.

6. Setu, "Christian Ministers," 83.

7. See Pobee, "Oral Theology." Note also the seminal research work done in Kenya
and Nigeria in Bowen and Bowen Jr., "Contextualization of Teaching Methodology."

theology in his own context, pioneering African Theologian, John Mbiti, affirms that, "Certainly within the foreseeable future, much of the theological activity in Christian Africa must be done as oral theology."[8] Kwame Bediako, one who built on the work of Mbiti, challenges the widespread assumption that anything recognized as real theology must take literary form. He asserts, "To speak of oral theology may be misleading as though all that we are dealing with is an oral phase, a transition phase, on the way to the academic or written theology, which then becomes real theology."[9]

Such struggles for the recognition of the validity of primary orality as a mode for "real theology," are keenly felt also among the women of Africa. Invited to address the 1996 Weavers consultation in Fiji, Kenyan Musimbi Kanyoro shares her own experience as an African woman theologian. With passion, she declares,

> There is a danger that we might think that the only theologians of Africa are the Western educated women who have gone to seminaries and universities. No, these are not the only theologians for us, because we define theology differently. We do not see theology as what we do to get our degrees. Neither do we see theology as what we are taught by someone, but we see theology as taking an experience that we have, and bringing meaning to that experience so that we can see God in what we do every day. Many women on our continent cannot read and write but they can sing, they can dance, and they can speak.[10]

Reflecting on the multi-layered context of suffering and pain in Africa, Kanyoro adds,

> These issues also weigh heavily on women who have received a formal theological education. Many simply have no time to sit and write long treatises with all the footnotes and quotations from a million other scholars. Many have no access to books and libraries as money is a problem and theological books are expensive on our continent. Those who pass judgement on African women as a people lacking in theological expression or reflection need to hear and read our choked silence.[11]

She anticipates that, sadly, the prioritizing of literate categories will continue to plague African cultural contexts, and to determine what constitutes

8. Mbiti, *Bible and Theology*, 229.

9. Bediako, *Jesus and the Gospel*, 17.

10. Kanyoro, "African Women's Quest," 80–81.

11. Kanyoro, "African Women's Quest," 85.

real theology. "Print media will, for a long time, marginalize the voices of African women. African rural women are singing songs, they are creating poetry, proverbs and dirges. Their reflections should challenge us to do theology in a different way. The method of sitting in comfortable offices, producing complete manuscripts in dominant languages will prevent so many of our own sisters from participating in theological reflection."[12]

The realities expressed by Kanyoro find their equivalent also in the story of contextualization of theology in the South Pacific, particularly, but not only among women. While this tension about "real theology" has been expressed regularly, the heart of the problem is inadequately appreciated. One key reason for this is that, "fully literate persons can only with great difficulty imagine what a primary oral culture is like, that is, a culture with no knowledge whatsoever of writing or even of the possibility of writing."[13] In other words, the heart of the problem rests with the fact that primary orality and primary literacy are not simply two different modes of communication; they constitute two different worlds.

The World of Primary Orality

Well-known teacher in the field of orality, Charles Madinger, noting that more than 70 percent of the world's population are oral preference learners, speaks of "the holistic model of orality," which he defines as the way in which oral cultures receive, process, remember and replicate news, important information, and truths. Literate cultures, he asserts, operate in a fundamentally different world.[14]

Referring to Walter Ong's groundbreaking work on orality, cultural anthropologist Michael Rynkiewich comments, "We have come to appreciate that orality is not just the lack of literacy. Orality and literacy both presuppose a mind-set, a way of experiencing the world that is not commensurate one with the other."[15] In other words, "oral cultures are not second-best cultures to literate cultures; rather, they are uniquely ordered in a way that sustains and perpetrates orality."[16] The consequence of this is critical for the contextualizing of theology:

> It is not simply that people in oral cultures lack the ability to
> read and write and that if such people were to give attention to

12. Kanyoro, "African Women's Quest," 87.

13. Ong, *Orality and Literacy*, 31.

14. Madinger, "Literate's Guide," 16.

15. Rynkiewich, "Mission," 50.

16. Prior, "Orality," 147.

overcoming this inability, then they would catch up with their sisters and brothers in more literate communities. Nor is it the case that the forms of theology emerging from oral communities are simply an oral equivalent of what is produced in literate communities.[17]

Importantly, Rynkiewich then identifies three essential elements that distinguish the "mind-set" of primary oral cultures from that of literate cultures. Each of them is relevant to South Pacific cultures.

First, says Rynkiewich, those things worthy of the community's learning and permanent memory are embodied. "Oral cultures employ particular means of ensuring that important things are held in memory—in particular, by repetition and the involvement of the whole body rather than simply the mind. Thus, oral cultures are marked by the use of ceremony, dance, art, poetry, and so on."[18] The "and so on" would commonly include song, drama and story.

The cultural realities of the South Pacific are illustrative of this first distinctive oral feature. For every stage of human life—from birth to death—and for every event of significance in family life, in the community, and at national level, there is some form of embodied ritual. The ritual may be elaborate (as in the case of some traditional custom ceremonies like the Toka Festival on the island of Tanna that lasts for three days and involves the killing of five hundred fattened pigs, and is accompanied by festivity of dance and song), or it may be modest and involve little more than a shaking of hands or the exchanging of mats (as in the case of a routine greeting or a farewell).

It is notable that in the early stages of the evolution of a defined Pacific theology, the significant consultation in 1985 resolved to "urge the churches to initiate action by which the local congregations will be helped to reflect theologically through various art forms such as song, dance, drawing and decorating."[19] Fifteen years later, Philip Manuao encouraged his own church not to look outside for foreign methods that are irrelevant to Melanesia. "In a predominantly oral society, the church ought to minister and teach primarily through indigenous oral media." Any church in a "predominantly oral society," that prioritizes written media, "is not indigenous."[20]

17. Prior, "Orality," 147.

18. Rynkiewich, "Mission," 51. For a more extensive approach to the distinctive nature of memory in oral cultures, see Ong, *Orality and Literacy*, 67–77.

19. Recommendation 21 in Lang et al., "Towards," 147.

20. Manuao, "Communicating the Gospel," 45.

Numerous diary entries over my own period of ministry among the peoples of Vanuatu indicate this same feature of primary oral cultures. In the worship life of the church, priority was often given to song and choir contributions over everything else that took place. By way of illustration, there was a strong protest submitted to the Presbytery of Efate—in central Vanuatu—when, in the interests of reducing the length of a worship service, a decision was made that some of the choirs would make their contribution over the cup of tea which would follow the worship service, rather than being included within worship. The Presbytery was firmly over-ruled. The length of time taken by choir items, especially in worship events associated with important public occasions, far exceeded the length of time taken for preaching. It became clear that singing is profoundly part of the culture of the people, and the means by which their faith is learned and expressed.

As it was with song, so also was it with drama, but not to the same degree. Drama is not demanded as a form of participation in worship, but it became very clear to me during my time of ministry among the people of Vanuatu that the use of drama in worship, in preaching, and in teaching, was a most fruitful and engaging method of communication.

Dance, also, has an important place in traditional custom ceremony and finds its way into popular forms of entertainment, and in presentations made for visitors, being used to explain and display the culture of the people. Yet it has not yet found a place in the Christian life and worship of the Protestant church communities.[21]

The telling of stories has always been fundamental in handing on the traditions of a local community. Custom stories about creation, about the meaning of existence, about the important lessons of human life, are central to the life of the people. The period of wailing, which has such a prescribed and powerful place in the funeral ritual, is not simply a means of expressing grief; it is also a way in which the story of the dead person's life is told—in story, song and tears combined. Story telling is such a part of the psyche of the culture that I found that the telling of stories became a conscious and central means of communication in preaching and teaching.

Art in the forms of carving, sand drawing, cave drawing, decoration of the body or of various forms of dress belongs to traditional cultures across the islands of Vanuatu. The use of art is a standard form of communication, and is integral to traditional ritual.

The second essential feature of cultures of primary orality, says Rynkiewich, is that "oral communities are fundamentally communal, and the

21. For some interesting reflections on the absence of dance in the Christian church and how it might be incorporated into worship in the cultures of the South Pacific, see Johnson-Hill, "Towards a Theology of Dance," 53–66.

making of memory involves the whole community, often in action rather than in the use of words. Memory, then, has more of a social character in oral communities."[22]

The communal nature of South Pacific cultures is definitive for what it means to be human.[23] The people know themselves to be truly human only within community, and within that community they find their identity. Such community comprises an interdependent network of people whose life together as community enables and sustains "life" for each of its members. "Life is not only biological existence; it is health, wealth, well-being, good relationships, security, prestige, strength, etc. The community has been experienced as the only way to such 'life', and so it comes to share in the 'absoluteness' of 'life.'"[24]

The significance and impact of this feature of South Pacific cultures are almost impossible to comprehend for people from Western cultures, the latter being so powerfully premised on the sanctity of the individual. By way of illustration, the concept of "arranged marriage" is based on the fact that all important decisions, involving the life of members of the community, need to be made by the community, and are subsequently supported and sustained by the community. Marriage preparation includes communal discussions involving numerous members of the respective families of the man and woman, and the processes towards marriage need to take account of the way in which the marriage will impact on communal life. One of the consequences of this is that any subsequent marriage problems that may occur become a matter for the community to resolve.

From the point of view of Pacific anthropology, one of the affirmations inherent in this second feature of primary oral cultures, is that human beings are created for social existence, to be in community with others. In order to preserve and protect this assumption, a society needs to have an intricate set of clear and accepted social rules and regulations. To break any of these social rules and regulations is to threaten the life of the community, and therefore to threaten others within the community, so that breaches of social rules and regulations can carry severe penalties. For example, in the traditional practice of some tribal communities in Vanuatu, if a married person engages in an inappropriate relationship with another person, the punishment may be death. In traditional custom, often the best form of discipline in such societies was to separate people from the community, that is,

---

22. Rynkiewich, "Mission," 51.

23. Four of eleven chapters (4, 5, 9, 10) give attention to this in Whiteman, *Introduction*. See also Boseto, "God as Community"; Kamu, *Samoan Culture*.

24. Mantovani, "Traditional Values," 201.

to ex-communicate them, which was effectively to put them to death. Mantovani observes of the tribal communities of Papua New Guinea, "Should a member endanger 'life' for the community, he will be eliminated. . . . To be exiled means to be condemned to death."[25]

One of the fascinating consequences of this priority of community as the medium of "life" is that when it comes to ethical behavior, it is the impact on the community that is the single criterion that determines what is ethically "good" or "bad." Mantovani illustrates this point by referring to the act of theft, "To steal from a brother is ethically wrong because it spoils a key relationship and endangers the community as a result. But to steal from an enemy is ethically good if it helps the community. . . . In other words, the ethical value of an action is assessed according to the effect of that action on the community."[26]

One further aspect of this communal nature is that the cultures of the South Pacific are also relational. The importance of the community is that it places people in relationship with one another. If you ask ni-Vanuatu people to introduce themselves, or to tell you something about themselves, they will immediately tell you about the network of relationships to which they belong: "I am the son/daughter of, the brother/sister of, the cousin of. . ."[27] It is the network of their relationships that defines their humanity. "A community is a number of people kept together by a web of special relationships: the special relationships making a community. . . . Relationships are essential to community, and hence to 'life.'"[28]

Included in those important relationships are the ancestors, who "are as much part of the community as the living members. The dead have not gone away from the community, they live in a different existence within it, remaining part of the social unit."[29] In fact, explains Mantovani, such is the power and influence of the ancestors that, "it is essential for the community to have proper relationships with the dead, in order to avoid suffering, or even eventual disintegration."[30] On the island of Tanna, in southern Vanuatu, the daily ritual of kava drinking is observed among the more senior males at the time when the sun is about to set. The act of drinking kava

25. Mantovani, "Traditional Values," 202.

26. Mantovani, "Traditional Values," 206.

27. See the insightful chapter on "The Scattered Self," written about the cultural understanding of the human person as relational, in the tribal context of Africa. Taylor could well be writing about the cultures of the South Pacific. Taylor, *Primal Vision*, 48–58.

28. Mantovani, "Traditional Values," 202.

29. Mantovani, "Traditional Values," 202.

30. Mantovani, "Traditional Values," 202.

takes place in a particular sacred or taboo site. It involves the consumption of the prepared kava from a half-coconut shell, in such a way that the person who is drinking, consumes the whole of the contents of the coconut shell in silence, without interruption to the process. The consumption of the kava is the means by which those who drink are in communion with their ancestors; to interrupt the drinking part way through is to interrupt or break the connection with the ancestors.

A similar reverence for the presence of the ancestors is evident in the meeting of the chief and elders in the *Nakamal*.[31] In some Vanuatu cultures, the men sit down in a circle on the ground with their backs against the base of their ancestral totem. When they speak, they do not speak with their own voice or from their own insight and wisdom; they speak with the voice of their ancestral tradition, and impart the wisdom and insight of previous generations. When others in the gathering speak, their voices are attended to in the same weighty manner.

When the members of the workshop on Culture and Faith gathered in the New Hebrides in 1979, they worked on a liturgy for Holy Communion that was adapted into the context of their own traditional cultures. As part of that liturgy, a portion of each of the two elements, of the flesh and the juice of the coconut, is put onto the ground in front of the celebrant "as an offering to the ancestors who are the saints of other times and who are in communion with us."[32]

In this same vein, one of the little recognized but significant ways in which Pacific Islanders reflect on their missionary past, is that they view the missionaries as ancestors. "Many Islanders believe that the ways of expressing the gospel taught by the 'ancestor' missionaries was the correct way and must be strictly observed."[33]

A further feature of this relational life is that the cultures of the South Pacific are cultures of interdependence and mutual obligation. Again this point is closely connected with the two points already made, namely the communal and the relational, but is distinctive. This is illustrated by the very common practice of sharing food and exchanging gifts. "Within the traditional community, relationships are maintained through reciprocity, that is, a relationship tending towards equivalence is sustained between members by giving and receiving, by helping and being helped."[34]

---

31. A Nakamal is the village chief's meeting house.

32. Prior, *Contemporary Local Perspectives*, 149.

33. Fugui and Wright, *Christ*, 5.

34. MacDonald, "Melanesian Communities," 216.

In his article on the important and complex role of gift-giving in Melanesian cultures, Buabeti Tabe, lecturer in Christian Education at Bishop Patteson Theological College in the Solomon Islands, refers to "giving of sacrifices to ancestors" (in expectation of recipient benefits), social forms of giving (e.g., bride-price as an act of exchange), economic aspects of giving (trade exchanges with other communities or peoples), political aspect of giving (as with a chief who must provide signs of his wealth), noting that "giving is important to every aspect of life . . . it is fundamentally about relationships."[35] He speaks for the peoples of the whole of the South Pacific when he concludes, "In the thought of Solomon Islanders giving is not a one-way act—causing someone to have. It is a dynamic act, with meaning, conveying messages about the relationship between the giver and the receiver. . . . No Solomon Islander would give just so another might have. Giving is necessarily about relationships and responsibilities. If there is no giving, there is no relationship."[36]

Outsiders may be welcomed into some aspects of this relational exchange of gifts. A personal illustration will provide an example. Upon arrival in January 1983, on my first Sunday in Vanuatu, when sitting down to lunch, one of the children of my immediate neighbor arrived with a plate of ground-oven baked food. I received the gift with much gratitude and my family relished the food. Later that day, I returned the plate, expressing my gratitude. But I had made a mistake—the plate was returned empty. It should have been returned with food on it. I sensed that there was something wrong at the time it was returned, but it was not until I learned more of local customs that I understood. My initial response in learning that the plate should have been returned with food was to question the generosity of the initial gift. Was it a conditional gift? Later, I learned that the initial gift of food was an expression from our neighbors that my family and I were being invited into a wider community, a community of inter-dependence. In returning the plate of food empty, I was rejecting our family's responsibility within that community. To return the plate full of food would have indicated that willingness.[37]

The implications for theology of this key element of primary oral communities, is both simple and profound. Any contextualization of theology in the South Pacific must in essence be communal. "Our success depends

35. Tabe, "Stewardship," 66.

36. Tabe, "Stewardship," 67.

37. January 29, 1983 in Prior, *Diary 1*. For a more general reflection on a Missionary's obligations to give and to receive in cultures like those in Vanuatu, see Gittins, *Gifts*, 102–9.

entirely on our ability to make our theology a communal theology."[38] It is as simple, and as fundamental, as that. Any individualized form or content or methodology of theology cannot make claim to be culturally contextual in the South Pacific.

The third essential feature, according to Rynkiewich, is "the importance of the distinctive relationship between the teacher and the learners in an oral community."[39] The cultures of the South Pacific operate with forms of hierarchy, headed by a chiefly figure. The role of the chief is to oversee the life of the community, to give direction, to guard and protect, to maintain the truths of the tradition, to resolve conflicts. A good chief is one of the people, one with the people, and one who is for the people. He (and it almost always is a "he" in these mostly patriarchal societies) is a person of wealth, power and authority in the community, but his wealth, power, and authority are held for the sake of—and in the service of—his people.

Documented interviews with the two chiefs who, in the post-independent era of Vanuatu, have each held the esteemed position, as the President of the National Council of Chiefs, endorse this overall function of the chief in Vanuatu societies. Through a number of stories of local village life, Chief Willi Bongmatur[40] reveals the significant role of the chief as guide, as teacher, as peacemaker of his people, and as a model of ethical life.[41] The interview with Chief Noel Mariesua,[42] who was President of Malvatumauri from 1993–2001, is more explicit in describing the power and authority of the chief and the decisive role they played at the time of the arrival of the first missionaries. Such was the influence of the chief on the life of the community that it was the chief who, alone, determined whether a missionary would be permitted to enter the tribal land, and where this did happen, the people instinctively trusted the work of the mission. Indeed, according to Mariesua, they willingly received the missionary message, and responded to the missionary call.

> The missionaries understood that when they arrived on the shores of our islands, they needed to communicate with and gain the permission of the chiefs. Otherwise, they would not be able to come ashore. . . . The chief and the missionary would

38. Kanyoro, "African Women's Quest," 87.

39. Rynkiewich, "Mission," 51.

40. Bongmatur was President of Malvatumauri (the National Council of Chiefs) from 1980–93, and one of three signatrees to the National Constitution at the time of Independence.

41. Prior, *Contemporary Local Perspectives*, 26–32.

42. Prior, *Contemporary Local Perspectives*, 33–40.

then make an agreement about where the missionary was permitted to go. . . . Because of respect for the chief, all the people
were then happy to become Christian. The chief instructed the
people to pay attention to the missionary. And in subsequent
generations, the chiefs have continued to have this role.[43]

Mariesua goes so far as to claim that, "It was because of the role of the
chiefs that the mission was so successful."[44] That may be overstating the
case, but the influence of the chief in all matters of importance in the life of
his community, cannot be overstated. The implications for the contextualizing of theology are important.

Out of his own experience working with Vanuatu cultures, and his
observations about the dynamics of Vanuatu communities, Jon Paschke
proposes a list of guidelines for the way in which this third feature of oral
communities might be applied contextually in creating an effective learning community. He writes, "Respect for authority: ideally, then, the group
leader will be a culturally recognized 'big' man; leadership style: expect a
strong, controlling leader to maintain harmony and conformity; life example of leader: the leader needs to be a model/example for the group—an
important way of group learning."[45]

As has been noted already,[46] indigenous chiefly figures have made
a profound contribution to the movement of contextualizing theology in
the South Pacific. Leaders like Havea, Tuwere, Boseto, Finau and Meo are
the most notable. What is clear is that their influence as theologians has
not been because of their individual capabilities and powers of persuasion.
Rather, their influence has evolved from their chiefly status within their
communities, and the power and influence that accompany that status. In
that sense, this third feature identified by Rynkiewich, has been evident
in the localizing of theology in the South Pacific from the very beginning.
Having acknowledged that, it remains an important consideration for any
future developments of the contextualization of theology. It will continue
to influence, not only the matter of who might give leadership to this, but
also the dynamics that apply within the learning community. As Rynkiewich asserts, the relationship in oral cultures between teacher and learners
is uniquely defined and fundamental to the learning process.

---

43. Prior, *Contemporary Local Perspectives*, 33.

44. Prior, *Contemporary Local Perspectives*, 34.

45. Paschke, "Small Group," 70–71.

46. See the section on chiefs in chapter 2 above.

NOT ENLIGHTENMENT

There is a second key observation to be made in relation to the struggle within the South Pacific for the contextualization of theology. It is one that is strongly interconnected with the first, is of comparable significance, and is also inadequately appreciated in terms of its implications. It can perhaps best be stated in a negative way, and gathered under the one fundamental cultural and historical fact, namely that the cultures of the South Pacific are not post-Enlightenment cultures. In other words, the "paradigm shift" (Bosch's term) represented by the Enlightenment era, that is such a formative part of the cultural history of the Western world, has no parallel in South Pacific cultures, nor does it belong to their cultural history. This fact alone ought to suggest a profound contrast between the cultures of the South Pacific and the cultures of the Western world.

As a way of understanding those features that are the distinguishing marks of post-Enlightenment Western cultures, and absent from traditional South Pacific cultures, the insights of Lesslie Newbigin and David Bosch offer a helpful and concise overview. Newbigin's "profile of a culture" can be summarized in the following way:

1. The development of science focuses the meaning of life on the questions of cause and effect, replacing the understanding of life in terms of purpose. The world now becomes an object of investigation and exploration to be understood and explained; thus the separation of the creative human from the created world.

2. Cultural history is now understood in terms of progress and development towards a better life, rather than preservation of the past.

3. The post-Enlightenment age is an age of reason and rationality, focused on the individual human and the search for truth and happiness.

4. The explanations afforded by science usurp the place of religion; science that deals with public facts based on evidence is set in contrast to all forms of belief and values (including religion), which are now confined to a private world of personal options.

5. This leads to a dichotomy between private and public, between religion and science, between the natural and the spiritual, between belief and fact, between the subjective and objective.

6. It leads also to the defining of work in terms of the progress of the society, determined now by a mechanized industrial society, with the evolution of education as a formal means of understanding this new

world, and contributing productively to it. Urbanization of society is a logical outcome of this change in the defining of work.

7. In conceptual terms, the center of the culture is the rational human individual who seeks to understand the world scientifically through critical analysis. The God who was the center of the pre-modern Christendom world is marginalized to a private and irrational world of optional belief.[47]

Bosch's description of the paradigmatic cultural shift in the Western world, constituted by the Enlightenment, is entirely consistent with that of Newbigin. Bosch notes that the Enlightenment era was pre-eminently an age of reason. It operated on a schema of subject-object, with the subject being the rational human individual, and the object being the natural world, as something to be analyzed. In fact, the whole world became the object of exploration and discovery, to be subdued and occupied, manipulated and exploited for human ends. This led to the replacement of the purpose of life with the pursuit of cause and effect, and to a fundamental belief in social progress. Humans took up control of their own destiny, with the ability to achieve all things, and the individual now had the freedom and resources to pursue an ideal life. This paved the way for a culture of consumerism, of prosperity and of economic development, and the fundamental belief that all problems are solvable.[48]

This overview of the impact of the Enlightenment on Western cultures helps us to identify and understand some of the features of the cultures of the South Pacific that do not share this same cultural history. In its simplest form, it could be said that for each main feature of post-Enlightenment Western cultures, there is a corresponding and contrasting feature in South Pacific cultures. By no means is the following list complete, but it itemizes those features that are pertinent to the pursuits of the contextualization of theology within South Pacific cultures. It overlaps the contrasting elements that distinguish oral cultures from literate cultures, described earlier.

South Pacific cultures are not cultures of critical and analytical engagement in the pursuit of rational scientific understanding of cause and effect. Rather they are cultures that assume uncritically that all things—good and evil—are determined by the influence of spirits or deities (and for Christians, therefore, by the influence of God). Notably, freedom from the fear of spirits remains a common theme for preachers. There are numerous local community practices to ward off the spirits, and commonly the power of spirits dictate

---

47. Newbigin, *Foolishness*, 21–41.
48. Bosch, *Transforming Mission*, 270–73.

major decisions made by the community. My own diary entries include several references. For example, "interruption to a funeral of an eighteen year old man by the village chief who wanted to explain that the cause of death was not simply that the young man drowned after his canoe overturned in the ocean, but that the angry ancestral spirits incarnated as a shark and caused the boat to overturn and the man to drown"[49]; and again the entry, "No-one dies without reason or cause. Therefore at Malekula when a canoe overturned and a seventy-five year old man drowned, his village people actually moved the village to another location for fear of the spirits."[50]

The cultures of the South Pacific are cultures where education is not about an academic pursuit of knowledge and ideas, separated from the dimension of beliefs and values. Rather, they are cultures where education is life-based learning about what is necessary for the community's well-being, integrating all aspects of existence. In particular there is integration, rather than binary separation, of things political and things religious, of the natural and the spiritual, of fact and belief, of public and private. By way of simple illustration, those who are the leaders of their tribal communities are leaders of every aspect of the community's life, because all aspects are integrated into a single whole.[51]

The cultures of the South Pacific are not cultures of advancement and progress; rather they are cultures of tradition and preservation. In South Pacific cultures, matters of importance for the life of the society are contained in, and come from, the community's past. It is the past that is the source of wisdom and truth. The consequence of this is that the requirement placed upon the people is to preserve what comes from the past, and to ensure that it is passed on to subsequent generations. A failure to do this will jeopardize everything that is important for human life. Within such cultures, the people who are most closely identified with the past, namely the older generation, are revered for their wisdom. In contrast, younger people need to be formed into their past, in order to become wise.

Many of the dilemmas that have surfaced through the period of the last four decades in the agenda of the contextualization of theology in the South Pacific, are rooted in this fundamental reality that the cultures of the South Pacific do not share the Western world's heritage of cultural Enlightenment. Awareness of the many and diverse implications of this, and of the extent to which Western post-Enlightenment cultural categories have, from the beginning, impregnated their way into the theological agenda of the

49. Wednesday, May 21, 1986 in Prior, *Diary 3*.

50. Prior, *Diary: Cultural and Church Life*.

51. Lini, "Should the Church?," 176. Lini, "Christians in Politics," 183–85.

South Pacific, is fundamental to achieving a genuinely culturally-grounded theology within the South Pacific.

THE SEPARATION OF THEOLOGICAL COLLEGE AND LOCAL CHURCH COMMUNITY

The third of the key issues that constitute a stumbling block in the contextualization of theology in the South Pacific is the inherited structural dislocation between the theological college and the local villages. The former is the place where theology is learned and where theological leaders are educated, and the latter is where the church has its essential expression and where Christian life is lived out. At first, this issue may seem trivial, but in reality it is critical to the theological agenda. In a context like the South Pacific where communal life, grounded in kinship relationships, has been, and remains, at the very heart of the identity of South Pacific peoples, this separation constitutes a fundamental cultural anomaly. It is not merely a geographical separation, it is a cultural dislocation. As such it therefore provides a major obstacle to the contextualization of theology. It perpetuates ongoing dilemmas about the distance of theology from, and therefore the irrelevance of theology to, the life of the people; it prompts core questions as to who does theology, the mode of formation of theological leaders, and the very nature and purpose of theology.

As early as 1976 this key issue was already apparent. In January of that year, the gathering of the Pacific Conference of Churches in Papua New Guinea approved a resolution urging theological schools in the Pacific region "to seek a standard of excellence that united pastoral qualities with academic ability, having in mind the needs of all the laity and of the 'grass roots.'"[52] In 1980, calling for a "people-oriented theology," Albert Burua, Principal of the Rarongo Theological College in Papua New Guinea wrote, "Theology in the past has been the work of theologians. It has been the intellectual exercise of a few. It seemed at times to be an abstract issue to most people. Is it possible for theology to be people-oriented?"[53]

In the questionnaire summary reported at the 1981 Tongan Assembly of the PCC, "There was almost unanimous agreement that ministerial formation required the minister/pastor to integrate theology with faith and local understanding." The report then proposes a mutual engagement between theological colleges and "lay people," through theological colleges resourcing lay people, and lay people making aware to the colleges their

52. PCC, "Third Assembly."
53. Burua, "Theology and Melanesia," 12.

real-life problems.[54] The conclusions note the need "for a relevant theology, that is, a theology that is understandable in its expressions and credible in its concern for the life and problems of the people; for theological educational-ists to be in touch with the people whom they are training their students to serve."[55] In the Background Reading Book for the same gathering in Tonga, faculty member, Dr. Salesi Havea, expresses serious concern about the clash between the theology that is being learned in theological colleges and the faith of the church in the local communities.

> Theological knowledge and education are seen as being in op-position to the faith of the church. The claim is that theological education's interest does not focus on spirituality and nour-ishment of the religious life of the people of God but rather on critical knowledge that ends up in proclaiming that God is dead. . . . Although theologians may gain the confidence of some church leaders, the attitude of many church leaders towards theology and theological colleges is still of indiffer-ence and suspicion. The contention that theology is a scientific study of God is rejected because it creates vanity within those who pretend to be theological experts and makes people in the church suspicious of theologians.[56]

In the same Assembly documents,[57] Harry Tevi, Bishop of the Anglican Church of Melanesia, reflects first of all on his own dislocating experience in theological education in the Solomon Islands. He then offers his criti-cism of theological colleges: "The training we offer gives some satisfaction to the tutors, thinking of letters and decorations to come after the students' names. This gives worldly recognition but it does not help personal faith in Christ."[58] In response to the rather forthright views expressed by Tevi, there were several voices of agreement.[59] Prominent Melanesian, Bishop Leslie Boseto, in his background paper for the Assembly, writes, "Let us not forget that any theology the Pacific community may desire . . . must be the theol-ogy of the love of God in our community and from our community. . . . It

---

54. PCC, "Background," 219–20.

55. PCC, "Background," 220.

56. PCC, "Background," 62.

57. Tevi, "Faith," 28–30, reproduced in condensed form in PCC, "Fourth Assembly," 176–78.

58. Tevi, "Faith, Relevance, and Future Training," 30.

59. PCC, "Fourth Assembly," 27–28. See also the report back from the questionnaire that records the same concerns, expressed mainly by those who have not been to theo-logical colleges, PCC, "Fourth Assembly," 219.

must be a real and responsible love which feeds, clothes and shelters the school leavers and dropouts whom we call the unemployed."[60]

The concluding section of the deliberations on theological education sets out a telling summary under the heading, "What are Some of the Shortcomings in our Present Forms of Theological Education and Training?" They reflect the unresolved tensions already noted, namely programs based on Western ideas and concepts, oriented to institutions rather than to people, factual or theoretical rather than situational and practical, using literature written by foreigners rather than by Pacific Islanders, with much stronger emphasis needed on field experience.[61]

The same concerns and tensions persist through the 1980s. In the 1986 special consultation on theological education, the tension between theological colleges and grass-root communities was forcefully stated. Solomon Islander, Charles Koete, spoke out against the elitism of theology and the assumption that theology is the enterprise only of a select few, "In the Solomons there is a great barrier between the grassroots people and the church leaders. Our people think that only bishops and priests can be theologians . . . our theology must address itself to the issues that are real to the people. It must emerge from the whole community of believers, not just from the top people."[62] At the same occasion, Ralph Teinaroe claimed, "The early missionaries made decisions about Pacific cultures and traditions from their own point of view rather than from that of the people. I hope that in building a Pacific theology we don't make the same mistake. . . . As we go through colleges and universities we can easily lose contact with our own culture, so we must let the people share in building our Pacific theology."[63]

The vast chorus of voices expressing similar concerns over this period reflects the ongoing tensions created by the separation of theological colleges and the life of the church. This voice remained strident through the 1990s. "There is no doubt that a very real gap exists between theology and theological education on the one hand, and the churches on the other. And this gap can widen further if theology does not do anything to address the church's and society's real needs."[64]

In his 2005 survey, Charles Forman discerns two significant positive developments in the contextualization of theology in Oceania over the last generation. One of these is the deliberate commitment by local theologians

60. Boseto, "Challenges," 8.
61. PCC, "Fourth Assembly," 234.
62. Lange et al., "Towards a Relevant Pacific Theology," 34.
63. Lange et al., "Towards a Relevant Pacific Theology," 44.
64. Tuwere, "Agenda," 5.

to engage seriously with issues of social responsibility. The other is the strengthening of links between Christian belief and traditional Pacific cultures.[65] However, he then concludes with a sober critique:

> The men and women whose thoughts have been examined here are part of the new cosmopolitan elite, the ones who have travelled around the Pacific or to other parts of the world and are at home with the use of English as their international language. They are not, by and large, village people who are steeped in the traditional society, nor are they likely to be suffering personal heartache at the loss of traditional ways. . . . Rather, they are comfortable in moving outside traditional ways of life at the same time that they are filled with new confidence regarding those traditional ways. Their writings are not for the rank-and-file Christians but for the intellectually advanced.[66]

For Forman, it is not that these men and women have turned their backs on their traditional cultures (although there is a clear suggestion that they are no longer immersed in their traditional culture), but that their theology is neither grounded in village life nor aimed at serving village life. Their theology fits better in an international arena where the writing of articles and books is the primary medium of communicating, and where English is the language of communication. The challenge, represented by Forman's statement, is not simply that what counts as theology from the South Pacific is being done and being represented to the world by a "cosmopolitan elite." More fundamentally, it represents a challenge to the methodology of theology. Forman is describing a form of theology that is framed by, and within, Western cultural parameters. It is a framework that assumes that the task of theology belongs essentially to well-educated individuals, and takes literacy-based forms. It is a theology that has been given its shape by a nineteenth century missionary tradition, has been cultivated within theological colleges, and is recognizable and acceptable according to Western academic standards.

Any appropriate contextualization of theology in the South Pacific must arise from and be grounded within the cultural framework of indigenous islanders. For the South Pacific, this means that the theological task itself must be located and grounded, not within theological colleges, but within local church and village communities. It is not merely a matter of geographical preference, it is a cultural necessity.

65. Forman, "Finding," 118–19.
66. Forman, "Finding," 121.

5

A Case Study

The "Gospel and Culture in Vanuatu" Project

THE EARLIER SURVEY OF the voices of South Pacific Islanders has indicated that, while much attention has been given to, and much progress has been made in, the contextualization of theology in the South Pacific, fundamental dilemmas remain, especially in relation to the methodology of theology. I have asserted that, at the root of the challenges, lay the three key issues described in the previous chapter. It is clear from our examination that they each impact profoundly on the agenda of contextualization, and they illuminate the contours for any further pursuit in contextualization. In particular, they address the most problematic area of contextualization, namely the methodology of theology—the questions as to who does theology, what form theology takes, the essential location for the theological task, and the primary purpose of theology. We may now turn to what is the basic question: What are the consequences of this for the shape of theology in the oral cultures of the South Pacific?

In responding to this fundamental question, I want now to take up the particular project on "Gospel and Culture in Vanuatu." This represents one experiment in exploring the contextualization of theology within the cultural context of the South Pacific. It was motivated by, and had its birth, during the formative newly post-independent era of the 1980s. It offers an approach to theology in which the local people are the subjects (the "who" of theology), it is located in the local community of faith (the "location" of theology), it is communal and oral in its character (the "form" of theology), and it serves the life and witness of the local church community (the "purpose" of theology).

In other words, it is an experiment in grounding theology—its content and its methodology—within South Pacific cultures.

As a case study for the contextualizing of theology in the South Pacific, it is not something that, from the beginning, was thoroughly defined. While it originated in direct response to specific contextual challenges, its content and shape have evolved over a period of more than thirty years. This evolution has been in response to changing circumstances, unexpected events, deepening insights, and constant reflection. While the presenting challenge was the cultural contextualization of the gospel in relation to concrete issues, the project later developed into the wider framework of the contextualization of theology, with a focus on matters of both content and methodology. In this sense, it is only retrospectively that the "Gospel and Culture in Vanuatu" project has now become a case study in the contextualization of theology.

Because of its very nature, it is important to recount the story of the origins and evolution of this project, as a way of examining whether and how it constitutes an experiment that represents a valid response to the quest for a genuine contextualization of theology in the oral cultures of the South Pacific. Might it then pave the way for the future?

THE NEED FOR THE CONTEXTUALIZATION OF THEOLOGY IN VANUATU

Before independence in Vanuatu was achieved in 1980, the need for the contextualization of Christian faith in the context of Vanuatu cultures was becoming increasingly apparent. In the late 1970s and early 1980s, the Australian Council of Churches and the Pacific Conference of Churches jointly sponsored a series of workshops throughout the South Pacific on "Culture and Faith" . . . in Samoa (1978), New Britain Papua New Guinea (1978), Solomon Islands (1978), New Hebrides (1979), Tonga (1979), Kiribati (1981), Tuvalu (1981), and Fiji (1983). Similar workshops were also held at the Pacific Theological College in Suva and at Rarongo Theological College in Papua New Guinea. At all of these workshops, the question was asked, "What issues arise from traditional beliefs and practices that need attention in relation to the Christian Faith?" Participants were then invited to make a selection of a particular issue, and then to "describe carefully the traditional belief or practice and its purpose." After "making a comparison with Christian understandings," three options were given for categorising the issue: "(i) What should be retained or revived? (ii) What could be "baptised," fulfilled? (iii) What should be discarded?"[1]

---

1. Fugui and Wright, *Christ*, 5–6.

In terms of theology in the South Pacific, these workshops were breaking new ground in a concrete attempt to engage in a localized theology. "This (process) invariably led workshop members not simply to talk about the need for the development of Pacific theology, worship, and ways of living in community, but to actually attempt such work."[2] The approach met with welcome response from the participants. "Though only a beginning could be made in the time available, the workshop reports indicate the great significance of these attempts."[3]

As reported in the introduction to this book, following the particular workshop in the New Hebrides in 1979, a summary report was written up with the sub-title "Two Heads and Two Hearts." It indicated that the people of the New Hebrides lived two separate and parallel lives; on the one hand, they were Christian and did those things that were understood to display a Christian commitment, while on the other hand, they were people who continued to be shaped by their own cultural traditions and beliefs. However these two lives did not connect; the people lived two parallel lives, or rather one dis-integrated life.[4] The process and experience of the 1979 workshop acted as a catalyst for those New Hebridean workshop members to address this fundamental dilemma in their church.

When the yearning for national independence strengthened through the 1970s, and came to fulfilment on July 30, 1980, it gave rise to two concurrent movements that taken together were to act as a significant catalyst for the contextualization of theology. It led, on the one hand, to a committed rejection of things colonial and, on the other hand, to a renaissance of traditional cultures and identity of the Vanuatu people. On the occasion of the formal declaration of Independence, Prime Minister, Father Walter Lini, addressing his people about this new nation's future, spoke of the importance of "cherishing our ethnic, linguistic and cultural diversity," and of the need for guidance "not only from God but from our own custom and traditional values."[5]

Now proudly belonging to an independent nation, ni-Vanuatu people were no longer ruled by foreign powers, but openly reclaimed and celebrated their own national and cultural identity. Perhaps more than any other South Pacific nation that gained its independence in this period, Vanuatu was forthrightly anti-colonial. It asserted itself as a politically non-aligned

2. Fugui and Wright, *Christ*, 7.

3. Fugui and Wright, *Christ*, 7.

4. For particular local examples of this experience, see Prior, *Voice of the Local Church*, 17, 51, 95.

5. Lini, *Beyond Pandemonium*, 62.

country, it refused to establish diplomatic relations with Western allies, and, much to the concern of its neighbors Australia and New Zealand, it pursued formal connections with Cuba, with Russia and with Libya. Celebrating ten years of independence, Father Walter Lini comments on outside perceptions of Vanuatu's diplomatic involvements, that "coverage as reported in the foreign press has been very disappointing. We have often been unfairly reported and wonder why international press persists with its incorrect portrayal of us. . . . Vanuatu has stood consistently as a small independent state with its own opinions and convictions."[6] My own diary from 1985 reports on a meeting with the newly appointed Australian High Commissioner: "Afternoon visit to the new Australian High Commissioner, described himself as 'a Pacific Expert.' He was sent here to give a clear picture to Australian Govt of what is happening in the country and in the Govt. He said, 'Ideologically, Vanuatu is the most distinctive South Pacific country—others are more pragmatic. In Foreign Affairs too, Vanuatu is active—it is the least understood in Canberra of all the South Pacific countries. Its attitude to Australia is not entirely positive.'"[7]

This dual current of anti-colonialism and cultural renaissance was doubtless a powerful catalyst for the need to re-examine the missionary heritage of the Christian faith, and to forge a contextual approach to the content and methodology of theology.

The necessity for the contextualizing of theology was also motivated by local village life across the islands. Village pastors had to live and work with the fact that they and their parishioners were now encouraged to be proud of their cultural heritage. With this pride came a resurfacing of the cultural practices and cultural beliefs that in fact, had never really disappeared, but were merely covert or suppressed, even for the most fervent of Christians. As this cultural renaissance was occurring, local pastors became occupied with a new question, "How can we help our people to be faithful to the Christian gospel within our own cultural context?"

Consistent with the fact that the missionary heritage was never effectively integrated into their cultural life was the fact that the concrete issues that pastors were facing in village life, were the very same issues addressed by the Christian missionaries from the very beginning. These included belief in good and evil spirits, custom forms of healing, black magic, traditional conventions associated with various rites of passage—birth, becoming adult, marriage, death—kava-drinking, inter and intra-tribal conflict, and ancestor worship. Despite over a century of missionary intent, and the

6. Whyte, *Vanuatu*, 10.

7. Monday, April 15, 1985 in Prior, *Diary 3*.

establishment of the Christian faith across the islands, these practices were still dominant among local people.

By way of illustration, during my time at the Theological College at Aulua, Malekula, I witnessed people carrying a light with them at night time, not, as one might expect, in order to see their way, but, as they acknowledged, to act as a deterrent to evil spirits. Such spirits were active at night time but were repelled by the light. In the same manner, the village houses had only one door and no windows, so as to prevent the entry of unwelcome spirits.[8]

In every location across the nation, the question forcing itself upon the churches was now, "How can we be Christian and ni-Vanuatu in a way that is integrated?" The question addressed by Jesus to the disciples in his own time and culture, "Who do you say that I am?"(Mark 8:29), was now an unavoidable and welcome contextual question, where the "you" is now a nation of local church communities of excitedly independent ni-Vanuatu Christians.

Fiama Rakau from the island of Futuna was destined to play a key role in the localization of theology in Vanuatu and in the "Gospel and Culture" project. Following his involvement in the 1979 workshop,[9] together with his exposure to lively discussions about Pacific theology through his time at the Pacific Theological College in Suva, Rakau was enthusiastically committed to the exploration of the relationship between the Gospel and the Cultures in his own newly independent nation.[10] As time went on, it became clear that growing numbers of local people, in particular the younger generation of local pastors who had done their theological studies through the 1970s, and had been actively involved in the independence movement, were keen to explore this same issue.[11]

This agenda was also evident among the students of theology.[12] On occasions when I did some teaching at the local Theological College, I became aware of the enthusiasm among students to engage with issues of Gospel and Culture in a way which indicated a desire to embrace their own cultural heritage as integral to their identity. Under the umbrella title of "Parish The-

8. Monday, April 2, 1984 in Prior, *Diary 2*. Wednesday, May 21, 1986 in Prior, *Diary 3*. Note also the particular issues named in contents in Prior, *Contemporary Local Perspectives; Voice of the Local Church*.

9. See the published liturgy for the Lord's Supper and the poem, "Custom is Calling," Fugui and Wright, *Christ*, 111–14.

10. Prior, *Founding Missionary*, vii–viii, 3.

11. See Prior, *25 Tingting*. For example, see articles by each of Nafuki, Tali, Urtalo, and Oli.

12. Tuesday, April 3, 1984 in Prior, *Diary 2*.

ology," we conversed theologically on themes and issues which the students identified as important in local village ministry; many of these were focused on particular cultural practices and beliefs.

Throughout my time in Vanuatu, the theme of Gospel and Culture, in one form or another, was high on the church's priorities, and most especially so on occasions when pastors gathered for retreats and conferences. Accordingly, towards the time of my departure near the end of 1987, a group of four people (of which I was one) made a pact that we would continue to work together on the issues of Gospel and Culture in Vanuatu. This working group identified some thirty or more different topics that needed to be addressed, ranging across ritual practices through to basic beliefs about spirits, death and after-life. The group resolved to focus on one topic per year, with a view to developing study resources for the local church on the selected topic. On reflection, the subsequent failure to make any headway with this was due, not to a lack of desire, but to a failure to give adequate attention to a culturally appropriate methodology to pursue the task. That is to say, the requirement to use the means of writing, and technological forms of communication, proved an obstacle too great, even among these younger Western-educated leaders.

In 1991, the World Council of Churches held its seventh Assembly in Canberra, Australia. Quite unexpectedly, and instigated by a most powerful and challenging presentation of the Christian Faith from Asian theologian, Chung Hyun Kyung from Korea,[13] the issue of Gospel and Culture became a topic of significant public controversy. This was most especially so between the representatives of the Orthodox Church traditions, and those who wanted to articulate the Christian faith in what were considered to be "unorthodox" ways, but in fact were, from their own point of view, culturally contextual ways. Subsequently, the World Council of Churches established a three-year program on Gospel and Culture, under the direction of eminent South Indian theologian Christopher Duraisingh, and invited churches from all over the world to hold meetings and workshops on the topic of Gospel and Culture. A framework of guideline study questions and themes was provided as a basis for local groups around the world to submit their own reports and insights into this issue of growing international significance in Christian mission. Aware of the significance of this issue for the people of Vanuatu, an ad-hoc working group took the initiative to convene a series of workshops and to ensure that this tiny South Pacific Island nation would make its own distinctive contribution to the global process.[14] That was

13. Kyung, *Struggle*.
14. Prior, "World Council."

the first time that any written documentation of the issues of Gospel and Culture in Vanuatu had appeared. From here came the seeds of an idea of documenting and publicizing some of the local work being done in Gospel and Culture in Vanuatu.

THE EVOLUTION AND THE FORM OF THE EXPERIMENT— STAGE ONE

In 1998, five hundred copies of a book were produced under the title, *Gospel and Culture in Vanuatu: The Founding Missionary and a Missionary for Today*.[15] As suggested by the title, the book is in two parts. The earlier part is an abbreviated summary of the mission work of the founder of the Presbyterian Church, John Geddie, with a critique of the way in which this mission impacted on the traditional cultures of the local people. The second part of the book preserves a series of drawings, created by local young artist, Graham Louhman. While the artist's story is given in detail in the published volume,[16] it warrants brief summary here because of its unique importance to the pursuit of the contextualization of theology in Vanuatu, and the development of the experiment that was subsequently to unfold.

Graham Louhman was the son of the Principal of the Aulua Theological College,[17] and a very gifted although unschooled artist. When his father suffered a severe stroke in 1985, the family moved to Port Vila. Louhman became de-facto head of the family. He capitalized on his artistic gifts by gaining employment at a clothing shop, where he created designs to be applied to items of clothing. When his artistic gifts became known to members of the working group on Gospel and Culture, he was invited to work on a series of drawings that combined key themes of the Christian faith with local cultural motifs. The result was a series of ten sketches.

---

15. Prior, *Founding Missionary*.

16. The story is recounted in Prior, *Founding Missionary*, 63–64.

17. Aulua was originally the location of a mission station on the island of Malekula. In the 1970s, it became the site of the pastor training center.

THE TEN DRAWINGS BY GRAHAM LOUHMAN

1. CREATION

The picture illustrates the cycles of gardening in traditional culture, with a diversity of traditional foods represented.

Top, from left to right: Breaking back the bush, clearing the ground, getting ready to plant.

Middle Top, from left to right: The fire—annually the garden and its rubbish are burned to ashes to rejuvenate the ground.

Middle Right Preparing the ground and planting the yam.

Middle Left: Digging the holes and planting the banana.

Bottom Left: Establishing banana plants

Bottom Right: Yam plants growing

2. THE FALL

The scene is a traditional Vanuatu village. In the background, villagers are represented in casual activity—a couple talking around a fire, another couple standing outside the door of their hut, a man carrying a hunting bow and arrow. On the left, a common hen and chickens feed from the ground.

In the foreground, the principal theme is acted out. Three people are seated beneath a banyan tree, a common village meeting place. On the right is the village chief, sitting on a chiefly stone that represents a position of authority. He is wearing a chief's belt around his waist. He is giving judgment to a young couple sitting on a mat before him. Both of them have heads bowed and are sitting at a distance from each other, representing their shame for wrongdoing.

3. THE BIRTH OF JESUS CHRIST

The scene is inside a local village house, after the birth of the child. Four people are seated together on a mat. The mother is nursing the child, with the father immediately behind. The other two people, one on the right and one on the left of the mother are close relatives. Standing at the doorway are two other local people, probably relatives. They are not permitted inside. Although it is normally prohibited for any men to be attending the time of birth, this picture reflects the presence of Joseph as well as Mary at the birth of Jesus.

The baby has two symbols to represent his significance. On his left wrist is a pig's tooth. In Vanuatu cultures, the pig is a sacred animal of great value, and used only for important ceremonial occasions. This tooth has been specially grown in such a way as to form a complete circle and it represents great wealth and chiefly power. In the right hand of the child is a namele leaf. This leaf has various meanings and functions. Commonly it is a symbol of peace and is used on occasions of peace-making between conflicting parties.

4. THE LIFE OF JESUS CHRIST—THE CALL TO DISCIPLESHIP

Here, Jesus calls two disciples. The scene is at the seashore of a coastal village, with another island in the background. The empty canoe is lying still in the water. The two young men, owners of the canoe, are seated on a rock and are dressed in traditional clothing. Their attention is arrested by the invitation of a man, representing Jesus, to come and accompany him. On the left wrist of Jesus is a pig's tooth, representing chiefly power and wealth.

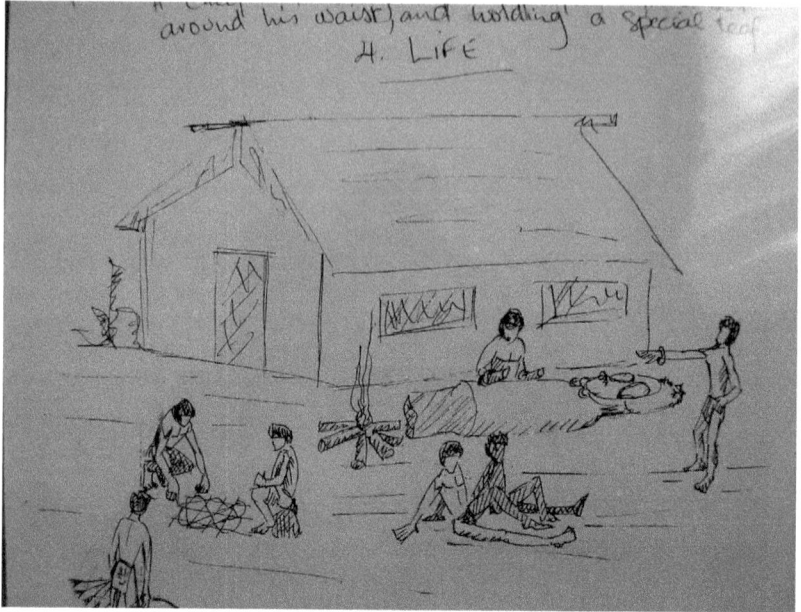

5. THE LIFE OF JESUS CHRIST—AMONG THE PEOPLE

Jesus is on the right of this sketch of daily village life. In his right hand he holds a special leaf indicating his authority, and on his right wrist is the chiefly sign of the pig's tooth. He is giving direction to a young man who is beating a message on the tam-tam. Village life goes on around this event. A fire burns, two men sit in conversation, two women are involved in sand drawing, and another man carries the hunting weapons of bow and arrow.

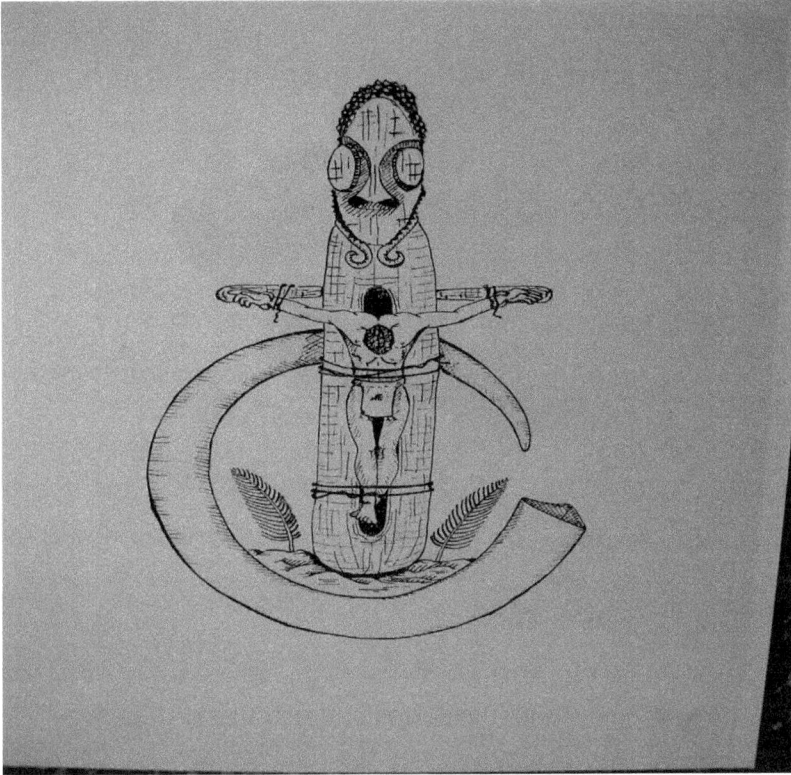

6. THE DEATH OF JESUS CHRIST

The cross itself is represented by a tam-tam, with a club as a horizontal piece holding the arms of Jesus. A tam-tam is a traditional totem symbol from the northern island of Ambrym. It represents the voice of the ancestors, the voice of wisdom and authority. When hollowed out, the tam-tam is used for sending messages around the local area of the village. The club is used for killing pigs, or traditionally, in warfare; it symbolizes power to conquer. Jesus' arms, body and feet are held by rope made from a local vine, representing the involvement of the people in the killing of Jesus. Around Jesus' wrists are circular teeth from a pig, a symbol worn by tribal chiefs and representing power, authority, wealth. A large pig's tooth covers the lower half of the picture and surrounds the cross. At the foot of the cross are two namele leaves, used in traditional culture for the ceremony of peace-making. The leaves are set in the ground, indicating the localizing of the message of the gospel into local soil. The figure of Jesus is depicted as a traditional ni-Vanuatu.

7. THE RESURRECTION OF JESUS CHRIST

The lower half of the drawing represents death. Inside a cave are symbols of warfare, superstition, and destruction (mask, spears, clubs and fire). On the right is a large stone that has been rolled away from the cave entrance. The upper half of the picture represents resurrection, victory over death. It is dominated by a young, newly shooting coconut tree which seems to be both on top of the cave and floating on the water. Such a shoot comes from a coconut that has fallen from a tree and been left to lie on the ground. The dormant coconut undergoes an internal change and sends out a new shoot from one end, while establishing roots into the ground from the other end. In this way, an old coconut produces a new tree, and produces coconuts of its own. The coconut in this picture has gone through the process of becoming a new young coconut tree; it is a symbol of new life from death. The main stem shooting from the coconut has the features of a human face. One of the leaves on the right has the shape of a human hand with a pointing index finger. The finger points to the rising of the sun to mark the beginning of a new day. Early signs of life, in the form of birds, are scattered around the sky. Flames of fire, depicting the Holy Spirit dance across the top of the cave. The setting of the seawater and the distant island complete the local flavour of the picture.

8. THE ASCENSION OF JESUS CHRIST

The scene is on a hill overlooking a coastal village. Jesus is seated on a stone of chiefly authority, and is wearing a chief's belt. A namele leaf, a traditional symbol of peace and used for peace-making ceremonies, is strapped to the left arm of Jesus. On both of Jesus' wrists are pig's teeth, symbols of chiefly power and wealth. Surrounding Jesus at his feet is a cloud, indicating that Jesus is being raised into heaven. The right hand of Jesus is held out in a sign of blessing upon the people gathered below. The people are represented as a single crowd, united and looking heavenward to Jesus.

9. PENTECOST

The scene is an island surrounded by seawater. A bird, a local white pigeon, dominates the center of the picture. This pigeon is the equivalent of the dove, representing the coming down of the Holy Spirit. Around the neck of the pigeon is the pig's tooth, representing chiefly power and wealth, and in its beak is a namele leaf, a traditional symbol of peace and used in peace-making ceremonies. These two symbols are the same two symbols that have consistently been found on the figure of Jesus, thus indicating that the Holy Spirit is the Spirit of the incarnate, crucified and risen Christ.

Rays of light radiate from the heavens onto the earth, linking the two together. The island is primarily dark, but begins to shine in the light from heaven. The seawater in the foreground is darkened and also begins to glimmer with light. The work of the Holy Spirit is to bring the light of Christ to the whole of creation.

10. THE FINAL COMING OF JESUS CHRIST

In the center of the picture, at the top, is a representation of Jesus Christ in his final coming. He is seated on a stone of chiefly authority. The stone also has the appearance of an island. Jesus is wearing a chief's belt. On his wrists are pig's teeth, representing chiefly power and wealth. On his right arm is strapped a namele leaf, a traditional symbol of peace and used in peace-making ceremonies. Jesus is holding a nul-nul, a weapon of power, in his left hand. Rays of light radiate around Jesus. The local people are in two groups, brining to mind the reading from Matthew 25:31–46, where at the final coming of Jesus, the people are divided into two groups—the sheep and the goats. Here, the group on the left all welcome the coming of Jesus and worship him. On the right, the people do not look towards Jesus; some are blind to his coming, others are afraid, or even dread his coming.

When Louhman submitted the drawings, the members of the working group were struck by what they saw. Here before them was a creative and expressive representation of the Christian faith within the context of the cultures of the people of Vanuatu; it was theology in the form of art. At the time, this artistic work broke new ground in the integration of gospel and culture, and it broke new ground in the localizing of theology. Louhman was seen as a pioneering post-independent, indigenous Vanuatu missionary.

Shortly after this work was done, and before it could be completed to the artist's intentions, Louhman died tragically at the age of twenty-one years. His sudden and unwelcome death prompted the working group, with the permission of his family, to have these drawings permanently and publicly recorded in printed form so that their significance might not be lost. It was decided that, as a post-independent depiction of the Christian faith, they be set alongside the work of the very first missionary to Vanuatu, John Geddie, the acknowledged founder of the Presbyterian Church. This contribution to the book was included in order to set Louhman's artwork within an historical and missiological context, hence, the subtitle of the publication, "The Founding Missionary and a Missionary for Today." Some observations about these two missiological approaches are relevant.

While both sections have in common the centrality of major themes of the Christian faith, coming to a definitive point in Jesus Christ, and with a missiological purpose to declare the Christian gospel, they contrast starkly in the theological presuppositions about the local cultures. Geddie denigrates much of traditional cultures and calls for separation of Christian life and cultural heritage, while the artwork of Louhman offers an incarnational gospel that embraces and re-interprets the cultural heritage. They also represent a contrast in their response to the methodological questions: (i) What form does theology take? (ii) Who does theology? (iii) What is the primary location for the theological task? (iv) What is the purpose of theology? Geddie, as the authorized missionary, imparts a universal, culture-free gospel, and declares it as news to be received and appropriated, leading to a conversion away from traditional cultural identity into the Christian faith, and especially into its Western cultural expression. On the other hand, Louhman, an unauthorized local disciple, offers a message that is rooted within the cultural context, is expressed artistically, and invites a creative response that re-interprets the cultural motifs in the light of the gospel. In contrast to the dis-integration reported in the 1979 workshop on Culture and Faith, there is, in this artistic expression, a genuine integration of Gospel with Culture. It is a ni-Vanuatu confessional response to the question of Jesus to his disciples, "Who do you say that I am?"(Mark 8:29), and it represents an affirmative response to the question, "Can I be a Christian within my cultural context?" Furthermore, as an artistic representation, it sits well within the Vanuatu oral cultures.

The book was officially launched at the subsequent National Assembly of the Presbyterian Church of Vanuatu in 1998. The front cover of the book features Louhman's drawing of "The Death of Jesus Christ." By helpful coincidence, the year of its launching marked the celebration of the 150th anniversary of the arrival of John Geddie to the shores of Vanuatu. This coincidence gave to the publication of the book a particular significance. The launching itself took place as part of the public opening of the Assembly, and included a formal presentation of the book to the Moderator of the Church.

At the time the publication of this volume was considered to be a stand-alone enterprise. If publications had ceased after this first volume, as was assumed, the working group would have been content. To have reproduced the art work of Louhman would have been sufficient in itself. It brought honor to the family and, importantly, it stood as a significant expression of the contextualizing of theology, both in content and in methodology.

But the story did not finish there. What was unforeseen at the time was that this was to be just a beginning. What followed developed into a much more considered and robust engagement with the questions of the contextualizing of theology in the Vanuatu context. This came about because, at its launching, this first book received an enthusiastic reception, and served to awaken local people to the possibilities of their own theological expressions. While these would not take artistic form, they did integrate core features of Vanuatu cultures into the theological task.

THE EVOLUTION AND THE FORM OF THE EXPERIMENT— STAGE TWO

In August 1999, at the invitation of its staff, I spent one week in residence at the Talua Ministry Training Centre on South Santo. I was invited to present the annual lecture to mark the eleventh anniversary of the founding of the center, and to conduct a series of presentations on the now ubiquitous theme of "Gospel and Culture."[18] With other members of the working group, I saw it as an opportunity to pursue this pressing topic, and to do so in a manner that was informed by the cultural context.

Together with my colleague and mentor, Fiama Rakau (who was now the Principal of Talua), we discussed with students and staff the shape of our time together. By then, we had gained certain insights that were important in working with local people, and we knew that the method and the

18. Prior, "Introduction to Gospel," 141–46.

structure of the sessions were as important as the content. In setting up the process, we were mindful of the following elements:

i.   The people are passionate about issues of "Gospel and Culture" in their own local communities; methodologically the local context with its distinctive issues needs to be the starting point.

ii. The people are essentially communal, and so it is important that the work be done in community.

iii. The people belong to primary oral cultures, and this needs to determine the mode of working. Any literacy-based resources need to be minimal, and if there is to be a written documentation of the group's work, this must be arranged in a suitable manner. By circumstance, there were some students who had been well educated in French or English-speaking schools and were able to act as recorders for the group.

iv. The people have high regard for their past heritage, which includes not only their traditional cultural heritage but also the missionary heritage which has shaped their church communities.

v.   Language is fundamental in communication, so the groups need to be free to use a language of familiarity. In fact, in most cases, that meant using the language of Bislama, the lingua franca of the country, which is the language of communication across all local tribal languages; it was also the language of the subsequent written record of the discussions.

vi. There is a great diversity of cultures in Vanuatu, and so there are great differences between what is important to people and in how they approach particular issues.

vii. The people are accustomed to chiefly leadership, and so it is important to recognize a suitable form of leadership, to offer some direction, and to make clear what it is that they are being asked to do.

viii. The people are accustomed to allowing sufficient time for issues to be discussed and outcomes to be discerned, without any pressure of needing to meet deadlines. This suggests that the groups need to have generous time and space to go about their task.

In response to these elements, and with the aim of inviting the people into a culturally grounded approach to doing theology, a particular methodology was followed.[19] Its primary features, accompanied by some commentary, are set out below.

---

19. Prior, *Contemporary Local Perspectives*, 78–80.

Each group was as culturally homogeneous as possible. Such a sorting of the participants, into groups of sub-cultural homogeneity, recognized the fact that across the islands of Vanuatu there is, from the point of view of ni-Vanuatu people, significant variation in cultural groups, each with a distinctive language and cultural definition. While it was impossible to establish purely intra-cultural/linguistic groups, it was possible to gather people into regionally based groups where the cultural world-views were sufficiently alike. Any issue could then be chosen and discussed in such a way that there was a common understanding of the topic, and common cultural assumptions among group members.

A cultural anomaly in the workshop structure later became apparent. It was arranged that each group would have a mixture of men and women, and of candidates for ordained and for lay ministries. In that way there would be a good cross-section of perspectives and experiences represented in the conversations and in the subsequent workshop report. However, the fact that each group included both men and women immediately posed a serious issue as to the nature of the dynamics within the groups, and most especially the dominance of male members in the conversation. In traditional village life, discussions would commonly take place in mono-gender groups; in such groups, discussion flows more easily.[20] In the process to be later followed at the Assembly in 2002, the decision was made that there would be some mono-gender groups, with particular attention given to the need for women-only groups, recognizing that the presence of men commonly has the effect of suppressing the voice of women.

Each group had a coordinator or leader, chosen by the group from among its members, one who was recognized to have cultural status as a leader, and who would take up their role in the manner of a chiefly figure in local village communities. This person helped to guide the group through the process, and to encourage everyone to contribute. Each group also had a chosen recorder with literacy-based skills who noted the names of the members of the group, and who was responsible for facilitating the group's written report.

The groups sat on the ground and formed a circle, again in a manner familiar to cultural practices when village people meet together. In each case, prayer preceded the discussion, thus setting the subsequent task within the affirming and guiding presence of God, again a normal practice in the local Christian community.

The groups met through each day of the week, in the afternoons. This provided a generous amount of time, and permitted each group to

20. Paschke, "Small Group," 69.

move at its own pace in working through the guideline questions and the subsequent report.

The preliminary task of each group was to identify a particular focus for the discussion. This was achieved by inviting each group to name three issues within the life of their own local church community where there was conflict about the engagement between the gospel and their culture, or between the church and the customary life of the local community. It was acknowledged that these were issues that demanded engagement and response from the community of faith. Each group was then asked to prioritize the three issues, with the intention of beginning with their first priority, and if time allowed, moving onto the second and third. The fact that the different groups might choose the same topic was not a concern, given that each group would tackle a given topic in a unique way. In the end, very few groups chose the same topic, and a considerable cross-section of topics was tackled.

This first part of the actual process immediately grounded the conversation in the life and experience of the group members, gave them shared ownership and direction of the topic, and served to give the conversation a sense of immediacy and relevance for them and their communities.

In these various structural ways, both the content and the methodology were already beginning to embody a contextualization of theology within the life of the local church community, countering the legacy of theology as received through the missionary tradition. The process was communal, honored their primary oral identity, and was grounded in the experience of the group members and their local church communities.

In order to engage with the nominated issues as a theological task, and to assist the groups in their discussion, guideline questions were provided. The questions were designed by the working group to encourage engagement by all participants in the process, and to allow the discussion to go in a range of possible directions dictated by each group. At the same time, the questions were deliberately directive in order to give some focus to the conversations, to ensure that opinions were expressed about particular elements of the chosen topic, and to reach something of an outcome that was oriented to responsive action. While the groups were not bound to follow them, the guidelines at least indicated the sort of ground to be covered in discussion of the topic. Because the questions were intended to reflect a cultural contextualization of the content and the methodology of theology, further comment about each of these questions is warranted.

1. In relation to this chosen topic, what was the cultural situation in the past?

The intention of this question was

a. to acknowledge that the current issues of tension between Gospel and Culture have a heritage in the past traditions of the people. This applies even to those issues that may be newly introduced onto the cultural scene, for example by the impacts of globalization.

b. to acknowledge the cultural validity of the people and their past, thereby serving to counter any view that their traditional culture was to be rejected.

c. to uphold the view that the cultural identity of people is one fundamental element of the context within which they seek to express the Christian faith.

d. to acknowledge people's familiarity with and connection to their past. It thus indicated awareness that in Vanuatu cultures, people understand themselves to be heirs of the past and communally linked to their ancestral heritage. It would also enhance the awareness of people about their own traditional cultural heritage.

e. to recognize that the Christian faith is not to be individualized, that is, confined to the experience of the individual, nor is it to be privatized, that is, separated from the public life of the community.

2. In relation to this topic what has been the attitude of the church in the past?

The intention of this question was

a. to recognize the importance of church tradition as an essential element in the contextualization process for the people of Vanuatu. In this sense, the question honors the cultures of Vanuatu where the past is understood as the source of wisdom and truth. It also follows the pattern of village discussions and decisions that call upon the heritage of the past in finding resolutions and outcomes to current issues and questions.

b. to recognize the significant historical marker represented by the arrival of missionaries, and the impact of that arrival (positively or negatively) upon the cultures of the people.

c. to acknowledge that the arrival of the missionaries established the foundations for the subsequent policies and practices of the church.

d. to explore the impact of the arrival of the missionaries and the life of the church in relation to particular cultural practices.

e. to open up discussion on the origins of tensions between the Christian faith and the culture in relation to any named cultural issue.

3. In relation to this topic what is the cultural situation now?

The intention of this question was

a. to encourage the approach that the group's selected topic requires communal consideration and understanding.

b. to open up and to clarify some of the particular issues and challenges in relation to the topic as it presents itself in the current life of the community.

4. What are some insights from the gospel about this topic?

The intention of this question was

a. to recognize the centrality of the gospel message in the process of the contextualization of theology.

b. to acknowledge that the gospel, as witnessed in the Scriptures, is a living word that engages with every situation in every context.

c. to enhance people's insight into the message of the Scriptures through mutual learning.

d. to provide scope for the teachers in the group to share their wisdom and insight. This was particularly so where pastors formed part of the group.

e. to allow the people to explore the message of the gospel in ways that were familiar to them, and not to imagine that they needed to have formal qualifications or Western education to do so.

5. In the light of the gospel, what is the best way to deal with this topic now and in the future?

The intention of this question was

a. to require that the group engage with the interaction of the gospel and the particular presenting issue.

b. to acknowledge that the purpose of theology is essentially to resource the faithfulness of the local church, noting that the vocation of the church is to embody and witness to the gospel within their cultural context.

c. to allow the group to come to a communal discernment about a faithful response.

d. to indicate that contextualization of theology in Vanuatu cultures recognizes no separation between theory and practice, between reflection and action, between words and deeds, between head and heart, between faith and life, but these binary couplets belong together as an integrated whole.

e. to offer a way ahead which could be pursued.

Each group had a record-keeper who was, culturally, a part of the group and who had the requisite literacy skills to be able to document the points arising from the conversations. After the completion of the workshop process, the recorder's report was submitted to the group for consideration and amendment, before being finally submitted for publication. This ensured that the report would, as far as possible, be a faithful record of the views of the group expressed in their discussion.

In preparing the material for publication, the translation of the material from Bislama into English, or the editing of those reports submitted in English, was done in such a way that it attempted to honor both the content and the character of the original report. In this way, although there may be some awkwardness in the reading, the character of the work of the group as well as the contents of the discussions would, within the limitations of a written medium, be as well preserved as possible. The hope was that the voices of the people themselves would be heard, rather than the voice of the editor.

This part of the overall process offered important potential benefits to the project:

1. The written documentation may be of significant educational value for the church; it is available for local people as a learning tool for their own understanding and practice.

2. The material may help to resource and stimulate the process of contextualization in the local communities around the islands.

3. The content and methodology may serve as reference material for theological education among subsequent generations of theology students.

4. The material may offer a model for doing theology that informs the debates about theology, and theological education, among Pacific Island peoples.

5. The people may be further encouraged to own their own theology in the midst of other cultures, religions and beliefs.

6. The publications may be a means of making known to the wider church, within and beyond the South Pacific, something of the theological life, processes and insights of the people in cultures of Vanuatu.

7. The publications would preserve material of historical and cultural value.

8. The written record of an oral theology allows the possibility of some form of accountability and critique of this theology from the global church community.

However, limitations need also to be acknowledged. As an oral mode of theology, this experiment shares the limitations of theological expression in other primary oral cultures. John Mbiti comments in relation to the oral theologies of African cultures:

> The audience of oral theology is generally very limited, very confined to local groups and situations, as well as occasions to which it addresses itself. As long as it is orally disseminated, it cannot be easily put through the mill of scholarly and critical evaluation. It is difficult, if not impossible, to transport specific formulations of oral theology from one place to another, from one period to another, without changes and alterations that go with oral transmission.[21]

Whether or not Mbiti has it in mind, his comments link directly with the fact that the medium for sharing the message of the gospel in the very earliest Christian communities was an oral one, and that when the content of the teachings and life of Jesus were subsequently put into written form, they displayed the sort of variations to which Mbiti refers. In fact, the generations of scholarship since the early part of the twentieth century, exploring textual criticism of biblical material, has led to an awareness of the vast number of textual variants contained in the hundreds of early written manuscripts of the biblical material. Whilst this is due, in part, to the fragmentation and type of manuscript evidence available, it is the oral tradition of this early post-Easter era of the church that has had a major impact on

---

21. Mbiti, "Cattle Are Born," 50.

the variations apparent in the written versions of Jesus' words and deeds in the New Testament.[22]

In the processes of the Vanuatu project, written documentation and dissemination has evolved as an important element of the whole project. However, conceptually, there is an inherent problem about writing down something that took place in an oral mode and is grounded in an oral culture. Apart from the need for literacy skills in order to accomplish this task, any oral event clearly defies attempts to document it adequately in literary form. The content of a group conversation is more than can be recorded, and the group communication involves a complex mix of unrecordable data. For example, it is not possible to offer any information about the nature and impact of the dynamics that operate within each group, noting that such interactive dynamics form an integral part of the way in which Pacific Island people communicate. John Paschke writes: "Communication style tends to be indirect, with emphasis on non-verbal messages and body language."[23] In other words, the oral workshop process is a unique event that cannot be adequately shared or passed on in any written form.

Over the period of the week, the eight groups produced eleven workshop reports, covering a range of themes. Two topics of widespread interest across many of the islands, Kava and Black Power, were tackled by more than one group (Kava by three groups and Black Power by two groups). Other topics chosen were Land, Marriage, Death, Custom Spirits, Magic, and Naming.

In 2001, the second publication was completed and duly launched at the National Assembly. In addition to the workshop reports as described, this second publication also included transcribed interviews with five retired pastors, two prominent national chiefs, and the lecturer in Mission at Talua, as well as written articles submitted by five people with literacy capabilities. All contributions had in common an aspect of the theme of "Gospel and Culture." The cover picture for this book was the same as for the first publication, namely "The Death of Jesus Christ" by Graham Louhman. This particular picture, by now, had become the image connected with the evolving project, and featured also on the project's letterhead.

In the wake of this second publication, the Assembly resolved to invite the working group to lead the Bible studies at the following annual Assembly in 2002, and determined that the studies be on the topic of "Gospel and Culture," with a view to a further similar publication. This step marked a major development of the project within the national church.

22. Dunn, *Oral Gospel Tradition*, 277–82.
23. Paschke, "Small Group," 70.

The Assembly gathering at Makira in August 2002 provided a rare opportunity to involve members and leaders of the Presbyterian Church around the islands in engaging with issues of Gospel and Culture. Thereby it was certain to include a much greater number and diversity of people across a much wider spread of local cultures. What seemed to have been a fruitful structure and process among the community of around fifty staff and students at the Talua Ministry Training Centre in 1999, was now to be extended to the whole of the National Assembly and PWMU Conference in 2002.[24]

It was important to consider how best to manage the fact that this occasion would involve a much greater number of people. All ordained pastors are automatically members of Assembly and for each pastor, there is also an elder appointed to attend. In a similar manner, women are appointed to attend the Annual Conference of the PWMU which runs concurrently with the Assembly. The net result is that over 350 people, lay and ordained, gather together to meet.

On the assumption that each group would need some support and direction through the studies, it was important to provide assistance in the simplest possible way. To this end, there were several people who were asked to act as resource people to help the groups throughout the studies. Seven pastors of the church were chosen because of their ability to handle the task, the esteem with which the church held them, and the confidence that people would have to relate to them.[25] The role of these resource people was to be available during the study time to answer questions, to give advice and enable each group to do its work.

The one substantive change made to the earlier methodology used at Talua was in the list of guidelines by which the groups tackled their chosen topic. It was embodied in the additional question that preceded all others, namely, "Share your experience and describe the particular topic you have chosen."

The reasons for this addition were four-fold. First, it indicated that the theological process of contextualization begins with the experience of the people of God in relation to the contextual issue. Secondly, and correspondingly, it served to make clearer that the process of contextualization of theology appropriately belongs to the local community of God's people. Thirdly, it represented the "incarnational" character of the Christian gospel, namely that every aspect of human life and cultural experience is embraced and addressed by the incarnate Word of God, and belongs to the scope of theology. Finally, it provided a way by which everyone within the group could offer

24. The process is explained in Prior, *Voice of the Local Church*, 3–7.
25. See the list of names in Prior, *Voice of the Local Church*, 5.

their own narrative into the community, and so have a sense of contributing. In this way it served the pastoral function of allowing people to name their experience, and of helping to counter a group dynamic whereby only some voices may be heard.

Altogether, by the end of the study program, twenty-seven reports were submitted. Topics chosen covered a wide range of issues.[26] Groups from the Southern Islands covered Language, Spirits, Land; groups from Efate covered Dress, Custom Medicine, Marriage; groups from Central Islands covered Ordination, Dress, The Role of Men and Women; groups from Ambrym and Paama covered Burial of the Dead, Death and Afterlife, and Marriage; groups from Malekula covered Respect through Giving, Feasting, Kava, Burial of the Dead; groups from Santo-Malo covered Land, the Taboo Nagkalat Tree, Giving, Dress, Bride-Price, Death, Marriage and Youth.

Because of its importance to this project, a representative selection of reports produced out of the workshop is documented below.[27]

Workshop Reports from the 2002 Assembly in Makira

The following reports are included:

1. Native Language

2. Spirits

3. Marriage (1)

4. Marriage (2)

1. Topic: Native Language (Group from Southern Islands Presbytery)

Introduction

Language is a fundamental topic when it comes to considering the issues of Gospel and Culture. As many of our group are pastors, and wives of pastors, from various islands around Vanuatu, all now working in Southern Islands Presbytery, we are acutely aware of language issues, and therefore have chosen this as our topic.

As soon as we begin to talk about culture, we are already talking about language, as language is integral to cultural identity. Within our own group alone, we represent several different languages, several different modes of

---

26. Prior, *Voice of the Local Church*, s.v. "Contents."

27. The text here is the verbatim report produced by the group. The text of all the Assembly workshop reports is recorded in Prior, *Voice of the Local Church*.

talking. We are each aware that when we work in another island context, where the language is different, plenty of time must be spent getting to know the language and culture, before our work can be effective. It is not possible to deal with every aspect of this important and large topic within the framework of this study, but we shall attempt to address the following:

a. A comparison of language in Vanuatu in the past and language in Vanuatu today.

b. Communication

c. The language of story and picture

d. We shall do this following the six headings proposed for this study.

SHARE YOUR EXPERIENCE AND DESCRIBE THE TOPIC

As pastors who come from islands in the north and are working in the south, there are several challenges we face in relation to language and communication. It is clear that we need to know the language of the people among whom we work before we are in a position to share the message of the gospel in such a way that it can be understood. The passing of messages among ni-Vanuatu people is done in ways other than by talking. There are various other methods used, for example, with leaves, wood, fire, bubu shell and tam-tam. In the northern islands, a namele leaf is used for sharing peace, or to indicate a sacred or taboo place, while in the southern islands, the leaf of wild cane, or of the nangaria, is used.

It seems apparent to us that languages are in a constant state of change. One of the developments in more recent times in Vanuatu, with the mixing of people across language groups, is that some original languages are dying out, and some languages are being mixed with other languages. One other method of communicating messages is through stories ("picture-talk"). During some meeting occasions, stories are used to convey meaning, but at times these stories are not easy to understand or interpret. There are times, in the *Nakamal*, when one man may be speaking using a story, and looking forcefully in your direction, but in fact, through his story, he is actually addressing someone else. Custom songs are also a familiar means of communication and sending messages. Through such cultural songs and cries, messages are shared.

What was the situation in the past in relation to language?

In the past, languages were very rich. This was before the time of development and mobility brought through the impact of colonizers, traders and missionaries. Very few people had a formal education, there were very few inter-language marriages, there was almost no travel by men and women to other islands, there was little reading or writing, there was no television, video, telephone, radio, all of which today are contributing to the fading away of our languages.

It is our view that when language is strong, then there is respect and order in social life. People know each other well, and can build up good relationships. For example, in the time of tribal wars, or cannibalism, it was the norm for one tribe to make war with another tribe, where there was no common language across the two groups. Language was a distinguishing feature and identified a particular people in a particular time and particular place and with a particular culture. Every tribe had its own language and culture.

There are several traditional means of communication that have been important in the past, but are not well known, or not used very commonly today. Some examples of this would be "sign language," where signs are used to communicate, "picture-talk," where a person speaks to another using pictures or stories with images, with another person interpreting what is being said, and "language of respect." There is a special form of communication between some people, which indicates respect. When a man speaks with his father-in-law or brother-in-law, he is not permitted to speak freely, but has to use a particular form of address, which shows his respect. In days past each tribal group had its own distinctive language. When the missionaries and traders came, they introduced English, and then later Bislama was "born" as a language. Bislama spread very quickly throughout the islands, as a language of communication across tribal language groups.

What is the situation now in relation to language?

The situation today is very different from what it has been in the past. There have been many developments in language, and in general, language is not as "heavy" as it used to be. Language has changed, as life and culture have changed. The ways of talking by "sign," or objects, or movements, have been lost, and many new and modern forms of communication have taken their place. More and more people are living in the towns, and are being educated to be able to read and write. New forms of technology like radio, telephone, television, tele-radio, boat, truck, letter-writing, etc. are becoming prominent, and bringing about a major influence in communication and language, leading to the loss of older forms. The bubu shell or tam-tam for sending messages has long been replaced by a bell; people are moving about the island groups and can now pick up the languages of other places or sometimes replace one language with another. Through inter-marriage, couples are learning the languages of their partner, and children are growing up with two, three or four different languages.

Having identified all these changes, it is still the case that some people are not formally educated at schools, and remain in their traditional tribal community for the whole of their lives. Such people continue to use the language of their own culture in its traditional form, and remain close to the culture of their past.

WHAT HAS BEEN THE ATTITUDE OF THE CHURCH IN THE PAST IN RELATION TO LANGUAGE?

When missionaries first arrived in our land of Vanuatu (formerly New Hebrides), they came with the message of the gospel from the perspective of their own language and culture. They developed various ways in which to share the news of the gospel. Many of them realized that if they were to be effective in sharing the news of the gospel, they needed to give priority to learning the language of the people. In this way, the gospel message was spread quickly. They put the languages into written form and taught the people to read, to sing and to talk about the gospel in their own language. The local languages became like a door through which the gospel was shared. Missionaries who learned local languages in this way were then easily able to communicate their message.

In the past, the church has not recognized the place of sign language in traditional communication, and so has not explored this form of language as a means of sharing the gospel. Perhaps the church could consider this form of communication. The neglect of the church in this has meant that such forms of communication are not so commonly used. The manner of communication by "picture-talk" is far less common now than it used to be. The church has not encouraged this form of communication because such communication needs interpretation and can be very misleading or confusing. Communication of the gospel has required the use of clear language forms, and forms that may lead to confusion would not be helpful.

WHAT ARE SOME INSIGHTS FROM THE GOSPEL
ABOUT THIS TOPIC?

Language is a basic means of communication between people. It is the most suitable form of communication of the good news of the gospel. The theme of language is central to the message of the Bible. To illustrate this, consider the following . . .

1. God is a living God; he relates to man and woman in creation in a personal way. God considers the situation of man, he looks, he has compassion, and he helps. In the Genesis story (chapter 1), God creates the world and human life through speech (language). "And God said: let there be light, and there was light." (Gen 1:3) God continued his conversation with his creation through the voice of the prophets of the Old Testament. The prophets were like a "mouth piece" for God in various settings of Israel's history.

2. In John 1:1, "In the beginning was the Word and the Word was with God and the Word was God." Jesus is presented by John as the divine Word who was in the beginning and who is God. God has chosen to speak to humankind through the person of Jesus.

3. The Old Testament is full of different languages. Genesis 8:10–11 is part of the story of Noah, where Noah sends a dove from the ark to determine if the flood has abated; the dove flies back with a leaf in its mouth to communicate that the floodwaters have dropped and the boat may sit again on dry land.

4. Exodus 12:13 talks about blood being placed on the doorpost of the homes of Israelite families, as a sign to God to pass over the homes of these people, while punishing the remainder who were Egyptians.

5. Proverbs, Psalms, and other books, are full of poetry, another form of language used widely among the people of Israel.

6. In the early Gospel stories in Matthew, the wise men from the east, coming to find the baby Jesus who was born in Bethlehem, followed the "language" or "sign" of the star. It was a language of the people of the time, and in particular of wise men such as these.

7. The Book of Revelation has numerous forms of language, in the form of signs and images, which were familiar to the people of those days, and which John used to build the people up in their Christian faith.

IN THE LIGHT OF THE GOSPEL, WHAT IS THE BEST WAY TO
DEAL WITH LANGUAGE NOW AND IN THE FUTURE?

The church must encourage Christian people to explore local resources for the sharing of its message. Translation of the Scriptures into local languages, which has been a long-standing project supported by the church, must continue, and extend into the translation of songs and other documents. Preachers must be encouraged to preach the gospel in the local language of the people, and within the local culture. Pastors must learn the local language of the people among whom they work as pastors.

The national government has recognized some weaknesses in their education policy, and is now encouraging the introduction of vernacular language classes around the islands of Vanuatu. The church must support and encourage the Government in this commitment. Pastors and lay leaders of the church around Vanuatu must be encouraged to do special courses on language and translation. This can best be done at Talua Ministry Training Centre as part of the training program. The church must encourage the restoring of good traditional forms of communication, for example, signs, "picture-talk," and action.

GENERAL COMMENT

The best way to preserve our culture is to keep our languages. It would be best for the church to encourage the communities to start teaching language in the local pre-schools. It would be valuable also to teach the children communication by body-language, or sign-language, and to use some of the technical words in language. In this way, we can slow down the loss of languages and changes in languages.

CONCLUSION

Our workshop group feels strongly that "language" is a very important issue of Gospel and Culture for the church. The church ought to encourage every local congregation throughout the islands to give emphasis to the use of traditional cultural forms of communication, for example, signs, "picture-talk." In closing, we wish to restate the main points

a. Language is basic to every culture. To lose one's language is to lose one's culture, tradition and custom.

b. Language gives identity, status and privilege in community. If a person does not know their language, they become like a stranger within their own land.

c. Language is like a "door" for the effective communication of the gospel to local people within their culture or society.

For people to have a full understanding of the gospel, the gospel must be communicated to the people in the language of their understanding. This is the only really effective means of communication of the gospel. This is clearly illustrated in Jesus' own life. His incarnational ministry meant that in order to share his message, he used the language and the methods and the styles of communication that were familiar to the people around him. As a result of his effective communication about the Kingdom of God, everyone who heard him listened in amazement. Jesus is himself an authentic example for our own ministry, and the ministry of the church in the world today, in relation to the use of language.

---

2. Topic: Narimin (= Spirits) (Group from the Island of Tanna)

Introduction

Today, we are at a time when we, the churches, are taking steps to identify what it means for us to be Christian people within our culture. On the island of Tanna, there are various stones that are used for different purposes, and in such a way that the stones are thought to possess the power of certain spirits. Such is the power of these stones that the people of the island live in great fear of them. In early times, fear was normal to the social way of life, but with the arrival of the Christian Faith, this fear was challenged. The Gospel of Jesus Christ confronted men and women of Tannese society with the message of the One Spirit of God, the Creator of Heaven and Earth and of the spirits.

Definition

On the island of Tanna, across all the languages of the island, we have a common basic understanding of what we mean by the spirit we call *Narimin*. It means "shadow," something that cannot be touched; it is like the content of a photo. It has a second type of meaning as "reflection," like the reflection in a mirror. This spirit is thought to be everlasting, to have eternal life.

The Spirit World

Every man, woman and child on Tanna island is aware of, and may associate with spirits. Whether a person is a church member or not, has a good education or not, everyone knows stories about the reality of the spirit world.

What about the cultural situation in the past?

In the past, it was expected that every member of the community would give appropriate honor to the spirits. Three particular spirits of power on Tanna are named *Matiktiki*, *Karapanim* and *Kalpapin*. These are the three main gods who have authority over all the smaller gods. There is a man of special power we call *Nautipuni*, who intercedes between the gods and humans. He is able to talk to the gods and to communicate the rules and ways of the gods to the people. It is the responsibility of this man to help the whole community to know what is required by the gods, and to keep everyone obedient to the ways of the gods.

What is the cultural situation today?

When the Christian faith came to Tanna, it represented a huge challenge to the culture of the people. In those early days, the approach of the missionaries was to reject and oppose our culture; they claimed that the things of our culture were sinful. Today, the thinking of the people in relation to the spirits is the same as it always was. Although some people no longer give allegiance to the spirits of the world in the way they did in the past, the majority of people are still fearful of the spirits. But belief in the spirits is more hidden today than it used to be. Because people are aware that it is not acceptable to believe in the spirits in the same way that our ancestors did, they continue to believe in them and their powers, but no longer acknowledge this in public. In this way it is hidden.

When a person comes to accept and believe in the Gospel of Jesus Christ, they leave behind their beliefs in the spirits, and replace it with belief in the Holy Spirit, the Spirit of the God who created the world.

What was the thinking of the church in the past?

It is very sad to look back over the history of the church on Tanna and realize that from the beginning in 1839, and for a very long time afterwards, the approach of the Western missionaries towards our culture was one of rejection. They operated within, and promoted their own culture. When a local person became a Christian, and adopted the beliefs and life-style of the Western missionary, they recognized that there were some aspects of our cultural life that were captive to the worship of the spirits. This realization led them to reject the whole of our culture.

What evidence is in the Bible about this issue?

In Genesis 1–3, God creates the world, including culture, and everything God creates is good. God also creates man and woman in such a way that they are to have a lasting relationship with God. When Adam and Eve both disobey God, the order of creation and culture becomes fractured and disordered. The relationship between the man and the woman, within their cultural life, and with their God, is no longer strong and lasting. This leads to the development of inappropriate relationships between people and other aspects of creation. People no longer relate with the Spirit of God, but establish relationships with false spirits who are opposed to the one true God. In Romans 1:18–31, the apostle Paul challenges us to have a good relationship with the Holy Spirit of God within our own culture.

In the light of the Gospel, what is a faithful way of dealing with the spirits of our culture, both now and in the future?

Since the independence of Vanuatu in 1980, there has been a renewed emphasis on the tradition and customs of local people. This has led to a renewed importance of the issue of the relationship between the Gospel and Culture. The church is beginning to address the values and practices of each of our cultures, in the light of the gospel. Some examples of current issues are listed below.

    i. Kapiel (Stones): On Tanna, people have stones which are believed to possess the power of certain gods, for example, stones for yam, banana, taro, *nantau*, *namambe*, turtle, shark, fish, rain, sun, wind, and soil. All such stones are given to certain men by the three main gods, *Matiktiki*, *Karapanim* and *Kalpapin*. These men hold a special place in village life, and the people are fearful of them. They are like priests, who can make special sacrifices on behalf of the people, to bring good crops, or other good fortune. To illustrate this, when a new yam is ready, there must be a sacrifice offered to the spirit-god of the yam, in order for the yam to be good. The Christian gospel challenges such thinking and practice. In the light of the gospel it would be appropriate for the first new yams to be offered to the church for thanksgiving.

ii. Garden: Everything in the gardens of Tannese people is associated with the spirit-gods. There are clear processes that must be followed in establishing, planting and caring for the garden. *Nautipunis* man (that is, the man who especially is able to communicate with the spirits) must plant his garden first, and only then may the other people of the community plant theirs. If this practice is not followed, then the spirit-god can bring sickness or cause the crops of the garden to fail.

Today, it would be good for the Christian community to make the garden of the church pastor first. This practice does not yet happen in every village around Tanna, but it is something that we are currently talking about on our island. It is a big challenge to the traditional thinking of the people to change in this way. It is good too if the Church Session in each place develops a good relationship with the traditional *Nautipunis* man, because they are our "heathen priests." We can easily turn them into priests who will offer the first harvests to the Christian God on our behalf, or present the new yams to the pastors or elders in the church, for thanksgiving to God in prayer.

iii. *Kleva*

In both the past and the present, the place of the *kleva* in our culture is strong. Anyone who wants to become a *kleva* has to approach someone who has the power to communicate with the spirits. For example, such a man must drink kava and spit, and he must keep to certain rules that will please the spirits. Such people could be converted to Christianity and encouraged to become the church's "seers," to be able to foretell what God wants us to do or what will happen to us today or tomorrow. Maybe these people, if they become Christians, will know for sure that the spirit they are contacting is the Holy Spirit, who comes to us to teach us, and to reveal many good things about real life.

iv. Spirits of the Dead

It is common in the past, and even in the present, for our people to be afraid of the spirits at the time of someone's death. People believe that the spirit of the dead man is present. Sometimes people are able to hear the spirit, or even to see the spirit. Sometimes this spirit takes hold of someone, or chases them. When someone dies, the people are very afraid to walk around at night, or to go to their garden, for fear that they will see the spirit of the dead man.

v. *Narik* (Poison)

In the past, the people used *narik* as a means of punishment. Suppose a member of the community did something wrong, "narik" was able to make the person become sick, and to remain sick until they admitted the wrong they did, and then they would recover from sickness. When a person is angry, or makes a plan to harm or kill another, he carries a piece of food belonging to the other person, and puts it onto a stone, which is a sacred or taboo stone. He puts some special substance onto the food on the stone, and the man becomes sick and dies.

vi. Sickness

Sickness is closely associated with the spirits. People believe that the spirits are able to cause sickness. Therefore when someone in a family becomes sick, the other members must consult the special people of their community who can speak with the spirits, and get these special people to communicate with them, in order to prevent, or cure, the sickness afflicting their family member.

The Behavior of These Spirits

With all the examples given above and discussed in the group, it appears as if everything in our life is associated with the spirits. These spirits are independent and invisible. They cannot be seen by people, but they come to people in a variety of ways, in order to influence their lives at almost every level.

The Bible refers to the term "evil spirits," "unclean spirits," and "demons." These terms are common in the New Testament. All of these spirits are servants of Satan, and do the work of Satan. These spirits have the power to oppress people, and even to control their lives. The following provides a summary of the work of these spirits.

a. Evil spirits are the servants of Satan (Mark 3:22–27)

b. Evil spirits have a name (see Mark 5:9 where Jesus asks: "What is your name?" The reply is given: "My name is Legion, for we are a large number.")

c. These spirits are able to control human life.

d. They can cause a person to act violently (Mark 5:2–5); they can cause a person to have convulsions and foam at the mouth (Mark 9:51ff); they can cause dumbness (Matthew 9:32; Mark 9:17–27); they can cause a person who is under their control to attack others violently (Acts 19:16); they can speak and hold conversations with another person (Matthew: 29–32); they scream or shout loudly (Mark 5:7; Luke 9:39).

CONCLUSION

It is good that the studies on Gospel and Culture have helped us to realize that when sin came into the world, then evil spirits became involved closely in human life. These spirits influenced and shaped human life, leading to pride in the building up of different cultures. These various spirits have influenced and shaped each and every community, so that the community is captive to the spirits that have become so much a part of the life of the people.

It is clear to us that today that we should reject these ideas and beliefs about the spirits, and replace them with belief in the Spirit of God, who is the creator of all things, the Holy Spirit of God. Spirits of stones, garden, *kleva*, the dead, *narik*, sickness, and other things, began to influence people only when they turned their back on God at the time of creation, according to the story in the book of Genesis. However, in Jesus Christ, the Kingdom of God has come to reveal to us the truth about the Spirit of God, and the way of life of those who believe in this Spirit.

---

3. TOPIC: MARRIAGE (GROUP FROM MELE AND IFIRA VILLAGES)

INTRODUCTION

Marriage is a rather big topic—too big, in fact, to be covered in five sessions of a workshop. But our group has tried its best to do as much work as possible. First of all, we all shared discussion about the purpose of marriage. The purpose of marriage is to

a. bear children and keep our family lines (totem lines) alive and ongoing for the next generation.

b. companionship—providing love, trust and respect, and a sense of belonging, and it also satisfies sexual needs.

c. build up relationship between extended families. We all agreed that marriage can create peace between families, and cement relationships forever between families.

In describing this particular topic, three members described their marriages as being very different from those of today, and two others described their marriages to be very different from marriages of the past. The first three described their marriage rituals as being less expensive, that is, involving less spending to be married, and more families gave gifts with a happy and willing heart. But their own children's marriages have been much more expensive than their own. For example, Elder Sokomanu said his own marriage cost about $45 while his two sons' marriages cost about 2 million vatu (= $25,000). This difference is huge and very demanding on local people. It indicates that marriages today are very costly and can be of a more competitive standard than before. This is shown in the style of marriage dress which is worn, not only for the marriage but through the whole week, in the invitations to the buffet dinner held later in the evening, in the fact that, previously, copra and cocoa could be used to pay for marriage expenses, but now money needs to be saved over a long period of time.

Everyone agreed that marriage was, and is, a festive occasion, which involves all family members, family lines, friends, and relatives both near and far. It is a time of joy, regardless of the hard work needed; it is a once-in-a-lifetime event (if all goes well!). It is a part of a person's history, which will long remain recorded in the hearts and minds of family members. Those who witness the event are also part of the history that has brought all the family together. Preparation towards the marriage is also another important factor in the closeness of family relationships, and contributes greatly to the marriage event. In Melanesian culture, "no man is an island." Everyone works together to achieve their aim and purpose successfully.

WHAT WAS THE SITUATION IN THE PAST
IN RELATION TO MARRIAGE?

Long ago, going back about thirty to forty years, most marriages were arranged by the parents or families of both the bride and the bridegroom. If the parents of the girl agreed with the parents of the boy, that their children should marry, the young girl and boy had no choice but to agree to their parents' choice of partner. This choice made by the families usually came for reasons of the family line (totem). For example, a couple might have only sons and no daughters, but because totem lines pass or continue on the woman's side (matrilineal), the boy's mother and father can decide that one of their sons must marry a girl from that totem line, in order to keep the line going. Alternatively, the choice may be made because the parents had an account, or debt, which they could not settle, and so the marriage arrangement may be made to settle that debt.

A further reason for an arranged marriage may be that both sides are of good blood, and are wealthy, and want to keep that wealth within the family line. It is also possible that an arranged marriage involves the swapping of two sets of boys and girls, that is, a boy and girl in one family with a girl and boy in another. When the decision is made about who is to marry whom, both sides agree to a certain date for the marriage to take place, and the arrangement is sealed. Once the date is set, the whole family, including extended family members, move to discuss and prepare the details. The normal preparations include feeding of pigs (every-day feeding by the family), weaving of mats (coconut and pandanus), and preparing the garden (planting of yams, manioc, taro, and other useful crops).

Recently at Mele village, the engagement between a boy and a girl was legally announced on January 1, coinciding with the harvest of the new yams. On the day of announcement, the girl spends the whole day with the family of the boy. There are exchanges of food between the two parties, with singing and feasting throughout the whole day. After this event, while the freedom to see each other goes on, the boy and the girl are not permitted to sleep with each other.

The practice of weddings before the arrival of the missionaries was entirely in traditional local style. The feasting went on for twenty-five days. Polygamy was permitted. There was only custom dress, no wedding ring, no formal clothes, no shoes, etc. There was an exchange of the "bride-price," which included a big live pig with tusks. The couple-to-be were usually married at the *Farea* or *Nakamal*, by the Chief, and by those responsible in the Chief's *Farea*. There were special people set apart to perform on such occasions. The wedding program included,

a. *Tuki*, or the *tam-tam*. Usually there were many of these standing together in one place, at the *Nakamal*, and usually standing sloped or on a lean.

b. *Tepara*, which is a bamboo beat, which created the beat for the dancing.

c. *Sualele*, a chant to go with the beating of the drums and the bamboo.

d. *Bosui*, which is the *Tuki* Men's Dance (only for the men).

    After the wedding ceremony was over, there was a sort of reception, like that of today, but much simpler. The whole village would sing to the married couple, who were seated, and would present them with valuable gifts, such as mats, shells, yams, etc.

WHAT IS THE SITUATION NOW IN RELATION TO MARRIAGE?

Today the cultural situation has changed a lot, and so has the style of local marriages. They have become much more Western in style. There have been a lot of changes, for example,

a. Choice of partner is permitted for the boy and the girl (it is no longer the parents who choose).

b. Much more church influence, such as Christian marriage, where the marriage is held in the church and conducted by the church pastor; the church also conducts marriage studies.

c. Singing, food, dress, appearance, order of marriage service and general appearance, are all influenced by Western culture.

d. The economic system has made marriages much more dependent on money.

e. Twenty-five days of feasting has been reduced to five days, due to financial costs to feed so many people.

f. Bush marriage, which is not a legal marriage, but where the couple live together. This happens where the couple make their own choice to be partners and do not have family support, so they live together without the marriage ceremony taking place first. They may be married later, but if the couple have children, then the bride-price becomes higher when the marriage happens.

g. Civil marriage (where marriage is conducted by a person who has Government approval to do so), and custom marriage are both widely practised today. While both are legally binding, neither of them are blessed by the church, and unless this blessing is given, the couple can easily separate and become divorced.

    Furthermore, due to advances in education in the country, knowledge has introduced different thoughts to the generations of people today. Many want to make their own choice of partner, and when they do choose, it could be for reasons of appearance, of beauty, handsomeness, or for wealth, or position.

Although today we have reduced the period of feasting from twenty-five days to one week, it is still expensive, despite the fact that there is a mixture of Western and traditional food. During the week before the marriage takes place, the families get together to prepare the wedding shelter, to collect firewood, to gather food, etc. On Saturday during that week, a big bullock and large pig must be killed, to be eaten during the weekend at the start of the week of feasting. On Sunday, after the three o'clock worship service, there is the collection for money carried out by the groom's and bride's family lines. Sometimes there may be as many as five, or six, or seven times, when you have to give money, as each family name seeks a contribution for the wedding. For example, if my mother comes from three family lines, and my father comes from two family lines, then I have to contribute to five families if the couple marrying come from one of these five family lines. The contributions are recorded in a book that is kept. In earlier times, this event happened on Wednesday night, but it is now held on Sunday afternoon.

Throughout the following week, families and relatives come with their gifts of mats, clothes, food, etc. On the Monday night of the feasting week, the bride-to-be is invited to be with the groom-to-be and his family, for dinner. When the girl's parents and aunties and uncles go to celebrate with the bride-to-be and her family, they have to dress up in new shirts and island dresses, all in the same colored material. There is singing accompanied by speeches, until it is time to return the bride-to-be to her parents' home. Gifts are brought back with her, to be shared later or kept for her future use. On the Tuesday of the feasting week, the bride-to-be is taken shopping in the town by the family of the groom-to-be. This is when the wedding ring, the shoes, and other necessary wedding clothing and decoration are bought. On the Wednesday, both parties go to their own big gardens, to harvest yam for the wedding feast. At night, the groom and his close relatives are invited for a meal by the bride's family (as on the Monday night). After the meal, when the bride and bridegroom are taken back to their respective places, there is dancing and singing on the way. On Thursday, there is the preparation of the "bride-price" on the side of the groom. There is the *tasokia tafura* or *tejiji*—the collection of yams tied together with a long pole. There may be as many as ten of these, depending on where the bride comes from.

There is the collection of mats with wool or feathers, calico (i.e., sewing or dress material) and amounts of money. There is the pig (a big live pig) and a bullock. Extra payment is made if the couple already have a child or children. In the village of Mele, the Chief and the Pastor check on the "bride-price"—if, in their opinion, it has been set too high, some things are taken out; if it is too low, some things are added.

On the bride's side, there is the *Supelea Balai* (mats rolled up), where there is the girl's *moeraga* (sleeping items, including mat, mattress, pillow cases and pillow, blanket, sheets, etc.). There is also a collection of the useful tools and kitchen utensils, pots and other necessary items, prepared and packed ready for her to move out when she leaves the day following the marriage and the custom ceremony. Usually on the Thursday night, there is local singing, which goes on until the next day, the day of the wedding.

Normally Friday is marriage day. About three o'clock in the morning, the pig is killed, and at four o'clock, there is the *teumu* (preparation of the local oven for laplap, using hot stones). At about eight o'clock in the morning, the groom's sisters go to bring the bride to their house, to be dressed to go to church for the wedding. At the church, the couple are married by the Pastor, who gives them God's blessing. Straight after the church service, everyone moves to the *Farea* (or Chief's meeting place), where the exchange of custom gifts, including the "bride-price," takes place. The bride then goes to lunch with her new husband, but she later returns to her own family, then to be brought back by her own family to her husband's home, and left there to start a new life with her husband. This is often an emotional time, when speeches and singing are accompanied by tears.

On the Saturday, the *Sosori* takes place. This is the sharing of the mats, the calico, and the money. Other gifts are also given out to close relatives, such as aunties and uncles. With this comes the closing of the feasting week, with a large feast for all the families who have come together to take part, before they all go their separate ways again. It is a feast of thanksgiving to everyone.

WHAT HAS BEEN THE ATTITUDE OF THE CHURCH IN THE PAST IN RELATION TO MARRIAGE?

The Church has always opposed polygamy, living together before marriage, a very high "bride-price," the customary rites of marriage without a Christian blessing, "forced" marriages (which may be against the personal choice of the couple being married), and the neglect of study preparation for marriage. The church has encouraged the full agreement of the respective couple and their families before a marriage takes place.

With regard to the "bride-price," the church is in support of this practice, providing it is set at a sensible level. The church does not agree with the term "bride-price" because it implies the payment of the man for the woman as if the woman is being purchased. The woman has a right to live in her own way, to love her husband, to respect him and his family, to join his ways, but also to maintain her own dignity, talents, and confidence to bring peace and harmony to her new family. A better term would be "payment to the parents," or some other description of the exchange of gifts, which is what it is in traditional ni-Vanuatu culture.

But the cultural way of preparing for a big event, such as a marriage, should continue. This includes the planting of gardens for food, looking after pigs to be killed during the feast, weaving mats, and so on. Each party should create their own economic situation according to their needs, and in line with their circumstances.

Finally, if the Church had the opportunity, it should support the idea of having as many couples as possible married together on the one occasion. This would cut down the costs to the families, it would save time and it would keep our records clean. There should also be more teaching about marriage to guide the young people and young couples-to-be. If teaching and preaching go well with the blessing, this should reap a good harvest. Marriages today tend to be more flexible, with a mixture of traditional culture and Western culture. There is a lot of feasting and drinking involved, and it should be a time of happy celebration. However, with the drinking of alcohol, the opposite commonly happens; the happy celebration turns into a fighting one. The Chief and the Church together need to control the drinking of alcohol and the drinking too of kava.

What are some insights from the Gospel about this topic?

In relation to the gospel, our group members all agreed that Christian Marriage is for life, and there should be no polygamy. A Christian Marriage reflects God's love, which started in the Garden of Eden. God himself performed the very first marriage between Adam and Eve, the first two human beings that God created. In God's Holy Book, the Bible, God laid down the rules and the Law concerning marriage, but people have the choice whether to obey these rules or to disobey and face the consequences. For example, in Leviticus 18, there are laws concerning sexual relationships; verses 22–23 emphasise homosexuality and lying with animals.

The eighth commandment is, "Thou shalt not commit adultery!" Today adultery is common, and the consequences are broken homes, hurt, pain, hopelessness, tears, homelessness, unstable children, tension between families, disgrace, sexually transmitted diseases, Aids, and many other negative reactions and feelings. Our living God is the God of love; his promises are true and eternal. His covenant with Israel and with us today, holds us in faith and trust, obedience and humbleness.

a. Customary obligations must be minimised. For example, the reduction of feasting from twenty-five days to five days is good. Some expensive practices should be reduced, for example the *Kalakala* (dressing up the whole extended family in the same shirts and dresses).

b. Marriage should be a time of giving and of a non-competitive nature.

c. *Temalaranga*, or the community giving of money, should be done graciously, and only the real family members do that, not any outside the totem line.

d. Leaders of the Church and the *Nakamal* must meet to talk about these attitudes and high expectations, and the problems arising in the marriage feasting week. They must create some sort of rules and regulations, following the principles in the Bible, and enforce them in the community. The Chief and his counsellors must make their declarations of the rules from the *Nakamal* and stand firm to achieve them. They must not easily give in to the people's demands.

e. The Church should also make clear declaration of the rules and announce them in the pulpit, and run some Bible studies concerning the topics. It would be best to do this one-to-one in people's homes. The purpose of the study would not be to speak against someone, but to help people to see the need, and why there should be some changes to what is going on at present. There are already devotions being held in feasting places where people can hear the Word of God. It helps also if the drinking of alcohol and kava is discouraged, without being stopped altogether.

Our Action-Plan:

a. Parents teach their children about what the Church and the *Farea* have decided.

b. There should be cultural education once a week in the schools to guide the children. There must be Bible Teaching in the *Farea* and guidance in the system of *Nakamal* administration.

c. Bible teaching should be based on giving unconditionally with love for each other. In the schools and village life, we need to encourage the children to speak our own language in the correct way (with proper tenses, verbs, nouns, etc.). The Western way of life is not only changing our traditional cultural way of life, but it has also influenced the local language of the Mele and Ifira people. The children especially need encouragement to have this straightened out. Bible studies, preaching, prayers and hymns need to be done in our language.

d. If possible, our culture must be revived, especially those good things of our culture, for example the caring, sharing, giving and loving, both spiritually and physically. It has to be practised and upheld for the good of all, especially in the future.

e. Finally, with marriages of today, the local Church Session needs to guide families in their timing. Afternoon marriages, which allow the invitations to go on ahead of time, would be good and sensible. Five days could possibly be reduced to a one day marriage! However, this would need to be talked about in the *Farea* and in the congregation, until a certain agreement is reached for the benefit of all.

f. Finally, marriage is a gift and a blessing given by God. If we follow his Word, love him, and obey his command, then we will succeed in building strong healthy marriages, which are full of peace and happiness. The challenges and difficulties of this life would only make our marriages more faithful, trustworthy and keep to God's word, "until death parts us." John 13:34 says, "Love one another," but this is rooted in Christ at all times.

---

4. Topic: Marriage (Group from Paama and South-East Ambrym)

INTRODUCTION

In considering this topic, we will look at three aspects of marriage:

a. During the time of darkness, or in the times of heathenism, marriage followed family lines. The father of the boy chose a woman for his son to marry.

b. For the payment of a woman, the two parties, the families of the boy and of the girl, exchanged gifts. For example, the father of the boy paid for the woman with a pig, offering it to the mother of the girl, while the mother of the girl gave a mat to the father of the boy, to indicate that the girl must show respect to her *apu* (father-in-law).

c. With the arrival of the missionaries, "Christian marriage" was introduced, and as time passed, it wasn't long before the payment for a woman was in money, for example ten English pounds or two thousand vatu. But the practice of the father of the boy choosing a wife for his son was continued.

In the times before the missionaries came, in heathen times, the ceremony of marriage was very important to the community. Once everything had been arranged, the chief gave a speech, and then when he had finished, he announced that the couple had become united, and were now married. The ceremony did not include any prayer.

What was the situation in the past in relation to marriage?

In the times before Christianity, a man could be married to two or three or more women. It was also the general practice that the man was based at his family home, while the women did their work in the family home and in the garden. Only the man and not the woman had the right to talk at the *Nakamal*.

What is the situation now in relation to marriage?

The ritual of marriage today is very different from the past, and does not follow properly the tradition of our culture. Some people from our communities follow the examples from other islands or from overseas. Some people think only about becoming wealthy.

Furthermore, in the past, there was not the same type or level of education, and there was a greater sense of respect for traditional authority, for example, for the chief and the parents. Whenever there was a problem between a married couple, the people involved would be brought to the *Nakamal*, and the chief would sort out the problem with them, because they had respect for the chief. But today, schooling and education have become much more important. The effect of this is that many men and women no longer have respect for the chief. As a result, there is more violence and divorce in family life, around all of our communities. Life today has changed a great deal. Whenever a family wants to make a feast for a celebration, everyone in the community contributes in kind. It is also common now for a man to choose his wife from another island.

What has been the attitude of the church in the past in relation to marriage?

At the time when missionaries first arrived, they preached to us the same message that Jesus had preached when he came out of the wilderness after his time of temptation (Mark 1:15), where he declared, "You must repent, turn away from everything which is no good, and change your way of life." What then happened was that, while in the past it was the practice for a man to choose a wife for his son, when some of our people began to be taught by the missionaries, and went to study at the Teacher Training Institute on Tangoa Island, they came back and told us that what we were doing was not right; they told us that every man has the right to choose his own wife. However, the effect of this change was that it worked well for some people, but for others it did not. As a result, there is a high level of violence and divorce in marriage, and this has created a huge social problem.

What are some insights from the Gospel about marriage?

The main message of the gospel is a message of the love of God. This is what Jesus came to teach us, that we ought to love everyone (Luke 10:17). This is the foundation of marriage.

In the light of the Gospel, what is the best way to deal with marriage now and in the future?

It is the view of this group that it is important that there be a special meeting or workshop involving the leaders of the church, the chiefs, and the leaders of the community, in order to discuss together the whole process of marriage, both now and in the future. Church leaders need to run a series of studies to improve the way things happen in marriage preparation, and in the payment for the woman.

We think that the church must work hard to reduce the high "bride-price" which is now being expected, and the expensive gifts that are being given. We should look again at the best practices to follow, both now and in the future.

In 2003 the third publication was completed.[28] Its subtitle, "The Voice of the Local Church," mirrored the content of the book; there were contributions from men and women spread across a wide range of local Vanuatu village communities. The book was duly launched at the following National Assembly.

Summary Critique of Stage Two

The process used at both the Talua Ministry Training Centre workshop in 1999, and in the 2002 Assembly, offers valuable insight into a methodology of theology that is contextually grounded in the cultures of Vanuatu. The framework provided a means by which the primary oral character of the cultures was honored, where there was no expectation that the categories of the Enlightenment were required, and where theology and the local church were brought together. While assuming the centrality of Scripture and church tradition, together with the particular context of village community life as the location for theological engagement, the form of contextualization was essentially oral and communal; its purpose and its potential were to involve the members of the local community in a way that informed their ongoing faithfulness to the gospel in their community context. Thus it offers clear answers to the four methodological questions, (i) What form does theology take? (ii) Who does theology? (iii) What is the primary location for the theological task? (iv) What is the primary purpose of theology?

There remain questions as to whether these purposes were actually fulfilled, and how this may be measured. There are also outstanding questions as to how any group's affirmations resulting from this methodology might be accountable beyond their immediate locale. Nevertheless, in taking up the categories of primary oral cultures, these workshop structures suggest a potentially effective methodological approach to the contextualization of theology. While noting the limitations of any attempt at a written record of an oral process, the evidence provided in the workshop reports, now summarized, offers firm support for this claim for contextualization.

i. The addition of an opening question used for the Assembly workshops in 2003, which invited all participants to share their own experiences, drew such diverse and personal comments that it suggests active

---

28. In addition to the workshop reports, the publication also includes interviews with selected notable leaders of the church, with government leaders and with prominent chiefs, together with one article which was submitted for publication. Again, all contributions are on the topic of "Gospel and Culture." Again, the project motif, the drawing, "The Death of Jesus Christ" adorned the front cover.

involvement from a majority if not all of the group members, both men and women.[29]

ii. The second question, inviting insight into the traditions of the past, not only reflects a strong familiarity with traditional cultural practices, as is normal for oral peoples, but also displays a great respect for the value of many of these practices. As an additional benefit, the written documentation of these various features of traditional culture serves to preserve and to disseminate fascinating elements of cultural anthropology

iii. The invitation for groups to comment on the impact of the arrival of the missionaries displays, in most cases, an approach where the cultural practice was either prohibited[30] or significantly modified,[31] replaced in some instances by missionary mandates which were strictly applied.[32] Several of the groups offered blanket comments about the missionary rejection of all aspects of traditional culture,[33] with some observing a destructive fusion of the gospel with Western cultural practices.[34] In some cases, well-meaning missionary practices unknowingly instigated profound disturbances to significant traditional practices, leaving a subsequent legacy of community conflict.[35] For a small number of groups, there is testimony that the missionary approach to the cultural traditions was supportive or respectful.[36]

iv. The handling of the question about the way in which the gospel engages with the selected cultural topic drew responses that emphasized the strong heritage of the missionary era with its focus on the central place of the Scriptures. As a result, in the majority of cases, the approach

29. For example, see the material in Prior, *Voice of the Local Church*, on Native Languages (10–11), Dress (26–27), Marriage (34–35, 39–40), Death and Afterlife (64–65), and Feasting (86–87).

30. For example, see Prior, *Voice of the Local Church*, in the case of Spirits (17), Dress (55), and Kava (89).

31. As in the case of aspects of Marriage in Prior, *Voice of the Local Church*, 44.

32. A very clear example is in the case of Dress in Prior, *Voice of the Local Church*, 55.

33. For example, see Prior, *Voice of the Local Church*, for groups working on the topics of Roles of Men and Women (59), Marriage (76), and Respect through Giving (84).

34. See Prior, *Voice of the Local Church*, for comments from the groups about Spirits (17), Marriage,(76), and Respect through Giving (84).

35. See the comments in Prior, *Voice of the Local Church*, on the issue of Land (99) and the impact of Education on the role of youth, imposing a foreign culture, creating divisions, and changing the cultural identity of young people (122).

36. For more on Native Language, see Prior, *Voice of the Local Church*, 13.

taken was to identify a text or texts, whether from the Old or New Testament, that seemed to speak specifically about the topic concerned. Where no such text was identified, attempts were made to locate one or more texts that may have some connection.[37] This aspect of the responses raises key questions for the local church and its theological leaders about the role of Scripture as a witness to the gospel, and what might constitute an appropriate contextual interpretation of Scripture that serves the local church in its Christian life. This key element of the contextualization of theology requires further exploration.

v. Perhaps the most telling outcome of the theological process is the way in which the final question about the interchange between the gospel and the cultural topic was resolved. There is clear evidence, across the diverse workshop groups and topics, of ongoing pride in, and respect for, traditional cultural identity and customs, with an accompanying desire to retain, reinforce or even restore many of them.[38] In a minority of examples, the rejection of some traditional practices is also endorsed.[39] At the same time, the priority of the Christian gospel, and its central place in shaping the future of the local church community, is upheld across every group. What is evident is the genuine engagement between Gospel and Culture, in such a way that the cultural issue is critiqued under the magnifying glass of the gospel.[40] Notably, in some cases, cultural traditions offer certain insights into the gospel that have not been part of the missionary message.[41]

37. For example, see Prior, *Voice of the Local Church,* on the topics of Dress (29), Marriage (74), Feasting (88), and Bride Price (112).

38. One of the groups on Marriage speaks firmly for the retention of some, and revival of other, traditional cultural processes (Prior, *Voice of the Local Church*, 46–47). The same is true for the group discussion on the Ordination of Chiefs (52). One of the groups dealing with Land calls for a return to the traditional cultural approach, "in the time of our fore-fathers, which maintained social harmony" (24). The group dealing with Respect through Giving pleads for the restoration of the traditional place of respect (85), the group on Native Languages encourages the renewed recognition of non-verbal forms of communication such as signs, picture-talk, actions (15), and the group reflecting on the Role of Men and Women urges a return to the traditional structures of the mutually supportive extended family (59).

39. For example, see Prior, *Voice of the Local Church,* in the case of custom medicine designed to bring harm to human life (33) and certain spirits that hold people in states of fear (21).

40. The gospel acts as a corrective to cultural practices. For example, see Prior, *Voice of the Local Church,* in the case of Spirits (21), Custom Medicine (33), and Burial of the Dead (95–96).

41. See the notion of the land as "Mother," and the implications of this in the relationship between God, land, and humankind in Prior, *Voice of the Local Church,* 97.

In the light of the above summary of the methodology used in the workshop process, an interim, if not definitive, conclusion is that the participants in each group together took up the challenge of serious engagement between the gospel and their cultural context. The outcome of the process suggests a movement towards a creative interaction between the two, and a more integrated Christian life, lived within their own cultural context. This movement towards integration is well represented in the concluding reflections of a mixed-gender group of ten people from the Shepherd Islands who addressed the topic, "The Roles of Men and Women":

> Finally, but not least importantly, the best way to deal with this is to respect our Vanuariki culture, and to respect the gospel of Jesus Christ. Scrutinise both ways and let the light of the gospel prune what is not helpful or what is misleading in our culture, and replace it with the gospel way of life. Whatever we do to uphold the role of men and women in Vanuariki, we, the people of Vanuariki strive to equip the head, the hands and the heart—this produces a complete human being.[42]

THE EVOLUTION AND THE FORM OF THE EXPERIMENT— STAGE THREE

The official launching of volume three occurred at the occasion of the National Assembly of the Presbyterian Church and the Annual Conference of the PWMU, in August 2003. The publication was again greeted with enthusiasm. The Assembly promptly made a decision that a fourth volume be published, this time giving the responsibilities to their own staff at the Talua Ministry Training Centre. In addition, they proposed that this next volume focus on the topic of "Christology—how we understand the person and message of Jesus Christ within the context of Vanuatu cultures," and that it be completed by the time of the Assembly in 2005.

This decision constituted a significant endorsement of the project, and a desire to consolidate local ownership of it as a national movement. It also indicated confidence in their own theological teachers to provide the necessary leadership.

What then happened as a result of this decision?[43] By now, the Talua Ministry Training Centre had developed a vision to become an ecu-

---

See also the non-verbal elements of traditional language, in Prior, *Voice of the Local Church*, 14–15.

42. Prior, *Voice of the Local Church*, 60.

43. For details of the Assembly decision and its outcome, see Prior, *Local Voices on*

menical center, and had officially entered a partnership with the Church of Melanesia.[44] There were two teachers from the Church of Melanesia on the staff of Talua, and students for ordained and lay leadership of the Church of Melanesia were now being trained at Talua. This new development proved most important in extending the Gospel and Culture Project beyond the single tradition of the Presbyterian Church into an ecumenical arena. Under the guidance of the Talua Principal, Masia Nato, a working committee was established from staff members at the Centre. The chair of the committee was Father Stanley Ure from the Church of Melanesia.

At first the committee struggled with their remit. They were not clear or confident about their task. What they did know was that they had to gather sufficient material on the topic of "Christology" for a publication within two years. Without a background in the processes followed previously, the committee took the view that the publication would be made up of personal contributions in a written form, including articles of their own. Predictably, this proved to be a challenge, even for the educated Talua staff. Still deeply formed by the culture of orality, the task of writing was not an easy one for a number of them, and to prepare something that was to be published, was daunting.

Thus, twelve months after the Assembly decision, little progress had been made. However, three available sources had been identified for the publication. First, the staff met regularly for seminars, at which a staff member presented a paper on a topic of their own choosing, and within a field of their own interest or teaching; it was thought that this material might be well suited to form part of the publication. Secondly, Father Stanley Ure was conducting classes in "Gospel and Culture." The students were required to prepare a written assignment on "Who is Jesus Christ for us today?" This material too was considered a potential resource for the publication. Finally, as part of the responsibility of final year ordination students, a significant piece of written research was required. In perusing this material, it was obvious that there were some suitable contributions for publication. Apart from each of these possibilities, selected people from the wider church, for whom the writing of an article came more easily, also submitted contributions. So productive was the outcome that the material gathered, by word count, was more than twice that included in volume three. As a result, a decision was made to publish two volumes from this material, volume four in time for the 2005 Presbyterian Church Assembly, and volume five in 2006.

Jesus Christ, 4–6.

44. The Anglican Church of the Province of Melanesia was formed in 1975. It is commonly known as the Anglican Church of Melanesia or simply as the Church of Melanesia.

Because most of the material was provided in written form and already in English, the task of editing might have seemed to be straightforward. However, given that the language of English is, for many ni-Vanuatu, their fourth or fifth language, and given the challenges for oral people to use a literate medium, the task of editing was complicated. This was due in part to the frequency of errors in spelling and grammar. It was due also to the challenge of making the material easily understood, while at the same time seeking to preserve the content and style of the article. Some articles required significant rewriting in order to make them publishable, even in rudimentary form.

In sorting out which material would be used for volume four and which material would be used for volume five, it became clear that priority for the fourth volume would need to be given to those contributions that were clearly focused on the topic decided by the National Assembly in 2003, namely "Christology." The subtitle of volume four is therefore "Local voices on Jesus Christ and Mission." The material in this volume is dominated by two approaches to the topic: first, the use of particular local cultural symbols—chief, healer, canoe, dolphin, yam, octopus—to represent a particular understanding of Jesus Christ, and secondly, a focus on the meaning of Christian themes—hope, the cross, peace, love, mission, forgiveness—in the local context. Some attention is given also to current challenges in Christian mission, for example, globalism.[45]

Volume five is unique in its own way because it features four important articles on the role of women in leadership in the culture and in the church. Notably, two of the four articles come from women students in their final year of ordination training, one from the Presbyterian Church and one from the Church of Melanesia, at a time when the latter church did not ordain women. The remaining two papers come from indigenous faculty members who take differing approaches, and who come to different conclusions on this issue. This is the first time that this topic had appeared in the "Gospel and Culture" publications. It represented the questions and challenges now emerging with the changing role of women at all levels of society, both within and beyond the church. The subtitle chosen for the fifth volume was "Women in Culture and Church, and Other Issues."

The second part of this fifth volume gathers together eleven articles that, with one exception, were prepared as research articles by students in their final year of ordination training; the exception is the contribution from a student in his penultimate year.[46] They all address focal issues of Gospel and

---

45. For the list of articles and authors see Prior, *Local Voices on Jesus Christ,* 5.

46. For some explanation of the research requirements for students in their final

Culture in the contemporary context of Vanuatu communities—marriage, role of youth, migration, division in village communities, peace, sacrifice, the *Nakamal*, land, kava, heaven and hell.[47] These articles represent the diversity of the student community in terms of their cultural and language backgrounds, and their literacy capabilities (with article quality varying greatly and article length ranging from under three thousand words to over twelve thousand words). They have in common that the authors are men, and that the contributors are aged in their twenties and thirties. These contributors will be among the next generation of leaders in the church in Vanuatu, and as such, their perspectives indicate something of the viewpoint of the future generation.

Because of delays in the processes of compiling material, a final version of volume four was not completed in time for the National Assembly in 2005. However, it was sufficiently complete for ten copies of a "Draft Only Version" to be produced, and these copies were used for an official ceremonial launching to take place at the Assembly. Father Stanley Ure, who chaired the working group, and Pastor Masia Nato, the then Principal of Talua, were present and formally thanked. Volume five was also to be available by the end of the same year; it was not formally launched at any Assembly.

Summary Critique of Stage Three

The outworking of the decision of 2003 was illuminating for the experiment in the contextualization of theology in Vanuatu. It was so because of both the successes of its outcome, and the problematic nature of that outcome. On one hand, it clearly reflected a genuine contextualization of the content of a local theology. On the other hand, it displayed vividly the struggle to discern the core issues of a contextual methodology.

Any initial critique of this stage would affirm that the published outcome of the Assembly resolution displays a most successful result in the contextualization of theology.[48] The quantity of material compiled produced not just one publication, but two, prompting the recognition that "there is a lot of energy among the churches in Vanuatu for tackling the issues of the relationship between the Christian gospel and the cultures of Vanuatu."[49] The publications also broke new ground by broadening the

year, see Prior, *Women in Culture and Church*, 243.

47. For the list of articles and authors see Prior, *Women in Culture and Church*, xi–xii.

48. The following points are listed in greater detail in the introduction to volume 5 of Prior's *Gospel and Culture*. See Prior, *Women in Culture and Church*, x–xiv.

49. Prior, *Women in Culture and Church*, 242.

input to embrace other church traditions (several contributions from the Church of Melanesia, as well as a contribution from each of the Roman Catholic Church and the French Protestant Church). They gave scope also for first-ever contributions from young women, including the first woman in the Church of Melanesia in Vanuatu to have completed preparation for ordination. Further, they introduced a range of previously unaddressed topics, and recorded valuable new material. They included major research projects of final year students, some of which are quite detailed, and all of which engage with topics of importance. They contained the voice of the younger generation of ni-Vanuatu, and thereby offer some insights into the viewpoints of the future generation of leaders and of the church. They provided some input from people beyond the geographical and cultural boundaries of Vanuatu. These are all significant successes.

Set alongside the successes, certain limitations were also evident. In particular, the implementation of the Assembly decision illuminated some of the key issues and challenges in the contextualization of the methodology of theology in the South Pacific. Only in retrospect, and upon reflection, did these issues and their significance become apparent.

What was most notable was the decision by the Talua staff to gather the content in the form of articles written by individuals in the language of English. This seemed to be the instinctive pathway to follow, one undoubtedly determined by the framework of the college within which they worked, shaped as it was by the heritage of Western theological tradition. No apparent consideration was given to a communal workshop process, nor to oral interviews. The decision to confine the contributions to literacy-based material led to substantial and predictable difficulties.

It meant that not all staff at Talua would submit articles. Not all local staff were sufficiently schooled or confident in the manner of writing theology, and no arrangement was made to conduct interviews with them that would have allowed their voices to be heard. The fact that some faculty voices are absent from the two subsequent publications was a matter of personal embarrassment and cultural shame for them. The same was true for the college students.

It meant too that the editing process was labor-intensive, considerably more so than the previous two volumes for which the material had to be translated into English before editing it. Many of the articles were written in a form of English that required not only correction in grammar and spelling, but substantial re-writing; this was necessary in order to make the material comprehensible, especially to a wider reading audience. It is not an easy matter for people to write logically, or articulately, in a language that is perhaps their third or fourth or even fifth language of communication, and especially so when writing is itself alien to their own cultural identity.

Upon reflection, it became apparent that the pathway chosen, following the decision of the 2003 Assembly, deflected the project away from an appropriate cultural contextualization of theology, and from what is clearly a more authentic methodology for doing theology in Vanuatu. The experiences of this stage of the project came to illustrate well the struggles involved in pursuing the agenda of contextualization, in a situation where the Western cultural heritage continues to assert its influence so powerfully upon the processes of theology. This is precisely the struggle identified earlier in chapter 3.

Volumes four and five represent a form of doing theology that is at home in literate cultures, where categories of the Enlightenment provide the criteria, and where theology and local church remain distant. Rather than being communal and relational, it is essentially the work of individuals; rather than being oral in expression and then documented from this oral origin, it is expressed in written form; rather than the workings of a local Christian community, it is the product of an elite minority who have sufficient levels of Western literacy-based education to be able to produce material in accepted publishable form; rather than having an orientation to the faithfulness of a local Christian community in context, its only apparent intention is the availability of information.

THE NEXT STAGE

During the Assembly at which the official launching of volume four took place, there was a further meeting of members of the working group that now included Father Stanley Ure. There was a keenness to maintain the momentum of the Gospel and Culture project. In discussion, the working group resolved to produce a further volume, this time on the single topic of "land." This decision arose out of a serious concern about land disputes impacting upon people across all the island communities of Vanuatu; this made the suggested topic contextually urgent, both locally and nationally.

Importantly, in planning the process for this next stage, it was agreed to use the same methodology that had been so fruitfully used both at Talua in 1999 and at the Assembly in 2003. This agreement represented a conscious move to re-align the "Gospel and Culture in Vanuatu" project to what was now considered a more appropriate methodological approach to the contextualization of theology within the cultures of Vanuatu. A proposal was agreed whereby the Presbyterian Church, the Church of Melanesia, the Talua community, the Vanuatu Christian Council and the

National Council of Chiefs would be involved. The gathering of material from these various workshops would constitute the material for volume six. This decision constituted a further significant development of the Gospel and Culture project. While focusing on just the single topic "land," it aimed to embrace both a broad ecumenical constituency of church members and leaders, as well as political and cultural leaders. It would take the Gospel and Culture project to a new level.

However, despite all the energy that drove the decision in late 2005 towards this next significant development, there was no coordinated follow-up, and no published outcome. The subsequent failure to bring this next stage to fruition inevitably raises important questions about the extent to which the commitment to the contextualization of theology through this methodology has yet found its home within the life of the local church. While the commitment to engage in the task has remained strong, and the issue of land has remained an urgent priority, the very logistics involved in implementing a project of such scope have been a key factor in the lack of progress.

Despite this failure, a significant endorsement of the Vanuatu project came from an unexpected source. An invitation was extended by the Protestant Church in Timor Leste for the two key leaders of the working group to lead a series of workshops on "Gospel and Culture" in Dili in November 2005, with an indigenous group of young pastors and lay leaders.[50] The Protestant Church in Timor Leste had heard about the Vanuatu project, and it appealed to them as a valuable resource for their own context, also culturally Melanesian. Timor Leste achieved its political independence in May 2002 and, like Vanuatu in 1980, the achievement of independence prompted a resurgence of interest in, and commitment to, their own tradition and culture. In the wake of their national independence, the Protestant Church had identified four priorities to be addressed by the churches, the first of which was "Gospel and Culture." Reflecting the peculiarities of their own context, the remaining three were socio-political justice, ecumenism and other faiths. In order to begin the process of tackling the first of these issues, "Gospel and Culture," they decided to learn from the generation of experience of the Presbyterian Church in post-independent Vanuatu. Their invitation to the Vanuatu-based working group gave some wider recognition to the significance of what had been evolving as a movement towards the contextualizing of theology in Vanuatu.

---

50. Following the visit in 2005, a second invitation was issued in 2013.

NEW DIRECTIONS IN AN ONGOING CASE STUDY

In the meantime, another very different and important theme has emerged in Vanuatu, and has since claimed priority as the agenda for "The Gospel and Culture in Vanuatu" project. In August 2012, the issue of "Women in Leadership" was formally adopted by the Assembly of the Presbyterian Church as the approved topic for serious engagement, with the expected outcome of two or more publications.[51] This decision marks a new and different stage in the development of the project, with a focus on the particular context of women in Vanuatu. It is a project that was initiated from the national movement of Presbyterian women (the PWMU), and is under the auspice of the PCV Assembly Committee on Women. This shift of focus has generated a high level of national interest, especially, but not only, among the women of the church. Some of the lessons of the previous stages of the experiment have helped to give shape to this project. While this new stage of the Vanuatu project is beyond the scope of this book, it promises to offer its own contribution to the issues of the contextualizing of theology in the cultures of the people of Vanuatu. In the future, this will be worthy of commentary and critique.

51. Two volumes on this theme have since been produced under the auspice of the Presbyterian Church of Vanuatu.

6

Conclusions

CHRISTIAN LIFE IN THE South Pacific can be lived with "one head and one heart." That is, it can be lived in a way that is *not dis-integrated*. That is the claim and purpose of this book.

However, in order to do so, a fundamentally changed approach to the contextualization of theology is necessary, and in particular to the methodology of theology. This change is informed by certain distinctive features of the cultures that define the peoples of the South Pacific. When the force of these features is appreciated, the pathway is opened to a contextualization of theology that is rooted within the context of the South Pacific peoples.

This book was motivated by the starkness and urgency of the challenge arising from the 1979 New Hebrides workshop on "Culture and Faith," which concluded that Christians in the New Hebrides were essentially living a life of "two heads and two hearts." A summary report of several similar workshops claimed that this same reality applied across the whole of the South Pacific. The basis of this claim was that the Christian faith, introduced across the islands of the South Pacific through the nineteenth century, had failed to become integrated with the cultural context of the island communities. While the Christian faith was introduced, acceptance required also the acceptance of the cultural categories that accompanied the Western missionary message. Correspondingly, it called for the negation of much of the indigenous cultural heritage. Because dislocation from one cultural reality, and relocation into another and very different culture, is never achievable, the traditional cultural identity remained suppressed rather than extinguished. The legacy for the people of the South Pacific was seriously problematic—the Christian faith became accommodated in parallel with, but not integrated with, indigenous cultural identity. It was as if the people lived two separated lives, a Christian life publicly expressed, an indigenous life publicly suppressed.

The emergence of independence movements in the South Pacific through the 1970s gave permission for the suppressed cultural identity of the people to find public expression. The opportunity to do so was grasped enthusiastically. When independence was achieved in Vanuatu, the people proudly reclaimed their traditional ways of life. As a consequence, it brought to clear recognition the fact that Christians were living two parallel lives, both "faith" and "custom," both "gospel" and "culture." Thus it was that the reported workshop outcome in 1979 was sub-titled, "Two Heads and Two Hearts."

This public awareness of dis-integration led to an inevitable and challenging question, "What would it take for a Christian to live with 'one head and one heart'?" The question was not one of idle interest. It was one that constituted a challenge of highest priority for the life of the churches across the South Pacific, bringing with it the pressing questions as to whether and how the Christian gospel can genuinely be incarnate in the context of the cultures and peoples of this particular part of the world.

The movement of the contextualization of theology, although not formally defined as such at the time, was emerging onto the churches' agenda in Asia, Africa and Latin America, from the 1950s. In its own distinctive way, it was also emerging onto the theological agenda in the Western world. It began to sow its seeds within the South Pacific in the 1960s, a period that saw the establishment of the Pacific Theological College in Suva, and the commitment to localize theological education. Concurrently, the Pacific Conference of Churches came into being, creating opportunities for local church leaders to meet together on pressing issues, and providing formal ways for Pacific church leaders and theologians to engage with their colleagues in other regions of the world.

The movement towards the localizing of theology began to gain momentum across the South Pacific through the 1970s, at the time when the seeds of anti-colonialism and pro-independence were coming to flower in many of the island nations. The impact was to establish more firmly the quest in the South Pacific to take local ownership of the theological task, and in particular, to explore a theology that might genuinely represent a home-grown form of contextualization.

The 1980s witnessed a series of significant steps forward, including the development of Coconut Theology that came to be lauded as a unique Pacific expression of theology. In addition, two regional journals came into circulation—in 1985 the Melanesian Journal of Theology, and in 1987 the Pacific Journal of Theology, the latter being re-launched after its first launching in 1961 faltered. Both journals were committed to the enterprise of the contextualization of theology, and provided an important avenue for local people to utter their own theological voices. Other significant publications also came to birth during this same decade, including one made up entirely of contributions from indigenous South Pacific Islanders,[1] another with the pertinent title, "South Pacific Theology," and one with the telling and provocative title, "The Gospel Is Not Western." These publications reflected the energy with which the agenda for the contextualization of theology in the South Pacific was now being taken up. A change in the approach to the theological task in the South Pacific was now well and truly under way.

In addition, through the 1980s, several gatherings of church leaders and theologians were convened. At such gatherings there was an emphatic focus on questions of the contextualization of theology, and of the interaction between the gospel and the cultures of the local peoples. Institutions of theological education began to address the revision of the teaching curriculum, in order to ensure that greater attention be given to a theological agenda of more relevance to the South Pacific.

Significant to the further localizing of theology was the birth, in 1989, of the Pacific women's group, Weavers. Not only did this group create a unique venue for women to meet together to discuss common issues of concern, it had significant impact on aspects of the contextualization of theology. It announced the intention to speak a fresh theological voice into what had, until then, been a male world. With a plea for a narrative theology that begins with the suffering and oppression of women, their voice challenged both the content and methodology of theology. It drew attention to the captivity of theology within Western theological models and within Western-constructed institutions of theological education.

The momentum for contextualization was sustained through the early 1990s with the establishment of the Ecumenical Association of Third World Theologians—Pacific Chapter, leading to further major conferences being convened on theology in the South Pacific. This was now in more formal collaboration with colleagues from other parts of the Third World. Each occasion brought renewed pleas for contextualization, together with new suggestions as to what this might mean. It was during this period that the notion of an "Oceania theology" gained greater attention. This incorporated into theology the fundamental importance of land for the identity of South Pacific Islanders. Land was not simply another important local topic to come under the contextualization umbrella; it named a life-defining cultural element of Island peoples, and it demanded integration into the theological task.

---

1. May, *Living Theology*.

These events of the 1990s were followed up by the significant commitment of the Pacific Conference of Churches to convene a series of regional workshops on the topic of "Contextual Theology." The fact that these workshops were planned to take place in the first four years of the new millennium flagged a significant intention of South Pacific church leaders and theologians—the new millennium would constitute a new era. It would be one marked by the assumption that the theological task belonged to the South Pacific peoples, and that any genuine theology must now be contextual.

However, reviewing the process of contextualization over the decades since the 1960s reveals that it has been only partially successful. From the beginning, it faced daunting challenges, essentially because the starting point for the task was not a neutral one. Prior to any awareness of the importance of the contextualization of theology, and before any desire to pursue this agenda, the theological task in the South Pacific had already become deeply rooted within the Western cultural presuppositions and practices inherited from the missionary era. At the time when the agenda for contextualization first appeared, it was these that prescribed the lens through which theology was perceived, and the theological task understood.

The contextualization of theology in the South Pacific needed then to have a dual agenda. On the one hand, there was a need to break away from the alien-ness of what was inherited, while on the other hand, there was a need to give a culturally indigenous shape to both the content and the methodology of theology. This dual agenda has been running concurrently throughout the four decades during which the process of contextualization has been a priority in the South Pacific. It could be said that the effectiveness in managing the latter agenda, namely a genuinely indigenous contextualization, has been constantly thwarted by a struggle to deal adequately with the former, namely the deeply rooted Western cultural heritage.

The successes of the contextualization of theology have been witnessed most clearly in the definition and the content of theology. The churches have taken up the contemporary challenges and changes impacting on their own region of the world, so that these now constitute the issues to be addressed theologically. Influenced in particular by the way in which other Third World churches and theologians have addressed socio-political issues and cultural changes, the theological agenda in the South Pacific has been keenly addressing the pressing and emerging issues such as political independence, exploitation and climate change. At the same time, traditional cultural symbols and motifs now routinely provide the language and images for the expression of theology. While "Coconut Theology" is the most prominent of these, numerous other traditional themes have also found expression in local writings and in the assignments of theological education students. Women in particular have brought into this agenda a "women theology," marked by their unique experiences of dehumanization, and their unique gender images. The cultural heritage, which has authorized the exclusive role of men in public leadership, and has confined women to home and garden, has come under strong critique.

In these various ways the focal content of theology has moved away from the agenda of the Western world into the context of the South Pacific. These changes in the content of theology have also been apparent in the institutions of theological education, where matters of immediate relevance to the cultures and contexts of the South Pacific have entered the curriculum.

But there has been another and more perplexing side to the contextualization story. In the exploration that has been detailed through the chapters of this book, it has become clear that there are primary obstacles that continue to thwart progress in the genuine contextualization of theology in the South Pacific. These obstacles relate most directly to the methodology of theology, as defined in terms of four particular questions, (i) What form does theology take? (ii) Who does theology? (iii) What is the primary location for the theological task? and (iv) What is the primary purpose of theology? In reviewing the decades of contextualization, it has become clear that these questions of the methodology of theology have received comparatively little attention. As a result, the questions defining the methodology of theology remain inadequately addressed. I have asserted that, if the pursuit for theology in the South Pacific is to be genuinely contextual, then the responses given to these questions must themselves be culturally contextual. In other words, the issues of the methodology of theology require their own contextualization alongside the contextualization of the content of theology.

There is no such thing as a neutral or culture-free methodology. Thus, when it comes to the issue of the methodology of theology, what has not been recognized is just how deeply captive is theology in the South Pacific to the inherited Western cultural presuppositions. In other words, even through the period where there has been a deliberate focus on the need for contextualizing theology in the South Pacific, the fundamental categories of the methodology of theology have been those that have been shaped by Western cultural presuppositions. For this reason, the contextualization process in the South Pacific continues to stumble. The key to the further effective development in the contextualization of theology within the South Pacific therefore lies in the conscious shift to categories of methodology that are culturally contextual.

This is the focal issue addressed in this book. It has been made clear that any breakthrough in methodology becomes possible only with a more acute awareness of the profound differences between the cultural presuppositions that have informed the missionary heritage of theology, and the cultural worldview that has defined, and continues to define, the peoples of the South Pacific. In particular, I have established that such a breakthrough centers on three key elements.

The first and most critical of these cultural differences is the fact that the peoples of the South Pacific belong to oral cultures, in contrast to the literate cultures of the Western world. As explained, the implications of this are far-reaching. It is not simply a matter of a difference in capabilities. Neither is it the case that by teaching oral people to read and to write, they then become competent literate people, and can manage themselves well in the cultural framework of literacy. In fact, orality and literacy represent profound differences in worldview and in social make-up.

An appreciation of the scale of these differences is necessary in dealing with the dilemmas of the contextualization of the methodology of theology. It demands that for peoples of the South Pacific, the theological task must be engaged in communally, and expressed in forms that are oral, embodied, and ritualized. The processes of learning and teaching would also need to identify certain people within the community as mentors and teachers. The primary location must be within the local church community, and the primary purpose must be to sustain and nurture the local church community in its faithfulness to the gospel.

The second significant cultural difference is that the cultures of the South Pacific do not share with the Western world the history of the Enlightenment, with all the associated categories of reality that evolved from that era. Particularly relevant for the pursuit of the contextualization of theology is that, for the Western world, the theological task assumes an intellectual, critical and rational engagement with information, ideas and concepts, and engaged in by individuals sufficiently educated to manage the task. Such an approach is utterly alien in the cultures of the South Pacific, where learning is shaped by the questions of what it means to sustain the ongoing life of the community, within a worldview which is inhabited by spirits of influence. The associated processes of learning involve the passing on of the wisdom and the truth which is located in the past, and which is learned communally through such means as story, ritual, drama and song.

The consequences of this for the contextualization of the methodology of theology are again far-reaching. Consistent with implications drawn from the oral nature of South Pacific cultures, the theological task can only be effective if it is a communal task, grounded in, and responding to, the life and the experience of the local church community, and serving the purpose of the faithfulness of that community.

The third of the differences involves the separation of the centers of theological learning from the life of the local church communities. This third fundamental element must also be addressed in the contextualization of the methodology of theology. While this is not, in and of itself, a difference between the cultures of the South Pacific and the cultures of the Western world, the separation does constitute a fundamental cultural anomaly for the peoples of the South Pacific. Such is the assumption of human life as communal that, to locate the theological enterprise within theological colleges, and to require students of theology to relocate into classroom learning, constitute a cultural dislocation which reinforces the alienation of theology from, and the irrelevance of theology to, the life of the church communities.

When this third issue is added to the previous two issues already identified, the depth of the challenges faced in the contextualization of the methodology of theology in the South Pacific becomes strikingly apparent. This awareness opens up the possibility for more serious reckoning with the dilemma.

The local working group on "Gospel and Culture in Vanuatu" came to birth in the post-independence climate of the 1980s in Vanuatu, with the desire to engage seriously with the legacy of theology as introduced by the missionary era, and to explore the contextualization of theology. In the first instance, it did this by engaging with particular issues and themes in the relationship between the Christian gospel and the cultural realities that shaped the life of the local people. At this early stage, the project was little more than a local response to the challenging question that accompanied independence, namely what it might mean for proudly independent ni-Vanuatu people to be Christian within their local cultural identity, rather than needing to suppress or negate this identity. There was little awareness at the time of the distinctions between content and methodology that would later become important. However, due to the ongoing relevance of the project to the local church, and the energy that it evoked among the local people, the project began to take shape in clearly defined ways. The need to relocate the theological task into the life of the church, and in particular into the local communities of the church became a clear commitment. Alongside this commitment was the recognition that the worldview and practices that constituted the traditional cultures of the people, now being given renewed authorization by the achievement of independence, ought to become the ingredients for theological engagement. This led to explorations on a wide range of themes and topics familiar to village people, and also to those for whom cultural experience was more urban.

The most important development came as a result of the recognition that it was questions of a methodology for doing theology that lay at the forefront of the challenge. This arose from a growing understanding of the traditional cultural realities that define the peoples of the South Pacific, and a growing awareness that the approach to theology had become trapped in the cultural presuppositions of the Western world, and this needed to be confronted. What subsequently developed was a methodology that profoundly redefined the theological task. It moved the locus of theology into the community of the local church, it recognized the community of the church as the subjects of the theological task, it applied an oral medium within a communal setting, and it established a process facilitated by a recognized leader. The defined purpose was to invite a communal response of faithfulness in Christian life. The overall enterprise served to ground theology within the cultural context of the local Christian community.

Along the way the working group was challenged by its own dilemmas. The roots of the heritage of theology from the Western world run very deep, and can so quickly reassert their influence. This was the experience in the production of Volumes four and five. While the content of these volumes remained very much a part of the South Pacific experience, the methodology that was applied was culturally alien. It was the obstacles encountered in pursuing this alien methodology that sharpened perspectives for the working group on the specific approach to methodology suited to the peoples of the South Pacific.

What has become clear in this book is that the invaluable legacy of the work undertaken by the working group on "Gospel and Culture in Vanuatu," over a period of more than a generation, has been to identify an approach to the methodology of theology that can claim to be genuinely grounded within the cultural context of South Pacific peoples. It is not so much that the specific process used by the working group is to be copied in all its detail; in fact, it is not without its ambiguities. However, it offers one experiment in the contextualization of theology where the processes pursued have helped to illuminate the key categories in any contextualization of theology in the South Pacific, particularly in its methodology.

One clear conclusion is that any approach to the contextualizing task that is shaped predominantly by Western cultural categories, cannot be valid for the South Pacific. Only an approach that honors the validity of primary oral cultures, recognizes the alien-ness of Enlightenment categories, and acknowledges the cultural anomaly of distancing the theological task from the life of the local Christian communities, paves the way for a valid contextualization. This has been the insight derived from the experimental project of "Gospel and Culture in Vanuatu." If this insight has any substance and credibility, then serious consideration needs to be given, not only to the modes of theologizing, but also to the structures of theological education across the South Pacific.

There may be implications also for the contextualization of theology in other parts of the world, in particular in those regions that boast a strong primary oral culture, and where similar dilemmas in the theological task may also be experienced.

There may also be consequences for the ongoing shape of theology within the Western world. On the one hand, the four questions framing the methodology of theology that have been brought to bear on the context of the oral cultures of the South Pacific may be fruitfully introduced into the context of Western culture. How this may challenge and change the methodology of theology within the Western world has not been the agenda of this book, but is nevertheless a worthy agenda.

At the same time, important changes are taking place within the nations of the Western world that will impact on the shape of the theological task. Migration is changing the cultural shape of Western nations and the churches in those nations. Australia is a case in point. Statistics over the last generation indicate clearly that the percentage of church members from non-Western cultural backgrounds is increasing rapidly while the percentage of membership from Anglo-Celtic cultural backgrounds is declining rapidly.[2] What this means for the learning of theology, and for the formal structures of theological education in the Australian context, is in just the earliest stages of discussion. What seems clear is that the presuppositions of Western culture that have given shape to this in the past, are no longer adequate for the task of the formation of leadership for the future church.

In these ways, the implications of this book for the ongoing pursuit of the contextualization of theology and theological education, beyond the bounds of the South Pacific, may be substantial. However, these implications are all subservient to the primary intention and outcome of this book, namely that it may serve to enhance a more genuine contextualizing of theology within the South Pacific and the possibility that the Christian life in the South Pacific may be lived with "one head and one heart."

Insofar as this book contributes to this outcome, it responds to the call made many years ago for a localized theology for South Pacific Islanders—not the legendary call in 1976 made by Sir John Guise, nor the equally familiar call a decade later by "the father of contextual theology," Dr. Sione 'Amanaki Havea, but the call by one of the numerous South Pacific Islanders who have contributed to the contextualization of theology in the South

2. Hughes, "Impact."

Pacific, Jotama Vamarasi from Rotuma.[3] It is appropriate that such a little known voice, coming from a little-known volcanic island of the South Pacific, concludes this book. As such, it represents the voices of all South Pacific peoples. His was a heart-felt call, uttered at the formative consultation on theology held in Papua New Guinea in 1986. It has implications for both the content and the methodology of the contextualization of theology in the South Pacific.

> There is a great and urgent need for the indigenous Islanders to be doing the kind of theology that brings out the *mana* of the Word of God to contemporary needs—the theology that arises out of life and the people's struggle to create meaning in life. . . . The past historical Christ-event must become alive to illumine our present, with new possibilities for personal and social transformation. . . . Theology must be done out of a pastoral concern: with the well-being of persons in view, and not as a detached abstract exercise. It should help the Pacific people remain the "people of God" in the Pacific.[4]

Over the three decades following this plea, the quest for contextualization of theology in the South Pacific remains urgent. This book has attempted to take this quest seriously and to offer the essential elements of a response.

Promoting Theology
in the
South Pacific

3. Jotama Vamarasi did his theological studies at the Methodist College in Fiji and then at the Pacific Theological College. He was a lecturer before becoming a Translations Officer with the Bible Society of the South Pacific, and he served as a Methodist Minister of the Rotuman congregation in Suva.

4. Vamarasi, "Mana," 49–50. Mana is a traditional cultural word which refers to "artistic and imaginative power" (Vamarasi, "Mana," 46). It is common in the South Pacific to speak of "mana" in reference to the impact of the Word of God.

Bibliography

Abraham, K. C., ed. *Third World Theologies: Commonalities and Divergences*. Maryknoll, NY: Orbis, 1990.

Aerts, Theo. "Man and His World: Biblical and Melanesian Worldviews." *Melanesian Journal of Theology* 5.1 (1989) 27–51.

Afayori, Robert. "Book Review: Acting Missiologically through Contextual Theology: Paul Duane Matheny, Contextual Theology: The Drama of Our Times (Cambridge, UK: James Clarke & Co., 2012)." *Expository Times* 125.2 (2013) 97–98.

Ahrens, Theodor. "Doing Theology: The Work of the Minister as a Change Agent in Melanesia Today." *Point* 1 (1976) 68–73.

———. "Local Church and Theology in Melanesia." *Point* 2 (1978) 140–58.

Amirtham, Samuel, and John S. Pobee. *Theology By The People: Reflections on Doing Theology in Community*. Geneva: World Council of Churches, 1986.

Anderson, Gerald. "American Protestants in Pursuit of Mission: 1886–1986." *International Bulletin of Missionary Research* 12.3 (1988) 98–118.

Anderson, Gerald, and Thomas Stransky. *Third World Theologies*. Mission Trends. Grand Rapids: Eerdmans, 1976.

Andrew, M. E. *The Old Testament and New Zealand Theology*. Dunedin, NZ: University of Dunedin, 1982.

Apea, Simon. "Footprints of God in Ialibu." *Point* 8 (1985) 2018–55.

Arbuckle, Gerald A. "The Impact of Vatican II on the Marists in Oceania." In *Mission, Church, and Sect in Oceania*, edited by James Boutilier, et al., 275–99. ASAO Monograph 6. Ann Arbor, MI: University of Michigan Press, 1978.

Avi, Dick. "Contextualization in Melanesia." *Melanesian Journal of Theology* 4.1 (1988) 7–22.

Barth, Karl. "No Boring Theology! A Letter from Karl Barth." *South East Asia Journal of Theology* 2 (1969) 3–5.

Bartle, Neville. *Death, Witchcraft, and the Spirit World in the Highlands of Papua New Guinea: Developing a Contextual Theology in Melanesia*. Point 29. Goroka, PNG: Melanesian Institute, 2005.

Baum, Gregory. "Three Theses on Contextual Theology." *The Ecumenist* 24.4 (1986) 49–59.

Bediako, Kwame. *Jesus and the Gospel in Africa: History and Experience*. Maryknoll, NY: Orbis, 2000.

Bergmann, Sigurd. *God in Context: A Survey of Contextual Theology*. Ashgate Translations in Philosophy, Theology, and Religion. Aldershot, UK: Ashgate, 2003.

Bergquist, James. "The Theological Education Fund and the Uncertain Future of Third World Theological Education." *Theological Education* 9.4 (1973) 244–53.

———. "Theological Education in Ferment and Change: The Crisis of Third World Theological Education." *Point* 1 (1976) 5–15.

———. "Theological Education in Ferment and Change: Extension and Other Alternative Forms of Theological Education." *Point* 1 (1976) 183–98.

Bevans, Stephen, ed. *A Century of Catholic Mission*. Regnum Edinburgh Centenary Series 15. Oxford: Regnum, 2013.

———. *Mission and Culture: The Louis J. Luzbetak Lectures 2000–2010*. American Society of Missiology 48. Maryknoll, NY: Orbis, 2012.

———. *Models of Contextual Theology*. Maryknoll, NY: Orbis, 1992.

———. *Models of Contextual Theology*. Rev. ed. Maryknoll, NY: Orbis, 2002.

Bevans, Stephen, and Katalina Tahaafe-Williams, eds. *Contextual Theology for the Twenty-First Century*. Cambridge: James Clarke & Co., 2012.

Bevans, Stephen, and Roger Schroeder. *Constants in Context: A Theology of Mission for Today*. American Society of Missiology Series. Maryknoll, NY: Orbis, 2004.

Boff, Leonardo, and Virgil Elizondo. *Theologies of the Third World: Convergences and Differences*. Concilium 199. Norwich, UK: Hymns Ancient & Modern, 1988.

Bonnemaison, Joël. *Vanuatu: Les Editions du Pacifique*. Translated by William Reed and James Philibert. Singapore: Times Editions, 1986.

Bosch, David. *Transforming Mission: Paradigm Shifts in Theology of Mission*. Twentieth Anniversary ed. Maryknoll, NY: Orbis, 2011.

Boseto, Lesley. "The Challenges of the 1980s and the Pacific Churches." In *Fourth Assembly of the Pacific Conference of Churches (May 3–15, 1981): Background Reading Book*, 7–14. Suva: Lotu Pasifika, 1981.

———. "Do Not Separate Us from Our Land and Sea." *Pacific Journal of Theology* 2.13 (1995) 69–72

———. "Environment and Community in Melanesia." *Melanesian Journal of Theology* 1.2 (1985) 166–73.

———. "God as Community—God in Melanesian Theology." *Pacific Journal of Theology* 2.10 (1993) 41–45.

———. "Towards a Pacific Theology of Reality: A Grassroots Response to Winds of Change." *Pacific Journal of Theology* 2.12 (1994) 53–61.

———. "The United Church: The Will and the Gift of God." *Pacific Journal of Theology* 2.14 (1995) 41–45.

Bowen, Dorothy N., and Earle A. Bowen, Jr. "Contextualization of Teaching Methodology in Theological Education in Africa: A Paper Presented at Limuru, Kenya, 16–19 June,1988." In *Conference of Theological Educators of The Acrediting Council for Theological Education*, edited by the Educational Resources Information Center (ERIC), 1–11. Limura, Kenya: US Department of Education, 1988.

———. "What Does It Mean to Think, Learn, Teach?" In *Internationalizing Missionary Training*, edited by W. D. Taylor, 203–16. Exeter: Paternoster, 1991.

Bradshaw, John. "In The Beginning Was The Journal." *Pacific Journal of Theology* 2.6 (1991) 3–7.

Bujo, Benezet. *African Theology in Its Social Context*. Maryknoll, NY: Orbis, 2006.

Burdon, Adrian. "Editorial." *Pacific Journal of Theology* 2.20 (1998) 1–2.

Burtness, James H. "Innovation as the Search for Probabilities: To Re-Contextualize the Text." In *Learning in Context: The Search for Innovative Patterns in Theological Education*, 9–17. Bromley, UK: Theological Education Fund, 1973.

Burua, Albert. "Theology and Melanesia." *Point* 1 (1980) 9–12.

Bush, Joseph. "Claiming a Christian State Where None Exists: Church and State in the Republic of Fiji." *Pacifica* 12.1 (1999) 55–68.

Cameron, Heather, et al., eds. *Together in Ministry: Essays to Honour John Paver*. Melbourne: Uniting Academic, 2009.

Campbell, Frederick A., et al. *A Year in the New Hebrides, Loyalty Islands, and New Caledonia*. Victoria, Australia: George Mercer, 1873.

Carrington, Don. "Jesus' Dreaming: Doing Theology through Aboriginal Stories." In *The Cultured Pearl*, edited by Jim Houston, 261–72. Melbourne: Joint Board of Christian Education, 1988.

Carroll, Seforosa. "Weaving New Spaces: Christological Perspectives from Oceania (Pacific) and the Oceanic Diaspora." *Studies in World Christianity* 10.1 (2004) 72–92.

Chadwick, Henry. *The Early Church*. Vol. 1 of *The Pelican History of the Church*. Middlesex: Penguin, 1967.

Chandran, Russell. "Asian Perspectives for Doing Theology." In *Towards a Relevant Pacific Theology: The Role of the Churches and Theological Education*. A Report of a Theological Consultation held in Bergengren House, Suva, Fiji. 8–12 July, 1985, 32–45. Suva: Lotu Pasifika, 1986.

———. *The Cross and the Tanoa: Gospel and Culture in the Pacific: Report on the Consultation on Gospel and Culture held in Suva, Fiji, 27–29 July, 1987*. Suva: South Pacific Association of Theological Schools, 1988.

———. "The Work of the Holy Spirit in the Theological Community." *Pacific Journal of Theology* 2.5 (1991) 5–7.

Chao, John Paul. "Leadership." In *An Introduction to Melanesian Cultures: A Handbook for Church Workers*, edited by D. L. Whiteman, 127–48. Goroka, Papua New Guinea: Melanesian Institute, 1984.

Chiang, Samuel E., and Grant Lovejoy, eds. "Beyond Literate Western Models: Contextualizing Theological Education in Oral Contexts." Hong Kong: International Orality Network, 2013.

Chinchen, Del. "The Art of Hospitality African Style: An Indigenous Method of Discipleship." *Evangelical Missions Quarterly* 36.4 (2000) 472–81.

———. "The Talking Drums; What are They Saying about You?" *Evangelical Missions Quarterly* 37.4 (2004) 458–63.

Chou, Ivy. "Southeast Asia Graduate School of Theology: Advanced Theological Study in Context." *Theological Education* 9.4 (1973) 273–78.

Chowning, Martha. *An Introduction to the Peoples and Cultures of Melanesia*. Boston: Addison-Wesley, 1973.

Clarke, Sathianathan, et al., eds. *Dalit Theology in the Twenty-First Century: Discordant Voices, Discerning Pathways*. New Delhi, India: Oxford University Press, 2010.

Cobb, Kelton. *Blackwell Guide to Theology of Popular Culture*. Blackwell Guides to Theologians. Oxford: Blackwells, 2005.

Codrington, Robert Henry. *The Melanesians: Studies in their Anthropology and Folklore.* Oxford: Clarendon, 1891.

Coe, Shoki. "In Search of Renewal in Theological Education." *Theological Education* 9.4 (1973) 233–43.

———. "Text and Context: Keynote Address at NEAATS Inauguration." *Northeast Asian Journal of Theology* 1.1 (1968) 126–31.

———. "Theological Education: A Worldwide Perspective." *Theological Education* 11.1 (1974) 5–12.

Coote, Robert, and John Stott. *Down to Earth: Studies in Christianity and Culture: The Papers of the Lausanne Consultation on Gospel and Culture.* Grand Rapids: Eerdmans, 1980.

Crocombe, Ron. *The Pacific Way: An Emerging Identity.* Suva: University of the South Pacific, 1976.

———. *The South Pacific.* Suva: University of the South Pacific, 2001.

———. "Theological Education—Challeges of the 80s." In *Fourth Assembly of the Pacific Conference of Churches (May 3–15, 1981): Background Reading Book.* Suva: Lotu Pasifika, 1981.

Crocombe, Ron, et al., eds. *The Pacific Way: Social Issues in National Development.* Suva: SPSS, 1975.

Davis, Kortright. "Third World Theological Priorities." *Scottish Journal of Theology* 40.1 (1987) 85–105.

Devasahayam, V. *Frontiers of Dalit Theology.* Madras: ISPCK, 1997.

Donovan, Vincent. *Christianity Rediscovered.* Maryknoll, NY: Orbis, 1982.

Dunn, James. *The Oral Gospel Tradition.* Grand Rapids: Eerdmans, 2013.

Dunstone, Alan S. "Rarongo Theological College: Teaching by Themes in Papua New Guinea." In *Learning in Context: The Search for Innovative Patterns in Theological Education,* 81–93. Bromley, UK: Theological Education Fund, 1973.

Dyrness, William A. *Invitation to Cross-Cultural Theology: Case Studies in Vernacular Theologies.* Grand Rapids: Zondervan, 1992.

———. *Learning about Theology from the Third World.* Grand Rapids: Zondervan, 1990.

Edonie, Ledimo. "Syncretism in the Milne Bay Province of Papua New Guinea." *Melanesian Journal of Theology* 16.2 (2000) 5–43.

Elwell, Walter A., ed. *Evangelical Dictionary of Theology.* Grand Rapids: Baker, 1984.

Enari, Sotiaka. "A Theological Approach to Samoan Understanding of Man." BDiv thesis, Pacific Theological College, 1971.

Erickson, A. "Search for Alternatives: The Training of Pastors." *Catalyst* 4.3 (1974) 53–58.

Ernst, Manfred. *Globalization and the Re-shaping of Christianity in the Pacific Islands.* Suva: Pacific Theological College, 2006.

———. *Winds of Change: Rapid Growing Religious Groups in the Pacific Islands.* Suva: Pacific Conference of Churches, 1994.

Everi, Martin. "Eco-theology and Its Application to the Pacific Context." *Pacific Journal of Theology* 2.26 (2001) 69–94.

Fa'asi, Urima. "Gospel and Culture in the Ava Ceremony." *Pacific Journal of Theology* 2.10 (1993) 61–63.

Fabella, Virginia, and Mercy Oduyoye. *With Passion and Compassion: Third World Women Doing Theology. Reflections from the Women's Commission of the Ecumenical Association of Third World Theologians.* Maryknoll, NY: Orbis, 1988

Fabella, Virginia, and Rasiah Sugirtharajah, eds. *Dictionary of Third World Theologies.* Maryknoll, NY: Orbis, 2000.

Ferme, Deane. *Third World Liberation Theologies: A Reader.* Maryknoll, NY: Orbis, 1986.

Finau, Patelisio. "Confessing Jesus Christ in the Pacific Today." *Pacific Journal of Theology* 2.11 (1994) 69–72.

———. "Prayer, Persuasion, and Politics." In *The Pacific Way*, edited by Ron Crocombe, et al., 166–67. Suva: South Pacific Social Sciences Association, 1975.

Flemming, Dean. *Contextualization in the New Testament: Patterns for Theology and Mission.* Downers Grove, IL: InterVarsity, 2005.

Forman, Charles. "Finding Our Own Voice: The Reinterpreting of Christianity by Oceanic Theologians." *International Bulletin of Missionary Research* 29.3 (2005) 115–22.

———. *The Island Churches of the South Pacific: Emergence in the Twentieth Century.* Maryknoll, NY: Orbis, 1982.

———. "The Pacific Conference of Churches Looks at Theological Education, May 1981." Unpublished report. Yale Divinity School Library, New Haven, CT.

———. "Theological Education in the South Pacific Islands: A Quiet Revolution." *Journal de la Société des Océanistes* 25 (1969) 151–67.

———. *The Voice of Many Waters: The Life and Ministry of the Pacific Conference of Churches in the Last Twenty-Five Years.* Suva: Lotu Pasifika, 1986.

Fountain, Jenny. "Literacy and Establishing Churches in Melanesia." *Melanesian Journal of Theology* 14.1 (1998) 5–56

Frei, Hans W. *Types of Christian Theology.* New Haven: Yale, 1992.

Freire, Paulo. *Education for Critical Consciousness.* New York: Seabury, 1973.

———. *Pedagogy of Freedom: Ethics, Democracy, and Civic Courage.* Lanham, MD: Rowman & Littlefield, 1998.

———. *Pedagogy of the Oppressed.* Translated by Myra Bergman Ramos. New York: Continuum, 1970.

Freire, Paulo, and Ira Shor. *A Pedagogy for Liberation: Dialogues on Transforming Education.* Westport, CT: Greenwood Group, 1987.

Fugmann, Gernot, ed. *The Birth of an Indigenous Church.* Point 10. Goroka, PNG: Melanesian Institute, 1986.

———. "Melanesische Theologie." In *Papua–Neueguinea Gesellschaft und Kirche: Ein Oekumenisches Handbuch*, edited by H. Wagner, et al., 229–46. Neuendettelsau/Erlangen: Friemund-Verlag, 1989.

Fugui, Leslie, and Cliff Wright, eds. *Christ in South Pacific Cultures.* Suva: Lotu Pasifika, 1986.

Gaqurae, Joe. "Indigenization as Incarnation—The Concept of a Melanesian Christ." *Point* 1 (1977) 145–52.

———. "Indigenization as Incarnation—The Concept of a Melanesian Christ." *Point* 8 (1985) 207–17.

Gardner, Helen. "Praying for Independence: The Presbyterian Church in the Decolonisation of Vanuatu." *The Journal of Pacific History* 48.2 (2013) 122–43.

Gaudi, Haraka. "One Gospel: Globalization and Pacific Regional Theology." *Pacific Journal of Theology* 2.17 (1997) 54–64.

Germon, C. H. "What Can the Pacific Contribute to Theology?" *Pacific Journal of Theology* 1.7 (1963) 5–7.

Gibbs, Philip. "Conference Report: Doing Theology in Oceania: Partners in Conversation." *Melanesian Journal of Theology* 12.2 (1996) 62–66.

———. "Grass Roots in Paradise: Contextual Theology for Papua New Guinea." *Melanesian Journal of Theology* 21.1 (2005) 37–55.

———. *The Word in the Third World. Divine Revelation in the Theology of Jean–Marc Ela, Aloysius Pieris, and Gustavo Gutierrez*. Rome, Italy: Pontifica Uneversita Gregoriana Roma, 1996.

Gilliand, Dean S. *The Word Among Us: Contexutalizing Theology for Mission Today*. Dallas, TX: Word, 1989.

Gittins, Anthony J. *Gifts and Strangers: Meeting the Challenge of Inculturation*. New York: Paulist, 1989.

———. "Kiribatizing Christianity: A Local Church Rediscovers Itself." *Mission Studies* 16.2 (1999) 71–99.

Gold, Jennifer. "Pacific Churches Urged to Bring 'Coconut Theology' to Global Platform." Press Release. September 6, 2007.

Graham, Elaine, et al. *Theological Reflection: Methods*. London: SCM, 2005.

Grenz, Stanley, and Roger Olson. *Twentieth-Century Theology: God and the World in a Transitional Age*. Downers Grove, IL: InterVarsity, 2006.

Gunn, Bill. *The Gospel in Futuna: With Chapters on the Islands of the New Hebrides, the People, Their Customs, Religious Beliefs, etc*. London: Hodder and Stoughton, 1914.

Gutierrez, Gustavo. *A Theology of Liberation: History, Politics, and Salvation*. London: SCM, 1979.

Hagesi, Robert. "Towards a Melanesian Christian Theology." *Melanesian Journal of Theology* 1.1 (1985) 17–24.

Haire, James. "Visions of the Spirit for the Church in the Great Southern Land." *Asia Journal of Theology* 6.2 (1992) 250–62.

Halapua, Winston. "Fakakakato: Symbols in a Pacific Context." *Pacific Journal of Theology* 2.20 (1998) 21–32.

———. "HIV/AIDS in the Pacific and the Injustice of Past and Current Theological Approaches." *Pacific Journal of Theology* 2.36 (2006) 46–55.

Hall, Douglas John. *The End of Christendom and the Future of Christianity*. Christian Mission and Modern Culture. Pasadena, CA: Trinity International, 1996.

Hannan, Larry. "From the SPATS President." *Pacific Journal of Theology* 2.2 (1989) 2–3.

Hanson, Doug. "Editorial Policy." *Melanesian Journal of Theology* 30.1 (2014) 2.

———. "Twenty–Four Years of the Melanesian Journal of Theology." *Melanesian Journal of Theology* 24.1 (2008) 89–95.

Harrison, Thomas Harnett. *Savage Civilization*. London: Gollancz, 1937.

Hassall, Graham. "Religion and Nation-State Formation in Melanesia: 1945 to Independence." PhD diss., ANU, 1989.

Havea, Jione. "The Cons of Contextuality . . . Kontextuality." In *Contextual Theology for the Twenty-First Century*, edited by Stephen Bevans and Katalina Tahaafe–Williams, 38–52. Cambridge, UK: James Clarke, 2012.

———. "The Politics of Climate Change: A Talanoa from Oceania." *International Journal of Public Theology* 4.3 (2010) 345–55.

Havea, Salesi. "Theological Education in the Pacific in the 1980s." In *Fourth Assembly of the Pacific Conference of Churches (May 3–15, 1981): Background Reading Book*, 62–66. Suva: Lotu Pasifika, 1981.

Havea, Sione 'Amanaki. "Christianity in the Pacific Context." In *South Pacific Theology: Papers from the Consultation on Pacific Theology, Papua New Guinea, January 1986*, edited by John D'Arcy May, 11–15. Oxford: Regnum, 1987.

———. "Church Unity in Diversity in the Pacific." In *Fourth Assembly of the Pacific Conference of Churches (May 3–15, 1981): Background Reading Book*, 67–71. Suva: Lotu Pasifika, 1981.

———. "Pacific Theology." In *Towards A Relevant Pacific Theology: The Role of the Churches and Theological Education: A Report of a Theological Consultation held in Bergengren House, Suva, Fiji, 8–12 July, 1985*, 21–4. Suva: Lotu Pasifika, 1985.

———. "The Quest for a Pacific Church." *Pacific Journal of Theology* 2.6 (1991) 9–10.

———. "A Reconsideration of Pacificness in a Search for a South Pacific Theology." *The Pacific Journal of Theology* 2.10 (1993) 5–16.

Herda, Phyllis, et al. *Vision and Reality in Pacific Religion: Essays in Honor of Niel Gunson*. Canberra: Pandanus, 2005.

Herenik, Vilsoni. "Representations of Cultural Identities." In *Tides of History: The Pacific Islands in the Twentieth Century*, edited by K. R. Howe, et al., 406–34. Hawaii: University of Hawaii Press, 1994.

Hesselgrave, David J. *Communicating Christ Cross-Culturally: An Introduction to Missionary Communication*. Grand Rapids: Zondervan, 1991.

Hiebert, Paul. "Critical Contextualization." *International Bulletin of Missionary Research* 11.3 (1987) 104–12.

———. "Sociocultural Theories and Mission to the West." In *Evangelical, Ecumenical, and Anabaptist Missiologies in Conversation: Essays in Honor of Wilbert R. Shenk*, edited by James Krabill, et al., 169–76. Maryknoll, NY: Orbis, 2006.

Hoiore, Joel. "Elements of an Ethic of Pacific Oceanic Theologizing." *Pacific Journal of Theology* 2.13 (1995) 49–59.

Hooper, Anthony, et al., eds. *Class and Culture in the South Pacific*. Suva: Institute for Pacific Studies, 1987.

Hovey, Kevin. *Before All Else Fails, Read the Instructions: Manual for Cross-Cultural Christians*. Brisbane: Harvest, 1986.

Howe, K. R., et al., eds. *Tides of History: The Pacific Islands in the Twentieth Century*. Hawaii: University of Hawaii Press, 1994.

Hughes, Philip. "The Impact of Recent Immigration on Religious Groups in Australia." *Pointers: Bulletin of the Christian Research Association* 22.4 (2012) 1.

Hunsberger, George R. "The Newbigin Gauntlet: Developing a Domestic Missiology for North America." *Missiology: An International Review* 19.4 (1991) 391–408.

Hwang, Chang Hui. "A Rethinking of Theological Training For the Ministry in the Younger Churches Today." *South East Asia Journal of Theology* 4.2 (1962) 7–24.

Idusulia, Penuel Ben. "Biblical Sacrifice Through Melanesian Eyes." *Point* 8 (1985) 256–303.

Inglis, John. *Bible Illustrations from the New Hebrides: With Notices of the Progress of the Mission*. London: Thomas Nelson, 1890.

———. *A Dictionary of the Aneityumese Language*. London: Williams & Norgate, 1882.

———. *In the New Hebrides: Reminiscences of Missionary Life and Work, Especially on the Island of Aneityum, from 1850 till 1877*. London: Thomas Nelson, 1887.

International Missionary Council. "Beyond the Reef: Records of the Conference of Churches and Missions in the Pacific." Paper presented at the International Missionary Council, Apia, West Samoa, April 22–May 4, 1961.

Irwin, J. "Towards a Maori Theology." *Colloquium* 16.1 (1983) 13–22.

Jenkins, Philip. *The New Faces of Christianity: Believing the Bible in the Global South*. Oxford: Oxford University Press, 2006.

———. *The Next Christendom: The Coming of Global Christianity*. Oxford: Oxford University Press, 2011.

John Paul II. *Post-synodal Apostolic Exhortation, Ecclesia in Oceania*. Rome: Libreria Editrice Vaticana, 2001.

Johnson, J. Boyd, ed. *South Pacific Theology: Papers from the Consultation on Pacific Theology, Papua New Guinea, January 1986*. Oxford: Regnum, 1987.

Johnson, Todd, and Kenneth Ross. *Atlas of Global Christianity*. Edinburgh: Edinburgh University Press, 2009.

Johnson-Hill, Lydia. "Beyond the Story: A Possible Future for Pacific Narrative Theology." *Pacific Journal of Theology* 2.7 (1992) 45–48.

———. "Editorial." *Pacific Journal of Theology* 2.8 (1992) 1–2.

———. "Editorial." *Pacific Journal of Theology* 2.10 (1993) 1–3.

———. "Towards a Theology of Dance in Christian Worship." *Pacific Journal of Theology* 2.9 (1993) 53–66.

Johnson-Hill, Lydia, and Joan Filemoni-Tofaeono, eds. *Weavings: Women Doing Theology in Oceania*. Suva: Weavers, SPATS, 2003.

Kadiba, John. "In Search of a Melanesian Theology." In *The Gospel is Not Western*, edited by Garry Trompf, 139–47. Maryknoll, NY: Orbis, 1987.

Kamu, Lalomilo. *The Samoan Culture and the Christian Gospel*. Suva: Donna Lou Kamu, 1996.

Kanongata'a, Keiti Ann. "Domestic Theology." *Pacific Journal of Theology* 2.15 (1996) 73–75.

———. "A Pacific Woman's Theology of Birthing and Liberation." *Pacific Journal of Theology* 2.7 (1992) 3–11.

———. "Pacific Women and Theology." *Pacific Journal of Theology* 2.13 (1995) 17–33.

———. "Why Contextual?" *Pacific Journal of Theology* 2.27 (2002) 21–40.

Kanyoro, Musimbi. "African Women's Quest for Justice: A Review of African Women's Theology: Address Given at the Second Weavers' Consultation on 'Women's Theology: Pacific Perspectives,' November 1995." *Pacific Journal of Theology* 2.15 (1996) 77–88.

Karie, Ann. "Leadership of Women in the Vanuatu Church." In *Foundations: Papers from the 'Women in Leadership' Conference held in Melbourne in 2011*, edited by Randall Prior, 117–32. Vol 1. of *Vanuatu Women in Leadership*. Melbourne: Gospel Vanuatu, 2015.

Kato, Byang. "The Gospel, Cultural Context, and Religious Syncretism." In *Let the Earth Hear His Voice*, edited by J. D. Douglas, 1216–23. Minneapolis: Worldwide, 1975.

Keesing, Roger M. "Creating the Past: Custom and Identity in the Contemporary Pacific." *Contemporary Pacific* 1 (1989) 19–42.

Ker, John M., and Kevin Sharpe. *Toward an Authentic New Zealand Theology*. Auckland, NZ: University of Auckland, 1984.

Keysser, Christian. *A People Reborn*. Translated by Alfred Allin and John Kuder. Pasadena, CA: William Carey, 1980.

Kiki, Gwayaweng, and Ed Parker. "Is There a Better Way to Teach Theology to Non-Western Persons? Research from Papua New Guinea that Could Benefit the Wider Pacific." *Australian e-Journal of Theology* 21.2 (2014) 108–24.

Kinsler, Ross. "Extension: An Alternative Model for Theological Education." In *Learning in Context: The Search for Innovative Patterns in Theological Education*, 27–49. Bromley, UK: Theological Education Fund, 1973.

———. "Relevance and Importance of TEF/PTE/ETE: Vignettes from the Past and Possibilities for the Future." Geneva: World Council of Churches, 2008.

Kirk, Andrew J. *Theology and the Third World Church*. Nottingham: InterVarsity, 1983.

Klem, Herbert. *Oral Communication of the Scripture: Insights from African Oral Art*. Pasadena, CA: William Carey, 1981.

Koria, Paulo. "Moving Towards a Pacific Theology: Theologizing with Concepts." *Pacific Journal of Theology* 2.22 (1999) 3–14.

Koyama, Kosuke. "Theological Education: Its Unities and Diversities." *Theological Education* 30.1 (1993) 87–105.

Krabill, James, et al., eds. *Evangelical, Ecumenical, and Anabaptist Missiologies in Conversation: Essays in Honor of Wilbert R. Shenk*. Maryknoll, NY: Orbis, 2006.

Kraft, Charles H. "The Contextualization of Theology." *Evangelical Missions Quarterly* 14.1 (1978) 31–36.

Küster, Volker. *A Protestant Theology of Passion: Korean Minjung Theology Revisited*. Vol. 4. Leiden: Brill, 2010.

Kyung, Chung Hyun. *Struggle To Be The Sun Again: Introducing Asian Women's Theology*. Maryknoll, NY: Orbis, 1990.

Lane, C. "The Breath of God: A Primer in Pacific/Asian theology." *Mission Studies* 8.1 (1991) 49–56.

Lange, Raeburn T. *Island Ministers: Indigenous Leadership in Nineteenth-Century Pacific Islands Christianity*. Canberra: Pandanus, 2005.

Lange, Raeburn T., et al., eds. "Towards a Relevant Pacific Theology: The Role of the Churches and Theological Education. A Report of a Theological Consultation held in Bergengren House, Suva, Fiji, 8–12 July, 1985." Suva: Lotu Pasifika, 1986.

Larkin, William J. *Culture and Biblical Hermeneutics*. Lanham: University Press of America, 1993.

Latourette, Kenneth Scott. *A History of the Expansion of Christianity*. 7 vols. London: Eyre and Spottiswoode, 1945.

Lee, Deborah, and Antonio Salos, eds. *Unfaithing US Colonialism*. Berkeley, CA: Pacific and Asian American Center for Theological Strategies: Dharma Cloud, 1999.

Lehmann, Paul. "On Doing Theology: A Contextual Possibility." In *Prospect for Theology: Essays in Honor of H. H. Farmer*, edited by Francis Healey, 117–36. Hertfordshire: Nisbet, 1966.

Lienemann–Perrin, Christine. *Training for a Relevant Ministry: A Study of the Work of the Theological Education Fund*. Madras, India: Christian Literature Society, 1981.

Lindbeck, George A. *The Nature of Doctrine: Religion and Theology in a Postliberal Age*. Westminster John Knox, 1984.

Lini, Walter. *Beyond Pandemonium: From the New Hebrides to Vanuatu*. Wellington, NZ: Asia Pacific, 1980.

———. "Christians in Politics." In *The Gospel is Not Western: Black Theologies from the Southwest Pacific*, edited by Garry Trompf, 183–85. Maryknoll, NY: Orbis, 1987.

———. "Should the Church Play Politics?" In *The Pacific Way: An Emerging Identity*, edited by Ron Crocombe 176–79. Suva: Lotu Pasifika, 1976.

Lokotui, Finau. "Theological Reflection on Gospel and Culture in the Pacific." In *The Cross and the Tanoa: Gospel and Culture in the Pacific*, edited by Russell Chandran, 34–38. Suva: South Pacific Association of Theological Schools, 1988.

Lomaloma, Sereima. "Women in Ordained Ministry." *Pacific Journal of Theology* 2.15 (1996) 49–52.

Lonergan, Bernard. *Method in Theology*. Canada: University of Toronto Press, 1990.

Lossky, Nicolas. *Dictionary of the Ecumenical Movement*. Geneva: World Council of Churches, 1991.

Luzbetak, Louis J. *Church and Cultures: New Perspectives in Missiological Anthropology*. Maryknoll, NY: Orbis, 2002.

MacDonald, Mary. "Melanesian Communities: Past and Present." In *An Introduction to Melanesian Cultures: A Handbook for Church Workers*, edited by Darrell Whiteman, 213–30. Goroka, Papua New Guinea: Melanesian Institute, 1984.

Madinger, Charles. "Coming to Terms with Orality: A Holistic Model." *Missiology: An International Review* 38.2 (2010) 201–13.

———. "A Literate's Guide to the Oral Galaxy." *Orality—The Journal of the International Orality Network* 2.2 (2013) 13–40.

Mafaufau, Kiliona. "Pacific Time and the Times: A Theological Reflection." *Pacific Journal of Theology* 2.6 (1991) 22–29.

Mantovani, Ennio. "Traditional Values and Ethics." In *An Introduction to Melanesian Cultures: A Handbook for Church Workers*, edited by D. L. Whiteman, 195–212. Goroka, Papua New Guinea: Melanesian Institute, 1984.

Manuao, Philip. "Communicating the Gospel in Meaningful Cultural Forms in Melanesia." *Melanesian Journal of Theology* 16.1 (2000) 57–91.

Matheny, Paul. *Contextual Theology: The Drama of Our Times*. Cambridge, UK: James Clarke, 2011.

May, John D'Arcy. "Editorial." *Melanesian Journal of Theology* 1.1 (1985) 1–3.

———, ed. *Living theology in Melanesia: A Reader*. Point Series 8. Goroka, Papua New Guinea: Melanesian Institute, 1985.

Mbiti, John S. *Bible and Theology in African Christianity*. Nairobi: Oxford University Press, 1986.

———. "Cattle are Born with Ears, Their Horns Grow Later: Towards an Appreciation of African Oral Theology." *Africa Theological Journal* 8.1 (1979) 15–25.

McIntyre, Roy. "Using Ceremonies to Disciple Oral Learners Among the Tribal People in Bangladesh." Phd Diss., Asbury Theological Seminary, 2005.

Melanesian Institute. "Melanesian Institute IPG." https://www.mi.org.pg/

Meleisea, Malama. "Ideology in Pacific Studies: A Personal View." In *Class and Culture in the South Pacific*, edited by Antony Hooper, et al., 140–53. Suva: Institute for Pacific Studies, 1987.

Meo, Jovili. *Developing a Liberation Education Model for the Methodist Theological College in the Fiji Islands*. Nashville, TN: George Peabody College, Vanderbilt University, 1989.

———. "Ecumenical Association of Third World Theologians." *Pacific Journal of Theology* 2.13 (1995) 1–3.

———. "How Do We Do Contextual Theology?" *Pacific Journal of Theology* 2.27 (2002) 41–60.

———. "An Introduction to the Second Consultation on the Quest for a Pacific Theology—EATWOT Pacific Chapter." *Pacific Journal of Theology* 2.17 (1997) 2–6.

———. "Pioneering New Perspectives in Pacific Theology." *Pacific Journal of Theology* 2.15 (1996) 13–15.

———. "Smallness and Solidarity." *Pacific Journal of Theology* 2.6 (1991) 91–95.

Meo, Lisa. "Advocacy for the Theological Education of Women." *Pacific Journal of Theology* 2.15 (1996) 45–46.

———. "Weaving Women and Theology." *Pacific Journal of Theology* 2.15 (1996) 11–12.

Miller, J. Graham. *Live: A History of Church Planting in the New Hebrides.* Vols. 1–2. Sydney: Committees on Christian Education and Overseas Missions, General Assembly of the Presbyterian Church of Australia, 1978–1981.

———. *Live: A History of Church Planting in the Republic of Vanuatu.* Vols. 3–7. Port Vila, Vanuatu: Presbyterian Church of Vanuatu, 1985–1990.

Miller, Robert. *Misi Gete: John Geddie Pioneer Missionary to the New Hebrides.* Launceston, Tasmania: Presbyterian Church of Tasmania, 1975.

Miria, Peter. "Christian Faith in Melanesia." *Melanesian Journal of Theology* 1.1 (1985) 14–16.

Moon, W. Jay. *African Proverbs Reveal Christianity in Culture: A Narrative Portrayal of Builsa Proverbs Contextualizing Christianity in Ghana.* American Society of Missiology Monograph Series. Eugene, OR: Pickwick, 2009.

———. "Builsa Proverbs and the Gospel." *Missiology* 30 (2002) 171–86.

———. "Should We Drum or Listen to the Teng Nyono?" *Missiology* 32 (2004) 203–15.

———. *Using Proverbs to Contextualize Christianity in the Builsa Culture of Ghana, West Africa.* Eugene, OR: Wipf & Stock, 2009.

Mott, John R. *The Evangelization of the World in this Generation.* New York: Student Volunteer Movement, 1905.

Mueller, Karl, et al., eds. *Dictionary of Mission: Theology, History, Perspectives.* Maryknoll, NY: Orbis, 1997.

Mullins, David. *Bishop Patelisio Finau of Tonga: He Spoke the Truth in Love: A Selection of His Writings and Speeches.* Auckland, NZ: Catholic Centre, 1994.

Muonwe, Michael. *The Dialectics of Faith-Culture Integration: Interculturation or Syncretism.* Indiana: Xlibris, 2014.

Naidoo, Marilyn. "Ministerial Training: The Need for Pedagogies of Formation and of Contextualization in Theological Education." *Missionalia: Southern African Journal of Mission Studies* 38.3 (2010) 347–68.

Naioca, Masulame. "The Danger of Losing the New Testament Pattern of Simple Lifestyle." In *South Pacific Theology,* edited by R. Boyd Johnson, 61–81. Oxford: Regnum, 1986.

Nemer, Lawrence. "Catholic Mission in Oceania and the Pacific 1910-2010." In *A Century of Catholic Mission,* edited by Stephen Bevans, 67–74. Regnum Edinburgh Centenary Series. Oxford: Regnum, 2013.

Newbigin, Lesslie. "Can the West be Converted?" *International Bulletin of Missionary Research* 11.1 (1987) 2–7.

———. *Foolishness to the Greeks: The Gospel and Western Culture.* Grand Rapids: Eerdmans, 1986.

———. *The Gospel in a Pluralist Society.* Grand Rapids: Eerdmans, 1989.

Nida, Eugene. *Message and Mission: The Communication of the Christian Faith.* New York: Harper and Brothers, 1960.

———. *Religion Across Culture.* Pasadena, CA: William Carey, 1968.

Nokise, Feleretika, and Holger Szesnat, eds. *Oceanic Voyages in Theology and Theological Education: Reflections and Reminiscences in Celebration of the Fiftieth Anniversary of the Pacific Theological College.* Suva: Pacific Theological College, 2015.

Oduyoye, Mercy Amba. "Contextualization as a Dynamic in Theological Education: Paper Delivered at the Meeting of The Association of Theological Schools in Pittsburgh, PA, June 1992." *Theological Education* 30.1 (1993) 107–20.

Olson, David R., and Nancy Torrance, eds. *Literacy and Orality.* New York: Cambridge University Press, 1991.

Ong, Walter J. *Orality and Literacy.* Padstow, Cornwall: T. J. Ltd., 1982.

Ormerod, Neil. *Introducing Contemporary Theologies: The What and the Who of Theology Today.* Newtown: Dwyer, 1990.

Otto, Ton, and Ad Borsboom. *Cultural Dynamics of Religious Change in Oceania.* Netherlands: Brill Academic, 1997.

Pacific Conference of Churches. *Beyond the Reef: Records of the Conference of Churches and Missions in the Pacific, Apia, Samoa. April 22–May 4, 1961.* London: IMC, 1961.

———. "Final Resolutions of the 10th Assembly of the Pacific Conference of Churches: 10th General Assembly, Honiara, March 2013." *Islands Business*, March 11, 2013. http//www.islandsbusiness.com/latestnews.

———. *Fourth Assembly of the Pacific Conference of Churches (May 3–15, 1981): Background Reading Book.* Suva: Lotu Pasifika, 1981.

———. *Report of the 2nd Assembly: Davuilevu, Fiji, May 1–14, 1971.* Suva: Pacific Conference of Churches, 1971.

———. *Report of the 3rd Assembly: University of Papua New Guinea, Port Moresby, January 10–21, 1976.* Suva: Pacific Conference of Churches, 1976.

———. *Report of the 4th Assembly: Nuku'alofa, Tonga, May 3–15, 1981.* Suva: Lotu Pasifika, 1981.

———. *Report of the 5th Assembly: Apia, W. Samoa, September 14–24, 1986.* Suva: Lotu Pasifika, 1986.

———. *Report of the 6th Assembly: Mele Village, Efate, Vanuatu, August 26–September 4, 1991.* Suva: Lotu Pasifika, 1991.

———. *Report of the 7th Assembly: Arue, Mahoi, Nuie, March 3–14, 1997.* Suva: Lotu Pasifika, 1997.

———. *Report of the South Pacific Consultation on Theological Education: Papauta, Samoa, January 10–17, 1978.* Suva: Pacific Conference of Churches, 1978.

———. *Towards a Relevant Pacific Theology: The Role of the Churches and Theological Education.* A Report of a Theological Consultation held in Bergengren House, Suva, Fiji. 8–12 July, 1985. Suva, Fiji : Lotu Pasifika, 1986.

Palu, Ma'afu'a Tu'itonga. "Dr. Sione 'Amanaki Havea of Tonga: the Architect of Pacific Theology." *Melanesian Journal of Theology* 28.2 (2012) 67–81.

———. "On Pacific Theology." *Pacific Journal of Theology* 2.28 (2002) 21–53.

———. "On Pacific Theology—A Reconsideration of its Methodology." *Pacific Journal of Theology* 2.29 (2003) 30–58.

Panikkar, Kavalam Madhava. *Asia and Western Dominance.* 2nd ed. London: Allen & Unwin, 1959.

Parratt, John, ed. *An Introduction to Third World Theologies*. Cambridge: Cambridge University Press, 2004.

Paschke, Jon. "The Small Group as a Learning Environment for Teaching Melanesian Christians: Issues for the Cross-Cultural Facilitator." *Melanesian Journal of Theology* 20.2 (2004) 54–78.

Paton, James, ed. *John G. Paton: Missionary to the New Hebrides: An Autobiography*. 2 Vols. London: Hodder and Stoughton, 1889.

Paton, Margaret Whitecross. *Letters and Sketches from the New Hebrides*. London: Hodder and Stoughton, 1894.

Patterson, George. *Missionary Life among the Cannibals: Being the Life of the Rev. John Geddie, DD, First Missionary to the New Hebrides*. Toronto: Campbell and Son, 1882.

Pears, Angie. *Doing Contextual Theology*. Abingdon: Routledge, 2010.

Pearson, Clive, ed. "Doing Theology in Oceania: Partners in Conversation." Paper presented at the Oceania conference, Dunedin, New Zealand, 1996.

Pech, Rufus. "The Name of God in Melanesia." *Melanesian Journal of Theology* 1.1 (1985) 30–46.

Perelini, Otele. "The Emancipation of Church Women." *Pacific Journal of Theology* 2.22 (1999) 15–18.

———. "Gospel and Culture: Biblical Perspectives." In *The Cross and the Tanoa: Gospel and Culture in the Pacific*, edited by Russell Chandran, 33–40. Suva: SPATS, 1988.

Philip, T. V. *Edinburgh to Salvador: Twentieth-Century Ecumenical Missiology: A Historical Study of the Ecumenical Discussions on Mission*. Delhi, India: CSS & ISPCK, 1999.

Plueddemann, James E. "Culture, Learning, and Missionary training." In *Internationalising Missionary Training*, edited by W. D. Taylor, 217–30. Exeter: Paternoster, 1991.

Pobee, John. "Oral Theology and Christian Oral Tradition: Challenge to our Traditional Archival Concept." *Mission Studies* 6.1 (1989) 87–93.

Pouesi, Victor. "Contextualizing Eucharist." *Pacific Journal of Theology* 2.6 (1991) 34.

Pratt, John. "Traditional and Christian Understanding of God in the Pacific." In *Christ in South Pacific Cultures*, edited by Cliff Fufui Wright and Leslie Fufui Wright. Suva: Lotu Pasifika, 1985.

Presbyterian Church of Vanuatu. *Development*. Vol. 2 of *Vanuatu Women in Leadership*. Melbourne: Gospel Vanuatu, 2018.

———. *Foundations: Papers from the "Women in Leadership" Conference held in Melbourne in 2011*. Vol. 1 of *Vanuatu Women in Leadership*. Melbourne: Gospel Vanuatu, 2015.

Prior, Randall, ed. *25 Tingting: Reflections on 25 Years of Independence in Vanuatu: A Project of the Presbyterian Church of Vanuatu*. Melbourne: Gospel Vanuatu, 2010.

———. "Book Review: 'Globalization and the Re-shaping of Christianity in the Pacific Islands.'" *International Bulletin of Missionary Research* 31.2 (2007) 104–5.

———, ed. *Contemporary Local Perspectives*. Vol. 2 of *Gospel and Culture in Vanuatu*. Melbourne: Gospel Vanuatu, 2001.

———. *Diary: Cultural and Church Life 1983–1987*. Unpublished. Personal Library, Melbourne, Australia.

———. *Diary 1: January 29, 1983–March 18, 1984*. Unpublished. Personal Library, Melbourne, Australia.

————. *Diary 2: March 19, 1984–April 13, 1985.* Unpublished. Personal Library, Melbourne, Australia.

————. *Diary 3: April 14, 1985–August 24, 1986.* Unpublished. Personal Library, Melbourne, Australia.

————. *Diary 4: August 25, 1986–September 21, 1987.* Unpublished. Personal Library, Melbourne, Australia.

————, ed. *Foundations: Papers from the "Women in Leadership" Conference held in Melbourne in 2011.* Vol. 1 of *Vanuatu Women in Leadership.* Melbourne: Gospel Vanuatu, 2015.

————. *The Founding Missionary and a Missionary for Today.* Vol. 1 of *Gospel and Culture in Vanuatu.* Melbourne: Gospel Vanuatu, 1998.

————. *The Gospel and Cultures: Initial Explorations in the Australian Context.* Melbourne: Victorian Council of Churches, 1997.

————. "I am the Coconut of Life: An Evaluation of Coconut Theology." *Pacific Journal of Theology* 2.10 (1993) 31–40.

————. "Introduction to Gospel and Culture: Memorial Lecture delivered on the eleventh anniversary of the founding of the Talua Ministry Training Centre, 9 August 1999." In *Gospel and Culture in Vanuatu 2: Contemporary Local Perspectives,* edited by Randall Prior, 141–46. Melbourne: Gospel Vanuatu, 2001.

————. "John Paver in the South Pacific: Theological Reflection in the Context of Vanuatu." In *Together in Ministry: Essays to Honor John Paver,* edited by Heather Cameron, et al., 127–39. Melbourne: Uniting Academic, 2009.

————, ed. *Local Voices on Jesus Christ and Mission.* Vol. 4 of *Gospel and Culture in Vanuatu.* Adelaide: ATF, 2006.

————. "The Relationship between Gospel and Culture: A Missiological Critique of the Historical Meeting of the Christian Gospel with the Cultures of the Peoples of Aneityum in Vanuatu, through the Missionary Work of the Rev. John Geddie." MA thesis, Melbourne College of Divinity, 1992.

————, ed. *The Voice of the Local Church.* Vol. 3 of *Gospel and Culture in Vanuatu.* Melbourne: Gospel Vanuatu, 2003.

————. "What is the Future for Our Church?" In *Creating a Welcoming Space: Reflections on Church and Mission,* edited by Ross Fishburn, 193–216. Melbourne: Morning Star, 2014.

————, ed. *Women in Culture and Church and Other Issues.* Vol. 5 of *Gospel and Culture in Vanuatu.* Adelaide: ATF, 2006.————. "Orality: The Not-So-Silent Issue in Mission Theology." *International Bulletin of Missionary Research* 35.3 (2011) 143–47.

————. "World Council of Churches Study Process on Gospel and Cultures: A Series of Six Studies by The Presbyterian Church of Vanuatu and the Talua Ministry Training Center, August 1–4, 1995." Vila, Vanuatu: Presbyterian Church of Vanuatu.

Puloka, Tevita Mohenoa. "An Attempt at Contexualizing Theology for the Tongan Church." In *South Pacific Theology: Papers from the Consultation on Pacific Theology, Papua New Guinea, January 1986,* 82–100. Oxford: Regnum, 1986.

————. "Evangelization: Culture and Communication." *Pacific Journal of Theology* Series 2.19 (1998) 42–54.

Rajkumar, Peniel. *Dalit Theology and Dalit Liberation: Problems, Paradigms, and Possibilities.* Surrey: Ashgate, 2010.

Rakau, Fiama. "Wholeness of Life." In *The Cross and the Tanoa: Gospel and Culture in the Pacific*, edited by Russell Chandran, 80–98. Suva: SPATS, 1988.

Ratuvile, Sitiveni. *Spiritual Bases for Rural Development in the Pacific*. Suva: Lotu Pasifika, 1979.

Ratzinger, Joseph, and Marcello Pera. *Without Roots: The West, Relativism, Christianity, Islam*. New York: Basic, 2007.

Rayawa, Josaia. "Pacific Theology." In *South Pacific Theology: Papers from the Consultation on Pacific Theology, Papua New Guinea, January 1986*, edited by R. Boyd Johnson, 16–41. Oxford: Regnum, 1986.

Regenvanu, Sethy John. *Laef Blong Mi: From Village to Nation: An Autobiography*. Suva: Institute of Pacific Studies, USP, 2004.

Reudi–Weber, Hans. "The Bible and Oral Tradition." *Pacific Journal of Theology* 2.2 (1989) 4–13.

Riecke, Kurt. "Why are Changes so Difficult to Make?" *Catalyst* 23 (1993) 17–38.

Robert, Dana L. *Christian Mission: How Christianity Became a World Religion*. New York: Wiley & Sons, 2009.

———. "The Origin of the Student Volunteer Watchword: The Evangelization of the World in this Generation." *International Bulletin of Missionary Research* 10.4 (1986) 146–49.

Robertson, Hugh A., and John Fraser. *Erromanga, The Martyr Isle*. New York: A. C. Armstrong, 1902.

Ropeti, Marie. "Women's Theology—Pacific Perspectives." In *Women's Visions: Theological Reflection, Celebration, Action*, edited by Ofelia Ortega–Nontoya, 172–76. Geneva: World Council of Churches, 1995.

Ross, Cathy. "'Often, Often, Often Goes the Christ in the Stranger's Guise': Hospitality as a Hallmark of Christian Ministry." *International Bulletin of Missionary Research* 39.4 (2015) 176–79.

Rounds-Ganilau, Bernadette. "An Assembly in Tahiti." *Pacific Journal of Theology* 2.17 (1997) 111–15.

Rynkiewich, Michael. "Mission, Hermeneutics, and the Local Church." *The Journal of Theological Interpretation* 1.1 (2007) 47–60.

Rzepkowski, Horst. "Stepping Stones to a Pacific Theology." *Mission Studies: Journal of the International Association of Mission Studies* 9.17 (1992) 40–61.

Sala, Ulisese. "An Attempt to do Pacific Theology." *Pacific Journal of Theology* 2.16 (1996) 7–13.

Sample, Tex, et al., eds. *Ministry in an Oral Culture: Living with Will Rogers*. New Haven: Yale University Press, 1994.

Sanneh, Lamin. *Disciples of All Nations: Pillars of World Christianity*. Oxford: Oxford University Press, 2007.

———. *Translating the Message: The Missionary Impact on Culture*. Maryknoll, NY: Orbis, 2002.

———. *West African Christianity: The Religious Impact*. Maryknoll, NY: Orbis, 2002.

———. *Whose Religion is Christianity? The Gospel Beyond the West*. Grand Rapids: Eerdmans, 2003.

Sapsezian, Aharon. "Theology of Liberation—Liberation of Theology: Educational Perspectives." *Theological Education* 9.4 (1973) 254–67.

Scheer, Gary. "How to Communicate in a Relational Culture." *Evangelical Missions Quarterly* 31.4 (1995) 470–75.

Schiller, Greg. "Cultural Anthropology, Teaching Methodology, and Theological Education." *Melanesian Journal of Theology* 15.1 (1999) 55–72.

Schineller, Peter. *A Handbook on Inculturation*. Mahwah, NJ: Paulist, 1990.

Schreiter, Robert. *Constructing Local Theologies*. Maryknoll, NY: Orbis, 1985.

———. "Contextualization from a World Perspective." *Theological Education* 30.1 (1993) 63–86.

Schreiter, Robert, and Clemens Sedmak. *Doing Local Theology: A Guide for Artisans of a New Humanity*. Faith and Cultures. Maryknoll, NY: Orbis, 2002.

Setu, Fa'atulituli. "Christian Ministers Should be Life-Long Readers." *Pacific Journal of Theology* 2.22 (1999) 82–86.

Silas, SSF. "Solving the Problem of the Pigs—A Case Study in Local Theology." *Melanesian Journal of Theology* 8.1 (1992) 59–64.

Siwatibau, Suliana. "A Theology for Justice and Peace in the Pacific." In *The Gospel is Not Western: Black Theologies from the Southwest Pacific*, edited by Garry W. Trompf, 192–97. Maryknoll, NY: Orbis, 1987.

Siwatibau, Suliana, and David Williams. *A Call to a New Exodus: An Anti-nuclear Primer for Pacific People*. Suva: Lotu Pasifika, 1979.

Smith-Christopher, Daniel. *Text and Experience: Towards a Cultural Exegesis of the Bible*. Sheffield: Sheffield Academic, 1995.

Snijders, Jan. "Religious Studies at Tertiary Level." *Melanesian Journal of Theology* 3.2 (1987) 6–9.

Solomone, Kafoa. "One Gospel: Contextually Inclusive and/or Exclusive." *Pacific Journal of Theology* 2.17 (1997) 7–23.

Southern Baptist Convention International Mission Board. *Worldview*. Richmond, VA: 2004.

Spriggs, Matthew. "Early Coconut Remains from the South Pacific." *Journal of the Polynesian Society* 93.1 (1984) 71–76.

Stanley, Brian. *The World Missionary Conference, Edinburgh 1910*. Studies in the History of Christian Missions. Grand Rapids: Eerdmans, 2009.

Steel, Robert. *The New Hebrides and Christian Missions: With a Sketch of the Labour Traffic, and Notes of a Cruise through the Group in the Mission Vessel*. London: James Nisbet, 1880.

Strelan, John G. *Search for Salvation: Studies in the History and Theology of Cargo Cults*. Adelaide: Lutheran House, 1977.

Sugden, C., and V. Samuel. *Sharing Jesus in the Two-Thirds World*. Oxford: Regnum, 1983.

Sugirtharajah, Rasiah. *Bible and the Third World: Precolonial, Colonial, Postcolonial Encounters*. Cambridge: Cambridge University Press, 2001.

———. *Interpreting the Bible in the Third World*. London: SPCK, 1991.

———. *Postcolonial Criticism and Biblical Interpretation*. Oxford: Oxford University Press, 2002.

———. *Postcolonial Reconfigurations: An Alternative Way of Reading the Bible and Doing Theology*. London: SCM, 2003.

———. *Voices from the Margin: Interpreting the Bible in the Third World*. Rev. ed. Maryknoll, NY: Orbis, 2006.

Tabe, Burabeti. "Stewardship and Giving in the Western Solomon Islands." *Pacific Journal of Theology* 2.23 (2000) 63–67.

Talapusi, Faitala. "The Future of Theology in the Pacific." *Pacific Journal of Theology* 2.13 (1995) 39–46.

Taurakoto, Peter. *Fighting for a Proper Passport: An Autobiography.* Port Vila, Vanuatu: Sun Productions, 2015.

Taylor, John V. *The Primal Vision.* London: SCM, 1963.

Tevi, Harry. "Faith, Relevance, and Future Training for the Church's Ministry and Its Renewal." In *Fourth Assembly of the Pacific Conference of Churches (May 3–15, 1981): Background Reading Book*, 28–45. Suva: Lotu Pasifika, 1981.

Theological Education Fund Staff. *Learning in Context: The Search for Innovative Patterns in Theological Education.* Bromley, UK: Theological Education Fund, 1973.

———. *Ministry in Context: The Third Mandate Programme of the Theological Education Fund (1970–77).* Bromley, UK: Theological Education Fund, 1972.

———. "Theological Curriculum and Teaching Methodology: A TEF Staff Working Paper." In *Learning in Context: The Search for Innovative Patterns in Theological Education*, 141–54. Bromley, UK: Theological Education Fund, 1973.

Thorogood, Bruce. "After 200 Years—The LMS Legacy." *Pacific Journal of Theology* 2.14 (1995) 5–15.

Timakata, Fred. "Political Ethics in Vanuatu." In *Perspectives on Political Ethics: An Ecumenical Enquiry*, edited by Koson Srisang, 155–62. Geneva: World Council of Churches, 1983.

Tofaeono, Ama'amalele. *Eco-Theology: AIGA. The Household of Life: A Perspective from the Living Myths and Traditions of Samoa.* Erlangen, Germany: Erlangen Verlag fur Mission und Oikumene, 2000.

———. "Editorial." *Pacific Journal of Theology* 2.27 (2002) 1–6.

Tongamoa, Taiamoni, ed. *Pacific Women: Roles and Status of Women in Pacific Societies.* Suva: Institute of Pacific Studies of the University of the South Pacific, 1988.

Trompf, Garry W., ed. *The Gospel is Not Western: Black Theologies from the Southwest Pacific.* Maryknoll, NY: Orbis, 1987.

———. *Melanesian Religion.* Cambridge: Cambridge University Press, 2004.

Tutu, Desmond. "Whither Theological Education: An African Perspective." *Theological Education* 9.4 (1973) 268–72.

Tuwere, Illaitia Sevati. "An Agenda for the Theological Task of the Church in Oceania." *Pacific Journal of Theology* 2.13 (1995) 5–12.

———. "Emerging Themes for a Pacific Theology." *Pacific Journal of Theology* 2.7 (1992) 49–55.

———. "He Began in Galilee and Now He is Here: Thoughts for a Pacific Ocean Theology." *Pacific Journal of Theology* 2.3 (1990) 4–15.

———. "Justice and Peace in the Womb of the Pacific." *Pacific Journal of Theology* 2.1 (1989) 8–15.

———. "Theological Reflection on the Contextualization of Spiritual Formation." *Pacific Journal of Theology* 2.5 (1991) 8–14.

———. "Thinking Theology Aloud in Fiji." In *The Gospel Is Not Western*, edited by Garry Trompf, 148–56. Oxford: Regnum, 1987.

———. *Vanua: Towards a Fijian Theology of Place.* Suva: Institute of Pacific Studies, 2002.

———. "What is Contextual Theology?: A View from Oceania." *Pacific Journal of Theology* 2.27 (2002) 7–20.

Tuza, Esau. "Instances of 'God-Talks' in Melanesia." *Melanesian Journal of Theology* 1.1 (1985) 47–60.

Ukpong, J. "Contextualization: A Historical Survey." *African Ecclesial Review* 29 (1987) 278–86.

Umba, Benjamin. "Life Is An Equation." In *Moments in Melanesia*, edited by Tegis Stella. Oxford: Oxford University Press, 1994.

Uriam, Kambati. "Doing Theology in the New Pacific." In *Vision and Reality in the Pacific Religion: Essays in Honour of Niel Gunson*, edited by Phyllis Herda, et al., 287–311. Canberra: Pandanus, 2005.

———. *In Their Own Words: History and Society in Gilbertese Oral Tradition*. Canberra: The Journal of Pacific History, with the assistance of the Asian South Pacific Cultures Fund, 1995.

———. "Theology and Practice in the Islands: Christianity and Island Communities in the New Pacific, 1947–1997." PhD diss., Australian National University, 1999.

Vamarasi, Jotama. "The Mana of the Word." In *South Pacific Theology: Papers from the Consultation on Pacific Theology, Papua New Guinea, January 1986*, edited by John D'Arcy May, 48–51. Oxford: Regnum, 1987.

Van Gelder, Craig, and Dwight Zscheile. *Missional Church in Perspective: Mapping Trends and Shaping the Conversation*. Grand Rapids: Baker Academic, 2011.

Van Trease, Howard. *The Politics of Land in Vanuatu: From Colony to Independence*. Suva: Instititute of Pacific Studies, 1987.

"Vanuatu Population." *Worldometers*. http://www.worldometers.info/world-population/vanuatu-population.

Walls, Andrew F. "Structural Problems in Mission Studies." *International Bulletin of Missionary Research* 15.4 (1991) 146–55.

Walker-Jones, Carrie. "A Tribute to Bishop Patelisio Finau." *Pacific Journal of Theology* 2.11 (1993) 1–6.

Wasimanu, Earnestly. "A Biblical Evaluation of Prayer in Beagu Tradition." *Melanesian Journal of Theology* 15.2 (1999) 41–73.

Wasmande, Sebby. "A Critique of the Niu Laip Bilong Olgeta Movement." *Melanesian Journal of Theology* 15.2 (1999) 5–40.

Watt, Agnes Craig Paterson. *Twenty-five Years' Mission Life on Tanna, New Hebrides*. Paisley, Scotland: J. and R. Parlane, 1896.

Wea, Djoubelly. "An Education for Kanak Liberation." BDiv thesis, Pacific Theological College, 1977.

Werner, Dietrich. *Challenges and Opportunities in Theological Education in the Twenty-First Century: Pointers for a New International Debate on Theological Education*. Geneva: World Council of Churches, 2009.

———. "Theological Education in the Changing Context of World Christianity: An Unfinished Agenda." *International Bulletin of Missionary Research* 35.2 (2011) 92–100.

Wesels, Anton. *Images of Jesus: How Jesus is Perceived and Portrayed in Non-European Cultures*. Grand Rapids: Eerdmans, 1990.

Wete, Pothin. *The Development of the Political Awareness of the Kanak Evangelical Church in New Caledonia and the Loyalty Islands from 1960 to 1987 and Its Theological Implications-Possibility for a Kanak Liberation Theology*. Suva: Pacific Theological College, 1988.

Wheeler, Ray. "The Legacy of Shoki Coe." *International Bulletin of Missionary Research* 26.2 (2002) 77–80.

Whiteman, Darrell, ed. *An Introduction to Melanesian Cultures: A Handbook for Church Workers.* Point Series 5. Goroka, Papua New Guinea: Melanesian Institute, 1984.

Whyte, Jennie, ed. *Vanuatu: Ten Years of Independence.* Rozelle, New South Wales: Other People Pty Ltd., 1990.

Wilson, John D. "What it Takes to Reach People in Oral Cultures." *Evangelical Missions Quarterly* 27.2 (1991) 154–58.

Workshop Participants. "Pacific Indigenous Peoples' Struggle for Land and Identity: Statement from Participants of the Workshop held in Suva, Fiji, September 11–14, 2000." *Pacific Journal of Theology* 2.25 (2001) 96–98.

Workshop Participants. "Statement of the Ecumenical Dialogue of Third World Theologians (Dar es Salaam 1976)." *Occasional Bulletin of Missionary Research* 1.1 (1977) 16–21.

World Council of Churches (WCC). "Pacific Conference of Churches Resolutions." *Oikoumene.* https://www.oikoumene.org/en/press-centre/news/pacific-conference-of-churches-resolutions.

Wright, Cliff. "Christ and Kiribati Culture: A Report of the Workshop in Kiribati, July 12–24, 1981." Suva: Lotu Pasifika, 1981.

———. "Melanesian Culture and Christian Faith: A Report of the Workshop in Auki, Malaita, Solomon Islands. October 12–26, 1978." Vila: Pacific Churches Research Centre, 1978.

———. "New Hebridean Culture and Christian Faith—Two Heads and Two Hearts: Report of an Education Workshop in Aulua, New Hebrides, April 19–May 3, 1979." Vila: Pacific Churches Research Centre, 1979.

———. "Not to Destroy but to Fulfill: Southern Highlands Cultures and Christian Faith: A Report of the Workshop in Mendi, July 23–August 3, 1980." Edited by Bernie Collins. Vila: Pacific Churches Research Centre, 1980.

———. "Seeds of the Word: Tongan Culture and Christian Faith: A Report of the Workshop June 20–July 3, 1979." Vila: Pacific Churches Research Centre, 1979.

Index of Names

Ahrens, Theodore, 135, 136
Amirtham, Samuel, 101
Apea, Simon, 96
Avi, Dick, 84-85, 88, 103–5

Barth, Karl, 19, 80, 94
Bergquist, James, 26, 118–20
Bevans, Stephen, 40, 41, 117
Bongmatur, Willi, 154
Bonhöffer, Dietrich, 80, 94
Bonnemaison, Joel, 8
Bosch, David, 17, 18, 20, 21, 156–57
Boseto, Leslie, 64, 65, 80, 155, 160
Bouganville, Louis, 106
Brunner, Emil, 80, 94
Burdon, Adrian 145
Burua, Albert 119, 120, 159
Burtness, James, 37–38, 39

Chandran, Russell, 53, 81, 82
Chang Hui Hwang (see Coe, Shoki)
Chun Hyun Kyung 168
Coe, Shoki, 23, 26–32, 37, 39, 84
Cook, James, 8

Dahle, Lars, 16
Doom, John Taroanui, 97
Duraisingh, Christopher 168

Ernst, Manfred, 45

Finau, Patelesio, 64, 65–66, 75, 106, 155
Foliaki, John, 75
Forman, Charles, 50, 56, 57, 59, 64, 66, 67, 71, 72, 74, 106, 107, 161, 162
Freire, Paulo, 25, 35, 119, 127
Fugui, Leslie, 3

Gaqurae, Joe, 93, 95–96
Gaudi, Haraki, 127, 128, 130
Geddie, John, 9–11, 18, 169, 180–81
Gibbs, Philip, 128–29
Guise, John, 42, 92, 93, 232

Hagesi, Robert, 78–79, 82, 95, 120–22
Halley, Cyril, 58
Hannan, Larry, 59
Hanson, Doug, 61, 103
Harris, James, 9
Havea, Sione ʻAmanaki, 42, 43, 64, 65, 72, 75, 80–81, 83, 84, 88, 94, 96, 100, 101, 155, 232
Havea, Salesi, 74, 75, 93, 160
Hopewell, James, 30
Hovey, Kevin, 132

Idusulia, Penuel Ben, 96

Johnson-Hill, Lydia, 68, 89–90, 112, 138, 140

Kamu, Lalomilo, 66
Kanongata'a, Keiti Ann, 89, 90–91, 111–13, 114–15, 138, 139–41
Kanyoro, Musimbi, 146–7
Kinsler, Ross, 27n56, 35–37
Klem, Herbert
Koete, Charles 161
Koria, Paulo, 130–32
Koyama, Kosuke, 19, 23

Lealofi, Etuale, 75–76
Lehmann, Paul, 37, 38–40
Lienemann-Perrin, Christine, 29, 37
Lindbeck, George, 134
Lini, Walter, 52–53, 165–66
Louhman, Graeme 169–81, 189

Madinger, Charles 147
Manuao, Philip, 132–33, 148
Mariesua, Noel 154–5
Matheny, Paul, 39
May, John D'Arcy, 51, 60, 62, 77, 79, 122
Mbiti, John, 146, 188
Meo, Jovili Iliesa, 64, 66, 68, 87, 155
Miller, J Graham, 44
Miria, Peter, 78, 79, 82
Mott, John, 17

Nabetari, Baiteke, 75
Naidoo, Marilyn, 19, 24
Narakobi, Bernard, 123
Natapei, Edward, 6
Nato, Masia, 217, 219
Newbigin, Lesslie, 14–15, 18, 47, 56, 133, 156–57
Nokise, Feleretika, 3, 46n18, 66n100

Oduyoye, Mercy Amber, 23, 25
Ong, Walter, 4n10, 147, 148n18

Padilla, Rene, 114
Palu, Ma'afu 'o Tu'itonga, 64, 96, 116, 134–37

Paschke, Jon 155, 189
Patel-Grey, Anne, 7
Puloka, Tevita Mohenoa, 124–26, 129–30, 144

Quiros, Ferdinand de, 7, 8

Rakau, Fiama, 13, 167, 181
Ropeti, Marie, 113–14
Rynkiewich, Michael 147–48, 149–50, 154, 155

Sanneh, Lamin, 11n34, 21
Schineller, Peter, 18
Schreiter, Robert, 2–3, 17, 22, 25
Setu, Fa'atulituli, 145
Silas, SSF 144–5
Speer, Robert, 17

Tabe, Baubeti, 153
Teinaroe, Ralph, 161
Tevi, Harry, 160
Tillich, Paul, 37n106, 80, 122
Timakata, Fred, 52–53
Tofaeono, Ama'amalele, 66–67
Tupouniua, Mahe U, 123
Tutu, Desmond, 21, 23, 24
Tuwere, Sevati Ilaitia, 64–65, 66, 86, 87–89, 101, 108–11, 113, 115, 116, 126–27, 133–34, 136–37, 155
Tuza, Esau, 95, 122

Ure, Stanley, 217, 219, 221
Uriam, Kambati, 43, 44, 46, 50, 51, 54, 57, 70, 71, 76, 97, 98, 106, 107

Vamarasi, Jotama 233

Warneck, Gustav, 18
Wete, Potin, 66, 106–7
Wheeler, Ray, 26
Whiteman, Darrell, 11
Williams, John, 8
Wright, Cliff, 1, 3

Index of Subjects

adaptation, 61, 90, 115, 120, 139
adoption, 24, 115
Africa, 2, 11n34, 17n10, 20, 21, 22, 23, 24, 25, 34, 36, 44, 53, 56, 58, 69, 114, 145–47, 151n27, 188, 225
ancestors, 2, 95, 108, 110, 110, 151, 152, 153, 166, 175, 198
anthropology, 62, 150, 214
anti-colonial, 113, 165–66, 225
art, 133, 144, 148, 149, 169–81
Asia, 21, 22, 23, 27, 29, 30, 34, 36, 44, 53, 58, 69, 81, 82, 88, 114, 168, 225
Australian Council of Churches, 1, 164

Betel Nut Theology, 78
Bislama language, 12, 182, 187, 193
blackbirding, 8
black magic 2, 166; black power,189

Catalyst publication, 62–63
celebration: in culture, 113, 124; in theology, 81, 96, 99
chief, 152, 153, 158, 189, 204, 206, 208, 209, 211, 215n38, 218; chiefly character, 137, 154, 182; chiefly system, 102, 103, 109; chief's meeting house (nakamal or farea), 152, 152n31, 192, 204, 207, 209,

210, 211, 219; in Christology, 218; National Council of Chiefs (Malvatumauri), 154, 222; role in the South Pacific/Vanuatu, 63–64, 154, 155, 171, 172, 173, 174, 175, 177, 178, 179, 182, 211, 212
Christendom, 14, 44, 47, 157; collapse of, 20
Christian century, 16, 19
Christian Leaders Training College, 62
Christianity, 67, 200, 211; as alien, 2–3, 10, 18, 105; as biblical culture, 3; as culture-free, 135; as global, 19, 21; in the Third World, 22, 45, 80n32; as western, 18–19, 20, 24
Christology, 61, 86, 94, 216, 217, 218; church: independence of, 50–52, 53, 92–93; as indigenous, 93, 132, 148, 225; as local, 4, 14, 24, 26, 33, 51, 56, 57, 78, 119, 130, 167, 168, 215; as locus for theology, 26, 78, 83, 124, 137, 142, 144, 148, 163, 184, 187, 213, 215, 225, 229, 230, 231; in the New Hebrides, 1, 9; as pioneer of Vanuatu independence, 1, 52–53; and political struggle, 21, 22–23,

Christology and political struggle
(*continued*), 26, 27, 29, 41, 45,
53, 66, 69, 80, 82, 102, 105,
106, 110, 115, 222, 227; role of
women in, 111–12, 114, 218,
223; separated from theology,
5, 33, 36, 123, 126, 127, 128,
135, 141, 143, 159–62, 221, 222,
230; and social justice, 23, 29,
32, 45, 46, 49, 53, 80, 106, 107,
125, 139, 222; Third World, 21,
22–26, 36, 37, 81–82, 83, 125,
225, 227; western, 14, 15, 16–20,
25; western decline, 19–22
Church of Melanesia, 75, 160, 217, 218,
220, 221
climate change, 69, 107, 110, 227
coconut, as a cultural image for
theology, 81, 97–99
Coconut Theology, 73, 78, 81, 96–99,
225, 227
colonial: mission, 54; rule, 8, 12, 23, 27,
53, 59, 86, 104, 106, 110, 193
colonialism: theological, 33; western, 19,
20, 46; as world view, 1, 3, 102,
113, 165
colonization: 1, 19, in New Hebrides, 8,
193; in New Caledonia, 66; as
a contextual issue, 46, 86, 106,
114, 115; 166; decolonization,
21, 22, 46, 50, 106, 225; post-
colonization, 1, 8n23, 20, 28, 43,
50, 53, 93, 106, 118
community: as bearer of mission, 29,
33, cultural significance of, 108,
113, 139, 140, 149–54, 182, 184,
190, 221; of theology, 36, 58, 60,
65, 79, 82, 84, 88, 102, 118, 120,
121, 122, 123, 127, 128, 130,
134, 137, 141, 143, 159–62, 163,
165, 182, 184, 185, 213, 221,
229–31
context: importance for theology, 27, 32,
33, 36, 37–41, 56, 61, 78–79, 80,
81, 85, 104, 115, 121, 124, 131,
140, 142, 164–66, 181, 224, 228,
231; of the South Pacific, 41,
45, 55, 56, 61, 67, 71, 73, 74, 75,

76, 80, 81, 87, 89, 114, 140, 163,
224, 228; of Vanuatu, 6–12
contextual theology (contextualization
of theology): all theology is,
40–41, 80, 82, 85, 100, 227;
beginnings 42–44; catalysts for,
44–63; changing attitude to,
19–22; content of, 4, 8, 69, 92–
117, 166; consultations on, 42,
49, 86–87, 90, 108, 114, 123 227;
context-free theology, 16–19,
20, 22, 31, 40; criticisms of, 31,
116, 134–37, 140; definition,
72–92; evolution of, 3, 5, 15,
16–41, 38, 68, 71, 82, 103–5,
168, 215; language of, 5, 26–40,
85; methodology, 5, 6, 14, 33,
39, 117–42, 144, 154, 213, 219,
221–22, 224, 231; in the South
Pacific, 4, 41, 42–69, 71, 72, 73,
83, 84, 87, 93, 103, 111, 116,
117, 118, 123, 126, 128, 136,
143, 144, 147, 153, 155–62, 164,
225–33; terminology of, 28–31,
80; in Vanuatu, 6, 12, 163–69,
184, 186, 187, 190, 213, 219,
221; in the west, 37n106, 38–40;
women's contribution to, 68,
89–91, 111–15, 137–41
conversion 3, 10–12, 47, 111, 180
culture: definition 133; literate, 4, 34,
35, 41, 58, 60, 61, 131, 132, 162,
182, 183, 187, 189, 219, 220,
221, 229; Melanesian, 7, 61, 62,
121, 133, 153, 203; non-western,
3; oral, 4, 6, 34, 35, 41, 57, 58,
59, 61, 144–55, 213, 219, 231,
232; (South) Pacific, 4, 57, 63,
75, 87, 96, 100, 102, 105, 108,
111, 114, 115, 116, 129, 139,
142, 143, 148, 150, 156–58, 161,
162, 164, 229; Third World, 3;
Vanuatu, 10, 13, 152, 155, 164,
169–81, 182, 185, 187, 188, 208,
213, 216, 219, 221; western, 4,
10, 19, 34, 45, 71, 83, 94, 144,
150, 156–57, 205, 208, 232

Culture and Faith Workshops: in New
Hebrides, 1, 2, 3, 6, 99, 152,
167, 180, 224, 225; in the South
Pacific, 1, 164–65

dance, 129, 144, 146, 148, 149
dis-integration: of faith and culture, 1–3,
5, 165, 180, 224
duality of faith and culture, 2–3
dualism, 10

Ecumenical Association of Third World
Theologians (EATWOT), 50, 86,
87, 90, 101, 108, 110, 113, 126,
127, 128, 226
ecumenical movement: influence of, 28,
46–50, 119
Edinburgh 1910 World Missionary
Conference, 16–17, 19, 22n31,
46
elitism, 24, 26, 29, 33, 34, 126, 127, 130,
142, 161, 162, 221
Enlightenment, 4–5, 14, 37, 229;
categories of, 17, 143, 156–59,
213, 221 231
evangelization, 3, 16, 17, 61, 120, 129

farea (chief's meeting house), 204, 207,
209, 210

globalization, 17, 44–46, 87, 102, 127,
185
Gospel and Culture: consultations on,
50, 53, 100–103; relationship
between, 9, 12, 13, 101, 167, 199
Gospel and Culture in Vanuatu project,
6, 12, 14, 41, 133, 163–223,
230, 231; artistic form 170–79;
critique of, 183, 188–89, 213-16,
219-21, 222; methodology 182–
88, 190, 216, 221-22; project
beginnings 164–69; project
development, 169, 181, 189,
217, 222, 223, 231; publications
169, 181, 188, 213, 216, 217–19.
reports 191–212, report on
language 191–97; report on
spirits 197–202; report on

marriage 202–10, 210-12; topics
189, 191, 218-19; on women in
leadership 223; in Timor Leste
222
Gospel and Our Culture (GOC)
Movement, 14

Holy Spirit, 11, 49, 100, 121, 176, 178;
and the spirit world, 198–202
hospitality, 101, 129

incarnation: of gospel in culture, 3, 10,
88, 180, 190, 225; as theological
significance, 31, 81, 85, 87, 88,
93, 96, 105, 114, 125, 178, 190,
197; in coconut theology, 98
independence, 21 27; of churches, 25,
50–52, 52n41; of Island nations,
52–53, 92, 106, 222, 225, 227;
ongoing struggles for, 66, 69,
105, 106, 107, 115; of Vanuatu,
1, 3, 9, 12, 52–53, 109, 110, 154,
163–67, 180, 199, 222, 225, 230
indigenization, 18, 30, 32, 41, 51, 52,
65, 70, 80, 84, 88, 227; of Lord's
Supper, 99, 132, 152, 167
indigenous: church, 51, 52, 53, 56, 93,
106, 132, 133, 148; cultural
context, 4, 9, 20, 224, 227;
people, 56, 7n18, 18, 51, 52, 63,
64, 109, 110, 117, 162, 180, 226,
233; theology, 29, 41, 55, 60,
61, 77, 79, 89, 94, 119, 120, 131,
155, 227, 233
individual (individualism), 36, 57, 74,
78, 91, 111, 113, 127, 129, 130,
131, 139, 142, 150, 154, 156,
157, 162, 185, 220, 221, 229
integration: in culture, 158; in theology,
31, 33, 35, 36, 39, 40, 65, 85,
106-7, 117, 124, 145, 158, 159,
165, 167, 180, 187, 224–26
International Missionary Council
(IMC), 17n6, 22n32, 28, 47,
50, 54

justice, as contextual issue, 32, 106, 107,
125, 139, 222

Kanak, 66, 105, 106
kinship, 159

land (see also "vanua"): importance of,
    7, 108–10; in theology, 59, 65,
    66, 99, 108–111, 113, 129, 189,
    191, 214n35, 215n38, 215n41,
    219, 221–22, 226
language: as gospel and culture issue,
    182, 191–97
Latin America, 2, 21, 22, 23, 24–25, 26,
    44, 56, 69, 104, 105, 114, 127,
    128n240, 130, 225
Liberation Theology, 85, 104, 105,
    106–8, 127–28
literate (literacy): cultures, 4, 34, 35, 41,
    58, 60, 61, 131, 132, 162, 182,
    183, 187, 189, 219, 220, 221,
    229; vs orality, 36, 37, 41, 58,
    129, 144–57, 218
London Missionary Society (LMS), 8, 47
Lord's Supper (Holy Communion), 99,
    132, 152, 167

marriage: in culture; 59, 61, 103, 129,
    167, 189, 191; as gospel and
    culture issue, 202–12, 214, 215,
    219
Melanesian: Christ, 92, 93; culture, 7,
    61, 62, 93, 121, 133, 153, 203;
    theology, 60, 61, 71, 77–79, 95,
    104, 120–22; way, 12
Melanesian Association of Theological
    Schools (MATS), 60, 63, 77
Melanesian Institute, 60, 62, 77, 79, 93
Melanesian Journal of Theology, 51,
    60–62, 77, 95, 120, 132, 225–26
Melanesian Theology, 60, 61, 71, 77–79,
    95, 104, 120–22
methodology of contextualization: the
    four defining questions of, 117,
    141, 143, 163, 180, 213, 228, 232
Micronesian Christ, 92
Missio Dei, 29, 31
mission: heritage of, 4, 100, 104, 123,
    166, 182; history in New
    Hebrides, 8–12, 18, 194;
    International Missionary

Council (IMC), 17n6, 22n32, 28,
    47, 50, 54; London Missionary
    Society (LMS), 8, 47; mission
    theology, 3, 9, 11, 12, 71, 91,
    111, 125, 141; nineteenth
    century, 3, 8–9, 17, 18, 25, 45,
    53, 102, 144, 162, 224, 229;
    western, 16–19, 25, 54, 83, 91,
    93, 101, 103, 116, 144, 162, 199,
    224

nakamal (chief's meeting house), 152,
    192, 204, 209, 211, 219
narrative (story-telling): in theology,
    89–90, 91, 122, 123, 131, 132,
    133–34, 136–39, 140, 148, 149,
    191, 226, 229
New Hebrides, 44, 51, 52, 53; history, 8;
    mission, 8–12, 18, 194; in war-
    time, 44, 45
New Hebrides Cultural Association,
    109,

Oceania, importance for theology,
    86, 87, 128–29, 161; Oceania
    theology, 88, 95, 108–11, 116
oral (orality): as communal, 149–54; as
    embodiment, 148–49; primary,
    4, 6, 34, 35, 41, 57, 58, 59, 61,
    144–55, 213, 219, 231, 232;
    teacher and learner relationship,
    154–55; in Vanuatu case study,
    163, 164, 181, 182, 184, 188,
    189; vs literacy, 36, 37, 41, 58,
    129, 144–57, 218; world of,
    147–55

Pacific Conference of Churches, 1, 42,
    47–49, 64, 107, 164, 225, 227;
    meetings, 46, 49, 73, 92, 159
Pacific Ecumenical Council, 69
Pacific Journal of Theology, 49, 58–60,
    84, 105, 225–26
Pacific Theological College, 3, 43, 50,
    54–58, 103, 164, 225
pedagogy: in theology, 24, 26, 32–35,
    119, 120, 141
Pentecost, 100, 178

Point publication, 62, 93
polygamy, 61, 103, 207, 208
Polynesian, 7, 63, 82, 92
praxis: methodology, 94, 128, 130, 138, 139, 142
Presbyterian Church: of New Hebrides, 51, 180; of Nova Scotia, 9, 169; of Vanuatu, 12, 52, 181, 190, 216, 217, 218, 221, 222, 223;
Presbyterian Women's Missionary Union (PWMU) 190, 216, 223
Program on Theological Education (PTE), 50, 83
Protestant: church, 149; mission, 8–12, 17–19; Church in Timor Leste, 220
publications: in Gospel and Culture series, 169, 180, 181, 187, 188, 189, 213, 216, 217, 218, 219, 220, 223

Roman Catholic: mission, 8, 17–18; view of theology, 75, 78

Scriptures: in contextualization, 51, 79, 87–88, 94, 96, 112, 115, 116, 135–36, 213, 214, 215; in mission teaching, 11–13, 53; translation of, 11–12, 196
Selly Oak Colleges, 14, 15, 66
song, 129, 144, 146, 148, 149, 194, 229
South Pacific Association of Theological Schools (SPATS), 59, 60, 69, 83, 87, 90, 102, 114
spirits: in Vanuatu cultures, 2, 7, 10, 96, 103, 104, 157–58, 166, 167, 168, 189, 191, 197–202, 214n30, 214n34, 215n39, 215n40, 229
story-telling (see narrative)

Talua Ministry Training Centre, 181, 189, 190, 196, 213, 216–20, 221
theological education: communal approach to, 55, 70, 129, 140, 141, 143, 149, 153–54, 163, 184, 213, 221, 229, 231; conferences/consultations on, 49, 54, 55, 56, 58, 64, 96, 161; survey of, 43,

56, 57, 106, 118; separated from local church, 5, 33, 36, 123, 126, 127, 128, 135, 141, 143, 159–62, 221, 222, 230; survey of, 43, 56, 57, 106, 118
Theological Education by Extension (TEE), 35–37
Theological Education Fund (TEF), 28–32; two definitive publications, 32–37
theology (see also contextual) as academic, 24, 26, 29, 33, 34, 36, 37, 39, 55, 57, 58, 61, 78, 85, 87, 88, 90, 93, 99, 100–103, 114, 123–24, 126, 127, 128–29, 131, 139, 141, 142, 145, 146, 158, 162, 233; Betel Nut Theology, 78; of Celebration, 81, 96, 99; Coconut Theology, 73, 78, 81, 96–99, 225, 227; as communal, 141, 149–50, 153–4; conferences/consultations on, 26, 28, 42, 49, 50, 53, 69, 73, 77, 80, 81, 82–84, 86–87, 89, 90, 101, 103, 107, 108, 123, 128, 129, 226; content, 4, 8, 69, 92–117, 166; as context-free, 16–19, 20, 22, 31, 40; definition, 72–92; development of, 6, 26, 32, 39, 41, 44, 46, 48, 49, 51, 54, 56, 57, 60, 61, 62, 63, 64, 72, 77, 79, 85–86, 91, 95, 97, 115, 116, 119, 120, 122, 137, 141, 155, 161, 165, 225, 228, 231; as embodied 142, 148–50, 190, 229; Liberation Theology, 85, 104, 105, 106–8, 127–28; local/localized, 49, 56, 57, 58–63, 69, 70, 71, 86, 93, 106, 130, 144, 145, 165, 167, 219, 232; methodology, 5, 6, 14, 33, 39, 117–42, 144, 154, 213, 219, 221–22, 224, 231; mission theology, 3; as narrative, 89–90, 138–39, 140, 226; Oceania theology, 88, 95, 108–11, 116; (South) Pacific, 4, 5, 16, 34, 41, 42–69, 70, 71, 72, 74, 75, 77, 86, 89, 97, 99, 100, 101, 103, 106,

theology, (South) Pacific *(continued)*,
111, 114, 115, 116, 117, 118,
126, 130, 133, 134, 138, 140,
142, 143–44, 147, 148, 153, 155,
158, 159, 161, 162, 163, 164,
165, 220, 226, 227, 228, 230,
231, 233; as sure knowledge, 17,
40; Third World, 3, 7, 18, 19, 21,
22, 25, 28, 29, 82; western, 18,
19, 21, 24, 25, 45, 64, 71, 80, 81,
92, 93, 95, 115, 125, 126, 128,
138; 141, 220, 221, 225, 226,
227, 228, 229, 230, 231, 232;
Woman (Women's) Theology,
67, 68, 90n76, 91, 139–41, 146,
226, 228

vanua (see land), 65, 108–10
Vanuatu, 6–12; cultures, 63, 109, 149,
150–55, 165, 169–81, 183,
185, 187, 188, 191–212, 213,
216, 219, 223; history, 9–11,
independence, 1, 3, 9, 12, 52–53,
109, 110, 154, 163–67, 180, 199,
222, 225, 230, map, xviii; the
name, 7, 162,
Vanuatu Government, 1, 12, 52, 65, 196,
205, 213n28
Vanuatu islands: Ambrym, 191,
210–12; Aneityum, 9, 10,
97, 106; Erromanga, 9; Ifira,
202–10; Makira: PCV Assembly,
190–213; Mele, 202–10; Paama,
191, 210–12; Santo, 7, 181,
191; Southern Islands, 191–97;
Tanna, 8, 18, 148, 151, 197–200
Vatican II, 22

Weavers: contribution to
contextualization, 90, 108, 111,
112, 137, 138, 141, 146, 226;
founding of organisation, 67–68;
western culture, 156–57, 208, 232; as
Christian, 10; imposition of, 4,
19, 45, 71, 83, 93–94, 205; as
literate, 34, 144
western theology: context-free, 16–19;
domination of, 19, 21, 45, 95,
125; irrelevance of, 21, 24, 64,
71, 80, 89, 92, 93, 95, 115, 126,
128, 138
western theologians, 19, 31
Woman (Women's) Theology, 67, 68,
90n76, 91, 139–41, 146, 226,
228; as narrative, 89–90, 138–39,
140, 226; as liberation, 89, 107–
8, 112, 139, 141
women: role of, 66, 67, 102, 111, 211,
214n33, 215n38, 216, 218,
223; on defining theology,
89–91; on content of theology,
111–15, 116; on methodology of
theology, 137–41
workshops, 109, 129, 144, 168; on
Culture and Faith, 1–2, 3, 99,
152, 164–65, 167, 180, 224,
225; on Gospel and Culture in
Vanuatu, 183, 187, 189, 191–
212, 213, 214, 216, 220, 222; on
theology, 76, 91, 114, 133, 227
World Council of Churches 26, 50, 65,
83, 97, 118, 133, 168
World Vision International, 82
World War II, 3, 44, 45, 54

www.ingramcontent.com/pod-product-compliance
Lightning Source LLC
Chambersburg PA
CBHW060329100426
42812CB00003B/932